Generative AI

Scrivener Publishing
100 Cummings Center, Suite 541J
Beverly, MA 01915-6106

Publishers at Scrivener
Martin Scrivener (martin@scrivenerpublishing.com)
Phillip Carmical (pcarmical@scrivenerpublishing.com)

Generative AI

Disruptive Technologies for Innovative Applications

Edited by

N. Gayathri
Department of Computer Science and Engineering, GITAM University, Bengaluru, India

S. Rakesh Kumar
Department of Computer Science and Engineering, GITAM University, Bengaluru, India

Ramesh Chandran
Vellore Institute of Technology, Vellore, India

Pethuru Raj Chelliah
Reliance Jio Platforms Ltd., Bangalore, Karanataka, India

and

Danilo Pelusi
Faculty of Communication Sciences, University of Teramo, Italy

Scrivener Publishing

WILEY

This edition first published 2025 by John Wiley & Sons, Inc., 111 River Street, Hoboken, NJ 07030, USA and Scrivener Publishing LLC, 100 Cummings Center, Suite 541J, Beverly, MA 01915, USA

For more information about Scrivener publications please visit www.scrivenerpublishing.com.

Wiley Global Headquarters
111 River Street, Hoboken, NJ 07030, USA

For details of our global editorial offices, customer services, and more information about Wiley products visit us at www.wiley.com.

Library of Congress Cataloging-in-Publication Data

ISBN 978-1-394-30290-1

Front cover image courtesy of Adobe Firefly
Cover design by Russell Richardson

Set in size of 11pt and Minion Pro by Manila Typesetting Company, Makati, Philippines

Printed in the USA

10 9 8 7 6 5 4 3 2 1

Contents

Preface

In the fast-evolving landscape of technology, few advancements have generated as much excitement and curiosity as Generative Artificial Intelligence (AI). Once confined to the realm of science fiction, AI has rapidly transitioned into a tangible, transformative force, influencing industries ranging from healthcare to entertainment. Among the various branches of AI, generative models stand out as particularly revolutionary. These models possess the ability to create—whether generating text, images, music, or even entire virtual worlds—ushering in an era where machines are not merely tools but creators in their own right.

Generative AI: Disruptive Technologies for Innovative Applications explores this remarkable field, offering a comprehensive guide to its underlying principles, practical applications, and the profound implications it holds for the future. This book aims to bridge the gap between technical expertise and real-world implementation, making generative AI accessible to both seasoned professionals and curious newcomers alike.

The journey of writing this book has been one of both discovery and reflection. As generative AI continues to evolve at an unprecedented pace, it challenges us to rethink what is possible in the realms of creativity, problem-solving, and human-machine collaboration. This book is not merely a technical manual; it is a window into the future, showcasing how generative AI can be harnessed to drive innovation across diverse fields.

We sincerely appreciate the research contributions from the authors. Their dedication and ingenuity have not only pushed the boundaries of technology, but also inspired the content of this book. Furthermore, we are thankful to Martin Scrivener and the team at Scrivener Publishing for their continuous support in the preparation of this book.

N. Gayathri
S. Rakesh Kumar
Ramesh Chandran
Pethuru Raj Chelliah
Danilo Pelusi

1

Introduction to Generative AI

Ritika Lath[1]*, Renuka Patwari[1], Amit Aylani[1] and Deepak Hajoary[2]

[1]Vidyalankar Institute of Technology, Mumbai, India

[2]Bodoland University, Assam, India

Abstract

Generative AI (Gen AI or GAI) is becoming a greater player in the creation and consumption of content with expected ramifications across several industries. In 2025, GAI will account for 10% of all data as compared to less than 1% currently according to Gartner's 2022 Emerging Technologies and Trends Impact Radar. This machine learning subset can generate new forms of content, including text, audio, images, and video by using advanced neural networks like OpenAI's GPT models. The introduction of ChatGPT, which was built on the basis of GPT-3.5 showed GAI's capability in conducting coherent conversations, thus emphasizing its potential in automating the knowledge work delivery process. The applications for GAI are wide-ranging, from drug discovery to manufacturing, thereby challenging traditional notions of creativity as well as authorship. It is anticipated that as companies develop specialized large language models, GAI will eventually become an instrumental tool across different sectors, facilitating innovation and improving efficiency. Nonetheless, there are serious ethical, legal, and social issues that arise because it changes our manner of creating, interacting with, and comprehending various forms of content. In this chapter, we begin by examining Gen AI, starting from its definition, moving on through distinguishing it from traditional Artificial Intelligence (AI) and Machine Learning (ML) by emphasizing its novelty of producing outputs that resemble variety of human generated content. The history of Gen AI is traced, revealing the models that facilitated its progress, including Generative Adversarial Networks (GANs), Variational Autoencoders (VAEs), Transformer models, Recurrent Neural Networks (RNNs) and Long Short-Term Memory Networks (LSTMs), among many others. Besides, this chapter examines how Generative AI works through exploring the complex structure of Large Language Models (LLMs) and how they operate. It highlights the minute

**Corresponding author*: ritikalath3001@gmail.com

N. Gayathri, S. Rakesh Kumar, Ramesh Chandran, Pethuru Raj Chelliah and Danilo Pelusi (eds.) Generative AI: Disruptive Technologies for Innovative Applications, (1–28) © 2025 Scrivener Publishing LLC

differences between LLMs and broader Generative AI frameworks while illustrating LLM's position within the Gen AI paradigm. The chapter also discusses the consequences and prospects of LLMs, given their transformative abilities in creative industries, scientific research, and other areas. Details concerning how Gen AI can help improve productivity, reduce costs, and the dangers involved, such as invasion of privacy and AI cyber-attacks are elaborated. The performance of Gen AI is then evaluated based upon standards such as quality, diversity, and speed. Besides, applying them in practical life is not easy. The challenges are addressed under the section on Technical Challenges, and the paper concludes by showcasing Gen AI's real-life application through examples like Unilever and Be My Eyes for societal good.

***Keywords*:** Generative models, gen AI, neural networks, synthetic data, algorithmic creativity, variational autoencoders (VAEs), generative adversarial networks (GANs), diffusion models, transformers

1.1 What is Generative AI

Generative AI is an fascinating area of artificial intelligence that deals with the creation of new data that is inspired by the patterns it has learned from the existing data. If you're ever wondering how generative AI works, think of it as learning to draw a cat. You might start by studying several photographs of casts, noting features such as body shape, ears, and tails. Eventually, you will start to recognize the basic characteristics of a dog. When you try to recall a dog and draw it, you create a new image using the patterns that you've learned. This picture will not be identical to any dog you've ever seen, but it will be a completely new interpretation of the concept of a dog. Similarly, generative AI is trained on a vast dataset which can include images, texts, sounds, and more. The AI system studies these instances, then finds the similarities and shapes in the data. By absorbing prior examples, it gains the capacity to generate genuine content with a slight similarity to the training data. For example, a model of generative AI trained on pictures of cats could invent a new kind of cat. The same thing is true for a machine that has been taught to use textual data, for it can create a new paragraph that is almost indistinguishable from a human's writing style [1].

The most interesting aspect of Gen AI is that it doesn't merely copy pieces of data it had already seen. Instead, it creates entirely new kinds of content based on the patterns it has learned. This creative ability - generating something new rather than just providing existing data - is what makes GAI so illicitly attractive. For example, a Gen AI model trained on musical scores can produce new music that, though influenced by the training data, is also an original composition [2].

Generative AI has been the most prominent game-changing technology in the last couple of years, leading to a fundamental change in the way content is generated and consumed. According to the Gartner's Emerging Technologies and Trends Impact Radar for 2022, the GAI will be crucial in many sectors, with the tendency to be dominant in the near future. By 2025, GAI is expected to account for 10% of all data produced, a 1% increment from the current level, which is less than 1%. Moreover, the goal is to achieve a 20% share in the test data output for the consumer applications highlighting that not only data generation but also consumption is increasing its influence in this field. Generative AI, a subset of ML technologies, can produce various types of new content (text, audio, images, and video) from text prompts. This distinct trait has captivated the world, especially via dialogue systems that predominantly revolve around the text. In comparison to conventional chatbots whose capabilities are restricted by fixed rules and limited comprehension of context, generative AI models employ advanced neural networks like OpenAI's GPT which maintain certain level of contextual awareness [2]. These models are developed using large-scale data collection, which gives them the ability to create new content based on user prompts. The data acquisition phase consists of models getting an AI intelligence that attains a representative knowledge of the world, a capability that even AI experts find difficulty to explain fully due to the inherent uncertainty in the algorithms.

A powerful version of ChatGPT based on the neural network model Open AI's GPT-3.5 was introduced on November 30, 2022, revealing the true potential of the generative AI's to the world. It managed to showcase the technology's ability to engage in a human-like dialogue through the provision of socially correct and contextually relevant answers. Furthermore, the model's content generation ability has not only changed the conversational space but also revealed the generative AI's potential to provide solutions in knowledge work, an area that has long been resistant to automation. Being able to create virtually anything that looks like a human text and even images, audio, or video only from basic text prompts, therefore, generative AI tools can be a partner in the creative process of making practical work purposes. Automation industry is going to be revolutionized by this development, as it will open up new avenues for creativity and efficiency in different sectors [3]. With the generative AI technology, the possibilities are endless. According to the Gartner prediction, by 2025, the use of GAI technology in drug discovery and development initiatives will reach 50%, thus science research will be made faster and better. It is reported that in the manufacturing sector by 2027, 30% of manufacturers will use this technology to enhance the efficiency of product development. Such predictions point to a future in which generative AI is a crucial instrument in industries from pharmaceuticals to manufacturing as it will promote innovation and efficiency [4]. The pleasing effect of generative AI is not only about its technical aspects. It means that a new chapter in our relationship with technology and creativity is opening up. The generative AI's ability to produce never-before-seen content throws new light on traditional understanding of creativity and authorship; therefore, bringing about the question of the role of AI in creative processes. Although the businesses and individuals are searching for the technologies' possible advantages, there is an increasing recognition of the necessity to comprehend the ethical, legal, and societal implications of generative AI [5].

In the coming years, organizations will develop their own unique models for big language. Companies have always been at the forefront of AI technology, but now AI is becoming more and more tailored to fit specific use cases. This brings us a step closer towards AI systems that have unique characteristics capable of AI functions that are exactly matched with the needs and problems of a company. The more this technology evolves, the more it will become a household name which will give rise to new business models, services, and products [6]. The blooming of AI with a plethora of services and products is not stoppable, it is on its way to every household in the globe. Gen AI is not just a top-notch technology; it is a turner of the tides that improves content generation communications and understandings. It is its ability to adjust itself to diverse areas as well as rapidly substitute manual tasks which makes it an indispensable factor for future innovations. Nonetheless, while we keep on researching and deploying the power of GAI, it is crucial to address the challenges and advantages that it poses to emphasize that this innovation ought to be employed for the greater benefit of mankind [7].

1.2 Difference Between AI, Machine Learning and Generative AI

Generative AI is one of the many manifestations of AI, including reasoning, learning, problem-solving, perception, and language understanding. Computer programs and software which mimic human intelligence to execute tasks are what AI is about. This includes vocabulary areas such as natural language processing (NLP), computer vision, and robotics [1, 4].

AI is essentially a computer imitation of human intelligence. Among the most prominent parts of this area, machine learning, or ML for short, is a subfield, which mostly concentrates on providing systems with input data and letting them discover patterns and draw conclusions. The difference between the classical programming, where systems get specific rules taught to them, and machine learning is that in the latter, computers can enhance their predictive or descriptive capabilities over time by learning from data. An illustration is that of an email spam filter utilizing ML to distinguish between spam and non-spam messages [2, 7].

Generative AI is a specific area of ML that is engaged in the creation of new content. While routine machine learning models are mainly focused to classify, predict or make decisions, generative AI models learn the structure of the training data and then use these patterns to produce new data. Examples of this can be creating realistic images, generating coherent text, composing music, and designing products [4].

Creating new content with such a technology entails the emergence of models such as Generative Adversarial Networks, Variational Autoencoders, and large language models like GPT (Generative Pre-trained Transformer). A simple example is, GANs that employ two neural networks, the generator and the discriminator. They both accompany the work. The generator is tasked with creation of new data and the discriminator assesses the validity of the information given by the generator, and thus over time, the quality of the generated content improves [5, 9].

A generative AI is full of potential across industries. In the entertainment world, using AI artwork or creating new music or videos is possible. In the area of product design, it can help improve product ideas or even help architecture projects. It is utilized in chatbots, translation, and content creation which are mainly in NLP. Moreover, generative AI can advance scientific fields like medicine and drug discovery by generating new molecular structures or bionics simulations [7–9].

Synthesized AI, a niche domain among the various fields of AI, is concerned with the production of new content based on learned patterns. Generative AI is the original output creator tool that is distinct from other areas of machine learning and artificial intelligence. There is no limit to the applications of AI in human life whether it is art and entertainment or scientific research. AI is a thriving and promising field of research to follow [4, 5, 8].

1.3 History of Generative AI

Generative AI has a long history, spanning over 70 years, but it has come into the spotlight only recently. The trip started with the primitive machine's trying to simulate human thinking and process information in a way similar to humans. Over seven decades, technology has traveled from the 1950s, when researchers concentrated on producing content that made sense for individual sentences. To the present day, generative models enable interactions that are similar to humans, an impressive evolution of technology.

1950s: The Birth of AI and Text Analytics - The idea of Artificial Intelligence (AI) originated in the 1950s when researchers first started to think about machines that would be able to perceive the world as humans do. The first steps in text analytics were made by creating more or less simple computer programs capable to process and analyze the data, with a focus on tasks like information retrieval and keyword extraction [10]. Though rudimentary by today's standards, these initial efforts laid the foundation for the development of more complex AI systems.

1960s: Rule-Based Systems & Knowledge Bases - In the 1960s and 1970s, AI research shifted towards rule-based systems, such as the Rete algorithm, and the creation of knowledge bases. This era saw the rise of expert systems, which encoded human knowledge into programmatic forms that could be processed using explicit rules and logical reasoning [11]. These systems showed that computers could perform tasks requiring human-like intelligence, such as medical diagnosis and financial forecasting, although they struggled with adaptability and flexibility across different domains [12].

1980s: Advances in Natural Language Processing (NLP) - The 1980s and early 1990s were marked by significant advancements in natural language processing (NLP). Institutions such as Harvard applied more advanced methods for parsing and analyzing text, thereby attracting the development of software such as machine translation, speech recognition, and sentiment analysis [13]. While rule-based, these systems could deal with more complicated linguistic tasks, thereby laying the foundation for the future innovations.

2000s: The Machine Learning and Big Data Revolution - The early 2000s was a period of transformative change in AI research characterized by the emergence of machine learning and the continuous growth of digital data. Neural networks which are the basis of most machine learning models made it possible for AI systems to learn very complex patterns from huge data sets [14]. The "Big Data" period witnessed the development in deep learning due to the use of the multi-layered neural network which made a considerable improvement in the understanding and generation of human language [15].

2020s: Generative AI - Breakthroughs with GPT-3 and Beyond - The 2020s have been a landmark period for Generative AI, highlighted by the release of GPT-3 (Generative Pre-trained Transformer 3). The gigantic model, one which had been trained on a whopping amount of text data, showed remarkable capability in generating sentences that are structurally coherent and contextually appropriate [16]. Adding to this, further developments such as GPT-4 models and image generation technologies—like Generative Adversarial Networks (GANs), Variational Autoencoders (VAEs), and diffusion models—have made it possible to create realizations of photorealistic images [17, 18].

1.4 Key Milestones and Continued Progress

As the years passed by, Generative AI achieved great advancements. One of the most renowned breakthroughs was Ian Goodfellow introducing GANs in 2014. GANs opened up new avenues in the area of computer graphics by enabling stimuli with unrealistically similar images to actual ones. [19]. The transformer architecture introduced by Vaswani *et al.* in 2017 is another discovery that disrupted the whole of the NLP domain. This architecture has opened doors for such advanced models as BERT and GPT-2 that can comprehend and produce human language [20]. The availability of large language models (LLMs) has opened up new avenues for creative practices, like deep fake technology and Neural Radiance Fields (NeRF) for generating 3D scenes [21, 22].

Generative AI has gone far, from simple methods such as Hidden Markov Models (HMMs) to truly smart architectures. This technology promises to be used in a lot of areas such as personalized content creation and creating synthetic data for AI training in the future. The development of Generative AI is going on and it is affecting different fields; therefore, it is important to be aware of these technologies to take advantage of their full capabilities. In the next paragraph, we are going to talk about the various kinds of generative AI models, and their architectures, and we will also mention some of their practical use cases and how they work.

1.4.1 Generative Adversarial Networks (GANs)

Generative Adversarial Networks (GANs) are interesting types of generative models. GANs were introduced in 2014 and consists of a generator and a discriminator that are both neural networks, respectively. These two networks are trained concurrently using the adversarial method, where the

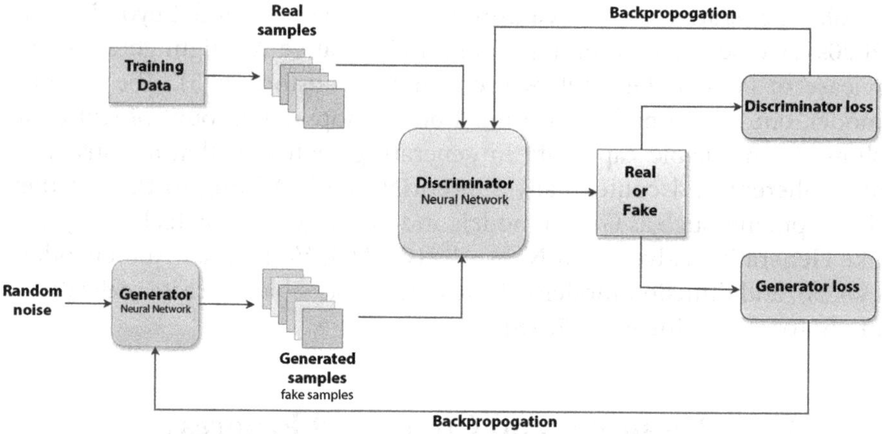

Figure 1.1 Generative adversarial networks architecture.

generator makes data and the discriminator checks whether they are real. The Figure 1.1 details the architecture of Generative Adversarial Networks.

a. **Generator:** This network creates new data instances, and continuously strives to produce outputs are indistinguishable from real data.
b. **Discriminator:** This is the other part of the network which tries to categorize how close fake data are from real data.

The generator aims at molding the data such that the discriminator misclassifies it as real, and the discriminator being the one who tries to distinguish it from the output. This back-and-forth technique is what leads to a situation wherein the generator produces data that a discriminator cannot differentiate from real data. The generator strives to reduce its loss function JG by conducting a data distribution that closely resemble those the discriminator real. The discriminator, nonetheless, plays its part by minimizing its loss JD through getting real and fake samples accurately [2].

Applications

a. A wide range of applications have since adopted GANs, including:
b. Image Generation: Generating realistic images (e.g. human faces, landscapes).
c. Video game development - Textures, characters, and worlds.
d. Art: Creating new modes of art or artwork.

1.4.2 Variational Autoencoders (VAEs)

Variational Autoencoders (VAEs) are probabilistic generative models that aim to model the underlying distribution of the data. Unlike GANs, VAEs focus on learning a latent representation of the input data, which can then be used to generate new data instances as demonstrated in Figure 1.2 [6].

VAEs consist of two main components:

a. **Encoder:** This part of the network encodes the input data into a latent space, represented by a mean and variance vector. This latent representation captures the essential features of the input data.
b. **Decoder:** The decoder generates new data from the latent representation, attempting to reconstruct the original input [5].

During training, VAEs minimize the reconstruction loss (difference between original and reconstructed data) and a regularization term that enforces a normal distribution in a latent space. This makes VAEs particularly useful for generating new, similar data based on the input distribution [6].

Applications

VAEs are used in various domains, including:

a. Image Generation: Creating new images based on learned features.
b. Data Imputation: Filling in missing data in datasets.
c. Anomaly Detection: Identifying unusual patterns in data.

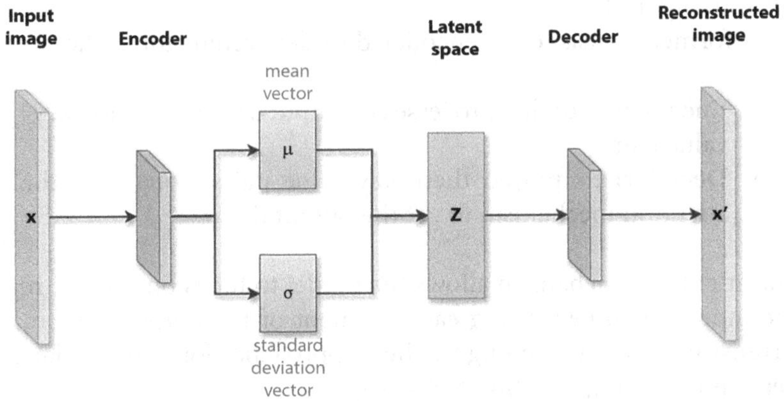

Figure 1.2 Variational autoencoders architecture.

1.4.3 Autoregressive Models

Autoregressive models generate new data one point at a time, whereby as each new data point is created, the model is conditioned on the already produced points. Such models work exceptionally well in the case of sequential data types, which are represented by text, music, or time series [8].

Autoregressive models' primary principle is the creation of a new data point being dependent on the preceding ones. This method is very prevalent in the field of natural language processing, where the words in a sentence are predicted according to the words preceding them [8].

Applications

a. **Natural Language Processing:** Text generation, machine translation, and language modeling.
b. **Music Generation:** Composing new pieces of music based on existing styles.
c. **Time Series Forecasting:** Predicting future values in a time series.

1.4.4 Transformer Models

Transformers employed in deep learning models like GPT (Generation Pre-trained Transformer) represent a big advancement in the area of natural language processing. The Transformer architecture employs an attention mechanism that allows it to prioritize the relevance of particular words in a sentence thereby modelling dependencies over distance detailed in Figure 1.3.

Transformers consist of an encoder-decoder architecture, where:

a. **Encoder:** Both first processes the input data and creates key-value pairs.
b. **Decoder:** Employed these key-value pairs along with the attention mechanism to get the output data.

The attention mechanism allows the model to focus on specific regions of the input, when generating each segment of the output, thus making the Transformers to be among the best approaches for complex language understanding and generation tasks [10].

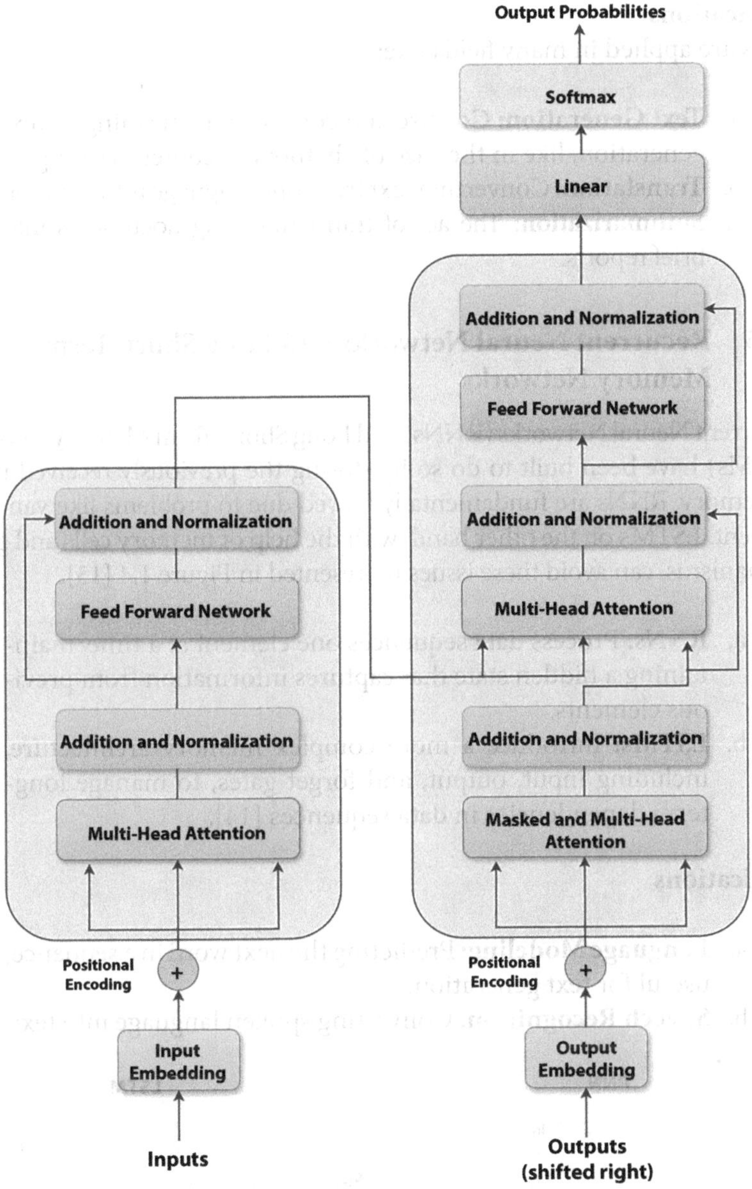

Figure 1.3 Transformer architecture.

Applications

VAEs are applied in many fields like:

a. **Text Generation:** Concise and contextually meaningful text generation, like in the case of chatbots or content writing.
b. **Translation:** Converting text from one language into another.
c. **Summarization:** The act of translating long documents into brief reports.

1.4.5 Recurrent Neural Networks and Long Short-Term Memory Networks

Recurrent Neural Networks (RNNs) and Long Short-Term Memory Networks (LSTMs) have been built to do so by storing the previously received inputs in memory. RNNs are fundamentally flawed due to problems like vanishing gradient. LSTMs on the other hand, with the help of memory cells and gating mechanisms, can avoid these issues represented in Figure 1.4 [13].

a. **RNNs:** Process data sequences one element at a time, maintaining a hidden state that captures information from previous elements.
b. **LSTMs:** Introduce a more complex memory architecture, including input, output, and forget gates, to manage long-term dependencies in data sequences [14].

Applications

a. **Language Modeling:** Predicting the next word in a sequence, useful for text generation.
b. **Speech Recognition:** Converting spoken language into text.

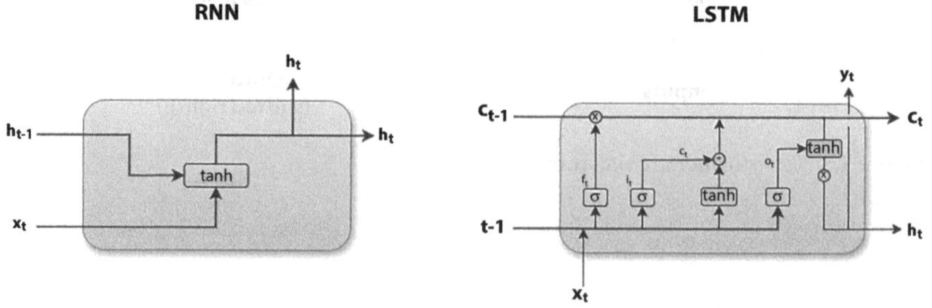

Figure 1.4 RNN and LSTM architecture.

c. **Time Series Analysis:** Forecasting future values based on historical data.

1.4.6 Energy-Based Models (EBMs)

Energy-Based Models (EBMs) are a distinct type of generative model which has an energy function that is defined over the input data and assigns lower energies to the more likely data configurations. EBMs are types of models such as Restricted Boltzmann Machines (RBMs) and Deep Boltzmann Machines (DBMs) [16].

a. **Energy Function:** Measures the compatibility between observed data and the model's parameters. The goal is to assign lower energy to real data and higher energy to unlikely configurations.
b. **Learning Process:** Involves adjusting the model parameters to minimize the energy of the observed data and maximize the energy of the unobserved data [17].

Applications

a. **Feature Learning:** Extracting useful features from raw data.
b. **Data Denoising:** Removing noise from corrupted data.
c. **Recommendation Systems:** Modelling user-item interactions for personalized recommendations.

1.4.7 Flow-Based Models

Flow-based models like Real NVP and Glow, which learn the distribution of data through a sequence of invertible transformations of data, are particularly good at generating high-quality samples and allow for exact likelihood computation, which is important in evaluating models [19]. The Figure 1.5 represents the architecture of Flow Based models.

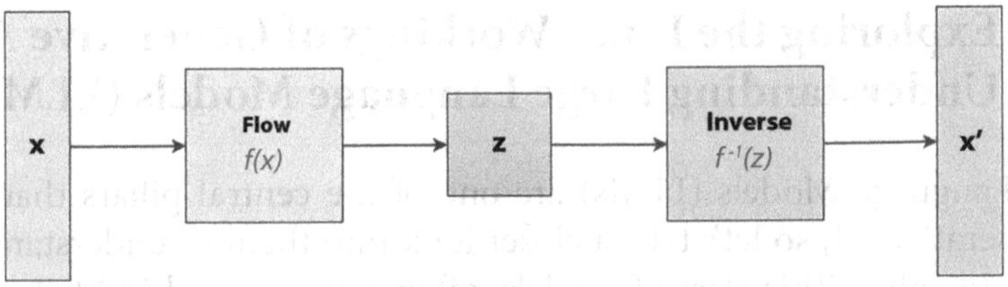

Figure 1.5 Flow based models architecture.

Flow- Flow-based models project the input data into the latent space via a series of one-to-one mappings (invertible functions). The model learns to map complex data distributions to simpler ones, thereby making it easier to generate new samples, and compute the likelihoods [20].

Applications

a. **Image Generation:** Creating photos that look like humans with specific wishes and modify them.
b. **Density Estimation:** Finding the probability density of data points in a specific space.
c. **Data Compression:** Reducing Enabling data to contain less information while keeping its most important features.

1.4.8 Diffusion Models

Diffusion models represent a newer generation of generative models which generate data through the reverse process of diffusion. They begin with noise and use an iterative approach to denoising which gives them very high-quality generation capabilities [22].

Diffusion models work by introducing noise to the data during the training phase and then the model learns to reverse the process during the generation phase. This method enables them to generate very close to real life and highly detailed samples [23].

Applications

a. **Image Generation:** Making the images high-resolution and super-realistic.
b. **Video Generation:** Producing fluid and life-like video sequences.
c. **Audio Synthesis:** Making realistic audio samples.

1.5 Exploring the Inner Workings of Generative AI: Understanding Large Language Models (LLMs)

Large Language Models (LLMs) are one of the central pillars that make up Generative AI, so let's take a closer look into them to understand how they fit together. This class of models, often simply called LLMs (workers use language-modelling neural networks) are central to the current capabilities new AI systems such as chatbots and text generators have [1, 2]. We shall check out what LLMs are, how they function and also their importance in the field of AI.

Large Language Models (LLMs), Who?

LLMs are larger AI systems, specifically designed for reading and writing human-like free text [2]. Those billions of parameters are trained on tons of data. In this case, a 'parameter' is something learned from the training data and utilized to predict [3]. For example, GPT-3 - one of the most well-known LLMs (*language model*) ever forged by OpenAI has about 175 billion parameters [16].

This set of parameters allows the model to learn intricate patterns from data which is later used in predicting next words -in sequence, making it easier to get sentence completions or even have complete paragraphs [5]. These models are trained with datasets, which may be open source e.g., The Wikipedia pages or proprietary like internal company documents [2, 4]. Essentially, the dataset is huge and rich in a variety of data which gives it this ability to learn a large variation on linguistic patterns and contexts [3, 7].

This is the core functionality of LLMs: The probabilistic predictions [1, 5]. Essentially, an LLM is a probabilistic predictor. It implies that the model not only memorizes text but also the probability of word sequences based on learning from its data. The model attempts to complete the sequence of words, with a designated starting string or text prompt that is provided when generating text [3, 4]. Another example could be the sentence: "Modern AI has been tipped as companies' newest weapon." An LLM produces this by determining the probability of each word given that "Modern AI has become the new...". "Predict: weapon," it decides, based on its training data. Instead, it compares the probability of "weapon" with alternative words for the given context and selects one that has been most probable in similar phrases during training [5, 16].

LLMs are able to consistently and pertinently piece together text because of this probabilistic approach. The objective of this assignment is to make it easier to forecast words as well as other situations in which tokens occur [1, 7]. For instance, while discussing methods or resources, an LLM may discover that terms like "weapon" follow the phrase "the latest"; this would make the text generation more pertinent [4, 6]. Adaptive Environments and Continuous Learning LLMs are dynamic; they are always learning and changing. To capture various levels of patterns, such as letters and words at the character level or sentences and paragraphs, a huge amount of text data is used to train the models [5, 13]. For example, following "w," it anticipates "x" to have a small probability and "y" to have a big probability [14]. It also has more intricate structures, such as idiom and phrase patterns [12, 13].

Additionally, LLMs can be tailored to a certain activity or domain. An all-purpose version of the model, such as GPT-3, may be trained on medical literature instead, and then it could be fine-tuned once again to focus on writing writings on medicine [5, 7]. This makes LLMs adaptable, and they may be tailored to meet variety of needs [15, 16].

Several LLMs have made significant strides in advancing AI capabilities:

a. **OpenAI's GPT Series (GPT-3, 3.5, 4):** Known for its text generating capabilities, the GPT series finds use in chatbots and creative writing tools, among other applications [16].
b. **Google's LaMDA and PaLM: LaMDA (Language Model for Dialogue Applications):** With an emphasis on dialogue creation, LaMDA seeks to develop conversational agents that are more engaging and natural. Another large-scale approach that promotes transfer learning and multitasking is called PaLM (Pathways Language approach) [2, 17].
c. **Hugging Face's BLOOM:** BLOOM is an open-source paradigm that allows developers to expand on its features and is designed to be transparent and accessible [19].
d. **Meta's LLaMA:** Customizable private models are the main emphasis of LLaMA, an open-source Large Language Model Meta AI. With this paradigm, developers may customize AI for certain domains or applications [5, 15].
e. **Nvidia's NeMO LLM:** Models developed by Nvidia with an emphasis on efficiency and scalability and tuned for Nvidia technology are part of their contribution to the LLM landscape [5, 14].

1.6 LLMs vs. Generative AI

LLMs are not the same as generative AI, but they are an important part of it. Generative AI involves more than just creating text. It can involve systems that generate images, music, video and other types of data [2, 4]. LLMs are a subset of generative AI with a specific focus on language [1, 7].

Generative AI includes such models as Generative Adversarial Networks (GANs), which are used for image generation in particular; and Variational Autoencoders (VAEs) that can fabricate information with certain attributes [18, 19]. The distinction lies in the type of data they generate: LLMs concentrate on text while other generative models might work with different media types [20, 21].

1.7 The Impact and Future of LLMs

LLMs of the future hold even greater prospects. When models are made bigger and better, they will start understanding human-like text words more [16, 18]. The results might facilitate what seem more human-like and responsive behavior for AI, fundamentally changing how we talk to machines. Such areas, in addition to the kind of problems discussed by me and colleagues here, reflect important ongoing challenges such as algorithmic bias from training data or ethical concerns around LLMs being misused [22, 23].

Large Language Models, in other words generative AI techniques for text have been the significant contributor behind advancements we see today. Since LLMs use large, real-world datasets as well as traditional predictive methods, they are able to produce fluid and relevant text with regard to context [16, 18]. With the maturation of these models, we are going to see them being applied in many more ways and disrupting the interaction that humans have with AI [5, 7].

Generative AI is one of the latest incarnations of artificial intelligence; it presents us with new strategies to automate data creation in many different domains, such as text, images, and music [2, 4]. The ever-evolving technology aims to revolutionize industries and workflows, offering a plethora of benefits. However, doing so also brings with its problems and risks that must be managed carefully [7, 23].

1.8 Benefits of Generative AI

a. Productivity Enhancement

Utilizing and creating reports, designs or even artistic works, with the help of AI software can significantly raise productivity. The introduction of the possibility of automating different aspects of work through this process will result in the saving of time and effort, and therefore humans can direct their concentration towards high-level and strategic tasks which require judgement and decision making [5, 7]. For instance, in industries like in the marketing and media sector, generative AI can quickly create personalized content for many different audience groups because of its versatility, so that, in turn, the creative department can concentrate on developing strategies and concepts [1, 14].

b. Complex Data Analysis

Generative AI's adroitness and correctness have outrun the old methods in different applications. In recommender systems, for example, generative models can give more proper and personalized suggestions to users by getting to know better user preferences and behaviors. More engagement and pleasure are frequently the results, as well as better user experiences. Furthermore, the application of generative AI in the fields of engineering and design may produce very realistic simulations and prototypes, saving time and money on iterative testing and development [5, 14].

c. Better Productivity and Precision

Gen AI is better than conventional methods in various tasks, such as recommending products. Generative models, in particular, can make recommendation engines produce more relevant and individual suggestions based on understanding user interests, needs and mapping them by characteristics. This whole process enhances the user experience and also has a positive effect on engagement and satisfaction. This results in a more involved and fulfilled user base [5, 14]. By reducing the time and resources needed to build iterative models and concepts, generative AI has made it possible to generate extremely realistic prototypes (whether you're making products or running simulations). For this reason, using generative AI to the design process greatly increases both efficacy and efficiency [5, 16].

d. Cost Savings

Customer service, advertising, journalism are some of the fields where content generation is an added benefit from the use of Gen AI. While artists and designers are free to focus on their creative side without feeling pressured to accomplish anything quickly, AI systems can produce this material in mass on their own, respond to simple questions, and create content that can be further developed thereby cutting down of the resources and the associated costs.

e. Innovation and Creativity

Artificial intelligence is known to be innovative through creativity. It can create art, music, and literature, which are new perspectives and new ideas that are not brought out by other directions [16, 20]. This capability serves as the creative engine behind these technologies, making problem-solving a straightforward process when AI models are developed to propose visionary solutions through designs such as drawing, 3D models, and simulation. For example, generative design in architecture and engineering can determine the optimal solution in this huge space of design possibilities, by considering parameters like material, aesthetics, and structural properties.

1.9 Risks of Generative AI

a. Data Privacy Issues
Training generative AI models on large datasets raises significant data privacy concerns. The datasets often include personal data, and users may not be fully aware of how their data is used. A lack of transparency can lead to the misuse of personal data and raise both ethical and legal issues. For example, aggregation and anonymization techniques used to protect data are often inadequate; re-identification of individuals from anonymized datasets has been successfully demonstrated in several studies [9].

b. Deep fakes and Misinformation
Generative AI technologies can create highly realistic content, including deep fake videos, which pose substantial risks. Deep fakes manipulate video or audio to produce convincing but synthetic versions of real people. This technology can be exploited by malicious actors to spread false information, tarnish reputations, or commit fraud [21]. The proliferation of deep fakes can erode trust in digital media and impact public perception and security.

c. Toxic Language and Harmful Outputs
Gen AI models, especially NLP ones, can at times produce toxic or harmful content. The biases in the training data or flaws in the model's design can cause such issues. For example, a language model might produce racist, sexist or inappropriate language if it has been trained on biased data. This highlights the importance of curating the training datasets carefully and implementing robust filtering and moderation mechanisms. Also, harmful outputs require ongoing monitoring and refinement of AI models to prevent perpetuation of societal biases and propagation of bad content [12, 13, 21].

d. Prompt Injections and AI Cyberattacks
Hackers can employ generative AI models as part of a cybercrime ploy by using quick injection techniques to cause AI behaviors that produce dangerous outputs or expose private documents. These dangers highlight

how important it is to safeguard AI systems and keep an eye on them at all times. However, because the attackers may modify their attack strategy it is challenging to defend against such attacks [18].

e. Data Leakage

One concern is that generative AI models could expose private data, especially if if they are trained on sensitive datasets. For instance, a trained model built on confidential financial data would result in an output revealing hidden assets, trade secrets or even personal information. Accidental breaches of sensitive data threaten the secrecy with which people entrust their information to AI, and destroy trust in AI systems [7].

1.10 Evaluating Generative AI Models

To use generative AI ethically, models should be evaluated based on the following criteria:

a. Quality

The quality of results matters most, especially with user interfaces. The text that has been produced needs to be coherent and contextually sound; furthermore, it should not have any errors. The image generated also need to have a similarity with the original one but no artifacts or inconsistencies should be present in them. For instance, the language model in a customer service chatbot must create grammatically correct sentences to make them contextually sensible [16].

b. Diversity

A good generative model should generate many outputs that capture different modes in its data distribution. By doing so, the model is protected from bias and is able to handle different types of input. For instance, an NLP model with diverse capabilities can generate texts in multiple languages or dialects while this diversity ensures new and varied results in creative applications [5].

c. Speed

Generative models must provide fast, real-time responses, especially in interactive environments. The efficacy of these models depends on their ability to produce high-quality outputs quickly. For instance, in Virtual Reality (VR), generative AI needs to generate complex scenes without delays to ensure a smooth user experience. Similarly, models used for algorithmic trading must operate in real-time to take advantage of market opportunities [15].

1.11 Technical Challenges and Limitations of Gen AI

Gen AI has made significant strides but it is still constrained by its data-driven algorithm. It is therefore crucial to understand the hurdles to develop practical solutions that solve real-life problems.

1.11.1 Continual Reliance on Data

Nivedhaa N. [24] demonstrates how data is used to create artificial intelligence models and why this leads to a number of complex issues.

a. Data Quality and Quantity:
The datasets used during training greatly affect the effectiveness of AI models since they are forecasting, optimizing and inferring from data. Therefore, high-quality data that comprehensively represents the real world is necessary for creating such a system that provides realistic answers. Besides, the diversity of data should also be considered because having biased or limited examples in training sets results in poor generalization and bad model performance.

b. Data Scarcity:
It is these algorithms, however, that cannot simply be "fed" with raw data even if data powers AI. The data needs to be properly labeled to give it context for AI; this process is called data annotation. This method takes a lot of time and resources, though. Artificial intelligence finds extensive application in medical imaging. However, IBM had to scale back its effort towards automating medical treatment due to the lack of information digitization, complex medical terminologies and language as well as high costs associated with turning unstructured text into semantically annotated data.

1.11.2 Hallucinations

Researcher Hrishitva Patel [26] notes that hallucinations occur when models create fake outputs in various forms, such as faked publications, citations and biography. Large Language Models often show this tendency since they produce and predict text that is statistically correlated with the input they get. As the AI field is evolving at a rapid pace, newer versions of models are frequently released. Consequently, it becomes challenging to reproduce content reliably and casts doubt upon research findings because the same prompts can yield different results over time or even across model versions. Also, ChatGPT models are not connected to the internet or do not have access to current information which poses difficulties in determining what information they generate is authentic enough. In fact, if these models refer to recent developments or events their information may become inaccurate or obsolete due to lack of up-to-date knowledge by which mode like this are characterized.

1.11.3 Lack of Creativity

Gen AI models can skillfully produce an accurate and relevant phrase for the context; however, they cannot match the complexity, novelty, and thoughtfulness that characterize genuine human creativity [25]. For example, Mark A. Runco [27] mentions AI creativity as "pseudo-creativity" to emphasize this distinction in creative capacity. It is fundamentally a matter of repeating terms, structures and patterns from its own training corpus. According to Lingaro [28], these models cannot draw inspiration from events, emotions and abstract concepts such as hope or purposelessness. The most important aspects of AI models are statistical associations and pattern recognition. They do not perform calculations in their minds but simply predict a word or sequence likely to come next based on input or training data unlike humans who would think abstractly or uniquely. This computational approach limits them from generating novel ideas beyond mere estimates of available data. In terms of individuals, artistic creations usually mirror the goals, feelings, and cultural background of the artist. Nevertheless, generative AI models do not have any motivation or sense of context in which they were created because they are not human beings with emotions that encourage creativity which is in turn influenced by experiences and cultural backgrounds. But generative AI models lack context awareness and motivation. They are devoid of feelings, life experiences, and cultural awareness that promotes creativity. For instance, they find it challenging to comprehend and communicate the ideas of irony, sarcasm, and comedy since meaningful answers to these concepts require an awareness of context and culture.

1.11.4 Ethics and Privacy

AI raises serious ethical and security concerns. Saharnaz Dilmaghani *et al.* [29] notes the challenges and risks in maintaining confidentiality and integrity of huge data in AI workflow and defines an adversarial model to secure it. Permissions, data collection, transparency issues, and bias are some of the challenges. So, protecting this data is critical. Privacy is breached when data is not managed well, or when there is risk of unauthorized access and compromised information. The data collected by AI systems can also infringe an individual's right to privacy. Obtaining informed consent for data collection and usage in AI applications is complicated. Since users do not know how their data will be used, shared or stored, it's hard to get their consent. Complexity of AI and opacity of data processing makes this problem worse. Deep learning-based AI systems are often termed as "black boxes," that is, it is difficult to understand and examine their decision-making processes. Because AI lacks transparency, it raises ethical concerns when used in critical industries like healthcare, criminal justice, and finance. It should be ensured that AI systems can convey information to humans in a comprehensible manner, including everything from their data processing methods to the reasoning behind their recommendation of a certain outcome. The potential for abuse of AI technology which includes monitoring, misinformation campaigns, and cyberattacks is one of the primary ethical issues. Misuse of AI should be prevented by creating strong legal and ethical regulations [30]. These systems share the environment with humans and therefore, it becomes essential that they act in a manner that aligns with human principles. If there is a value mismatch, it can cause difficulties in co-operation of autonomous systems and human-machine collaborative systems.

1.12 Real Life Use Case of Gen AI

Unilever's collaboration with Be My Eyes

a. Pre-Collaboration

The consumer goods corporation Unilever has put to aid the visually impaired, for instance, their inability to understand the product information or the cooking instructions written on them. They also noted a lack of options in the real-time support services to help them with product-related questions. Be My Eyes, a specialist in building apps that are accessible, and Unilever worked together to deal with these issues.

b. Post-Collaboration

Unilever and Be My Eyes united to set up an ambitious plan to enable those with visual disabilities to use generative AI for accessibility purposes.

Unilever operates a huge database of product information that the Be My Eyes platform utilized and improved through the integration of AI-powered functionalities.

Following are its implementation details:

i. **Application of Generative AI:**
   Be My Eyes app implemented a complex algorithm developed by Unilever using this technology. This technology was developed to give real-time, detailed product information, such as component lists, descriptions, and usage instructions, based on visual data that users gathered.
ii. **Real-Time Support:**
   The visually impaired individuals can connect to volunteers, customer service or even the Chat GPT-4-powered chatbot who communicate and describe the details or instructions to them. This AI-powered technology boosted these encounters by giving quick and precise product information.

c. Impact

Generative AI can solve real world problems; Unilever reported that the partnership with Be My Eyes had increased accessibility for the visually impaired. Unilever made shopping more accessible by integrating Generative AI into the Be My Eyes app. This AI tech allowed people to get full product details like ingredient lists, cooking instructions and usage guidelines. People could now make their own decisions and not have to ask for help. Additionally, Unilever's program shows the company's broader commitment to social responsibility and using technology to drive inclusivity thereby creating a positive influence. Maybe other companies will follow suit with similar AI based solutions because of this integration and positive feedback, and raise the bar for accessibility in the consumer products space. This program creates a more accessible and fairer market place and improves life for the visually impaired.

1.13 Conclusion

The Gen AI has become an important source of inspiration for modern artificial intelligence. This can be seen in the manner that machines communicate human-like text. Some models that rely on extensive data sets to generate meaningful, cohesive and diverse responses include OpenAI's GPT series, Google's LaMDA and PaLM, as well as Meta's LLaMA.

When complicated data set processing is automated it raises production capacity and growing creativity within areas such as fine arts or industrial design.

Though they are promising, generative AI systems also have a lot of drawbacks and challenges. The importance of having an abundance of quality data raises further concerns about privacy issues related to data and the ethical use of personal information. Additionally, these models still lack true originality or understanding of context as they evolve; thus, a constant need for improvement against the danger of producing deceitful or dangerous content such as deep fakes arises. Moreover; scarcity in certain types of data, hallucinations and ethical implications surrounding AI decisions indicate the importance of maintaining transparency and ensuring responsible use.

The sheer practicality of generative artificial intelligence is shown by Unilever's collaboration with Be My Eyes to show how it may enhance inclusion and accessibility. This partnership manifested a commitment towards the social responsibility as well as making shopping easy for visually impaired people. These kinds of creations indicate that generative AI can solve real-time issues and lead to further developments if used judiciously.

In conclusion, while there exist huge opportunities for growth in different areas due to Gen AI, there are also associated risks and limitations that should be put into consideration. On that note, the potentiality of generative AI should be maximized for the benefit of humanity although its unfavorable effects can still be reduced through constant research, ethical behavior as well as careful implementation.

AI disclosure statement: The author acknowledges the use of AI-based tools for minor language editing or grammatical correction. However, all intellectual contributions, analyses, and conclusions presented in this chapter are entirely the author's own.

References

1. Wang, X. and Zhang, L., Introduction to Generative AI, in: *Advances in Artificial Intelligence*, pp. 1–20, Springer, 2024, https://doi.org/10.1007/979-8-8688-0403-8_1.
2. Hsu, L. and Kuo, Y.-H., The impact of Generative AI on Supply Chain Management: A framework and research agenda. *J. Supply Chain Manage.*, 29, 2, 245–262, 2023, https://doi.org/10.1007/s12525-023-00680-1.

3. Vaswani, A., Shazeer, N., Parmar, N., Uszkoreit, J., Jones, L., Gomez, A.N., Kaiser, Ł., Polosukhin, I., Attention is All You Need. *Proceedings of the 31st Conference on Neural Information Processing Systems (NeurIPS)*, 2017, Retrieved from https://arxiv.org/abs/1706.03762.
4. Bengio, Y., Courville, A., Vincent, P., Representation Learning: A Review and New Perspectives. *IEEE Trans. Pattern Anal. Mach. Intell. (PAMI)*, 35, 8, 1798–1828, 2013, Retrieved from https://arxiv.org/abs/1206.5538.
5. Hacker, P., Engel, A., Mauer, M., Regulating ChatGPT and Other Large Generative AI Models. *FAccT '23: Proceedings of the 2023 ACM Conference on Fairness, Accountability, and Transparency*, Association for Computing Machinery, pp. 1112–1123, 2023, https://doi.org/10.1145/3593013.3594067.
6. Kingma, D.P. and Welling, M., Auto-Encoding Variational Bayes. *Proceedings of the 2nd International Conference on Learning Representations (ICLR)*, 2013, Retrieved from https://arxiv.org/abs/1312.6114.
7. Goodfellow, I., Pouget-Abadie, J., Mirza, M., Xu, B., Warde-Farley, D., Ozair, S., Bengio, Y., Generative Adversarial Networks. *Proceedings of the 2014 Conference on Neural Information Processing Systems (NIPS)*, 2014, Retrieved from https://arxiv.org/abs/1406.2661.
8. Radford, A., Narasimhan, K., Salimans, T., Sutskever, I., Improving Language Understanding by Generative Pre-Training, OpenAI, 2018, Retrieved from https://www.openai.com/research/generative-pre-training.
9. Banh, L. and Strobel, G., Generative artificial intelligence. *Electron. Mark.*, 33, 2023, 10.1007/s12525-023-00680-1.
10. Cao, Y., Li, S., Liu, Y., Yan, Z., Dai, Y., Yu, P.S., Sun, L., A Comprehensive Survey of AI-Generated Content (AIGC): A History of Generative AI from GAN to ChatGPT, arXiv, 2023, https://doi.org/10.48550/arXiv.2303.04226.
11. Al-Amin, *et al.*, History of Generative Artificial Intelligence (AI) Chatbots: Past, Present, and Future Development, arXiv, 2024, https://doi.org/10.48550/arXiv.2402.05122.
12. Ploennigs, J. and Berger, M., Generative AI and the History of Architecture, in: *Decoding Cultural Heritage*, F. Moral-Andrés, E. Merino-Gómez, P. Reviriego (Eds.), pp. 23–45, Springer, Cham, 2024, https://doi.org/10.1007/978-3-031-57675-1_2.
13. Dasgupta, D., Venugopal, D., Gupta, K.D., A Review of Generative AI from Historical Perspectives, TechRxiv, 2023, https://doi.org/10.36227/techrxiv.22097942.v1.
14. LeCun, Y., Bengio, Y., Hinton, G., Deep Learning: A Technical Review. *IEEE Trans. Neural Netw. Learn. Syst.*, 2015. Retrieved from https://ieeexplore.ieee.org/document/7384372.
15. Bommasani, R., Hudson, D.A., Adolphs, S., M.A., On the Opportunities and Risks of Foundation Models, arXiv preprint arXiv:2108.07258, 2021, Retrieved from https://arxiv.org/abs/2108.07258.

16. Brown, T.B. and Karras, T., Scaling Laws for Neural Language Models. *Proceedings of the 35th Conference on Neural Information Processing Systems (NeurIPS)*, 2022, Retrieved from https://arxiv.org/abs/2203.08952.
17. Sohl-Dickstein, J., Weiss, E., Maheswaranathan, N., Ganguli, S., Diffusion Models for Generative AI, 2015, Retrieved from https://arxiv.org/abs/2006.14884.
18. Goodfellow, I., Pouget-Abadie, J., Mirza, M., Xu, B., Warde-Farley, D., Ozair, S., Bengio, Y., Generative Adversarial Networks: A Review. *ACM Comput. Surv.*, 2016. Retrieved from https://dl.acm.org/doi/10.1145/3068300.
19. Vaswani, A., Shazeer, N., Parmar, N., Uszkoreit, J., Jones, L., Gomez, A.N., Kaiser, Ł., Polosukhin, I., Attention Is All You Need: The Transformer Model, 2017, Retrieved from https://arxiv.org/abs/1706.03762.
20. Chesney, B. and Citron, D.K., Deep Fakes: A Looming Challenge for Privacy, Democracy, and National Security. *Calif. Law Rev.*, 107, 6, 1753–1799, 2019, Retrieved from https://www.jstor.org/stable/26720671.
21. Li, H. and Zhang, Z., Generative Neural Radiance Fields for Scene Synthesis and Augmentation. *Proceedings of the IEEE/CVF Conference on Computer Vision and Pattern Recognition (CVPR)*, 2021, Retrieved from https://arxiv.org/abs/2104.07308.
22. Ooi, K.-B. *et al.*, The Potential of Generative Artificial Intelligence Across Disciplines: Perspectives and Future Directions. *J. Comput. Inf. Syst.*, 2023, https://doi.org/10.1080/08874417.2023.2261010.
23. Nivedhaa, N., A Comprehensive Review of AI's Dependence on Data. *Int. J. Artif. Intell. Data Sci. (IJADS)*, 2024, 10.13140/RG.2.2.27033.63840.
24. Patel, H., Bane and boon of hallucinations in context of generative AI, 2024, 10.36227/techrxiv.171198062.20183635/v1.
25. Runco, M.A., AI can only produce artificial creativity. *J. Creativity*, 33, 3, 2023, https://doi.org/10.1016/j.yjoc.2023.100063.
26. The Limitations of Generative AI, According to Generative AI, Lingaro Group, https://lingarogroup.com/blog/the-limitations-of-generative-ai-according-to-generative-ai.
27. Dilmaghani, S., Brust, M.R., Danoy, G., Cassagnes, N., Pecero, J., Bouvry, P., Privacy and Security of Big Data in AI Systems: A Research and Standards Perspective. *2019 IEEE International Conference on Big Data (Big Data)*, pp. 5737–5743, 2019, doi: 10.1109/BigData47090.2019.9006283.
28. Shachar, A., Introduction to Algogens, arXiv:2403.01426, 2023, https://doi.org/10.48550/arXiv.2403.01426.
29. Ray, P.P., ChatGPT: A comprehensive review on background, applications, key challenges, bias, ethics, limitations and future scope. *Internet Things Cyber-Phys. Syst.*, 3, 121–154, 2023, https://doi.org/10.1016/j.iotcps.2023.04.003.
30. Mishra, S., Exploring the Transformative Potential and Generative AI's Multifaceted Impact on Diverse Sectors, in: *Exploring the Ethical Implications of Generative AI*, 2024.

2

Generative Adversarial Networks (GANs)

Ankur Chaudhary*, Ritesh Rastogi, Aditee Mattoo, Punit Kumar, Tanvi Kumari and Devansh Dubey

Noida Institute of Engineering & Technology, Greater Noida, India

Abstract

Generative Adversarial Networks (GANs) have emerged as a revolutionary paradigm within the realms of machine learning and artificial intelligence, offering a fresh perspective on generative modelling. Originating from the collaborative efforts of Ian Goodfellow and his peers in 2014, GANs have demonstrated transformative potential across a multitude of domains.

In essence, GANs feature a dynamic interplay between two neural networks: the generator and discriminator. Engaged in a competitive interplay, the generator strives to produce synthetic data that mirrors the authenticity of real data, whereas the discriminator works to distinguish between authentic and generated data. This adversarial training process propels both networks to continuously refine their capabilities and establish a dynamic equilibrium.

The efficacy of GANs stems from their ability to comprehend and reproduce the intricate patterns inherent in complex datasets. This proficiency has profound applications in image generation, where GANs have shown unparalleled skills in crafting realistic, high-resolution images, such as the generation of lifelike faces, landscapes, and artworks, underscore the aesthetic potential of GANs, transcending the limitations associated with traditional generative models.

Beyond the realm of visual artistry, GANs have proven invaluable in addressing challenges related to limited datasets through data augmentation. By generating synthetic samples mirroring the distribution of real data, GANs enhance the robustness and generalization of machine learning models. In turn, this

**Corresponding author*: ankurchaudhary849@gmail.com; ORCID: https://orcid.org/0000-0002-8756-9157

Aditee Mattoo: ORCID: https://orcid.org/0000-0002-5978-5741

Punit Kumar: ORCID: https://orcid.org/0009-0007-6226-9944

N. Gayathri, S. Rakesh Kumar, Ramesh Chandran, Pethuru Raj Chelliah and Danilo Pelusi (eds.) Generative AI: Disruptive Technologies for Innovative Applications, (29–56) © 2025 Scrivener Publishing LLC

augmentation plays a pivotal role in mitigating issues such as overfitting and significantly elevating the performance of models across diverse tasks, ranging from image classification to natural language processing.

In the context of unsupervised learning, GANs excel at capturing the latent features of data without relying on explicit labels. The generator's learned latent space encapsulates the underlying structure of the input data, enabling applications such as style transfer, in which the essence of one image is transposed onto another. This versatility extends across various domains including fashion, architecture, and design, highlighting GANs as potent tools for fostering creativity.

Despite their remarkable achievements, GANs encounter challenges, such as mode collapse, training instability, and ethical considerations. Mode collapse occurs when the generator produces a limited set of outputs, compromising the diversity of the generated samples. Addressing training instability requires meticulous fine-tuning to maintain a delicate balance between the generator and the discriminator. Ethical concerns, notably regarding potential misuse in the deepfake generation and other deceptive practices, underscore the necessity for ethical guidelines governing GAN deployment.

The evolution of GANs involves advancements in conditional generation, allowing data synthesis based on specific attributes or constraints. This paves the way for personalized content creation, targeted image synthesis, and enhanced data manipulation. Ongoing research endeavors are dedicated to overcoming existing challenges, contributing to the maturation of GANs into more robust, reliable, and ethically sound technologies.

Generative Adversarial Networks epitomizes the ingenuity of contemporary machine learning. Their capacity to generate realistic data coupled with applications in data augmentation, unsupervised learning, and creative domains positions GANs at the forefront of AI innovation. As research and development progresses, GANs hold the promise of reshaping the landscape of generative modelling, unlocking new possibilities, and pushing the boundaries of what machines can create.

***Keywords*:** Generative adversarial networks, unsupervised learning, machine learning, Artificial Intelligence

2.1 Introduction

In recent years, breakthroughs have been made in artificial intelligence (AI), especially in the field of machine learning. Supervised learning is a fundamental technique that allows computers to learn the relationships between input and output instances by using prolonged training on labeled data. Although AI has advanced significantly owing to supervised learning, its scalability and adaptability to new situations are limited by its intrinsic reliance on massive datasets and intensive human supervision [1, 2].

The investigation of unsupervised learning strategies has become a viable approach for overcoming these restrictions. Unsupervised learning uses data to find latent structures and patterns without the assistance of labeled instances. Because they can produce fresh data samples that closely mimic data distributions in the actual world, generative models have attracted significant attention in this field. Generative Adversarial Networks (GANs), a ground-breaking framework that was unveiled in 2014 and has completely changed the AI landscape, are at the forefront of generative modeling [3].

With GANs, a revolutionary paradigm, two neural networks compete strategically: the discriminator and the generator. The discriminator looks for differences between actual and fake data, whereas the generator tries to generate realistic data samples. GANs have proven their unmatched ability to produce high-quality data through adversarial processes in a variety of fields, including computer vision, natural language processing, and time series data [4].

Time-series data pose distinct problems and potential for GANs, as they consist of vector sequences that are contingent on time. GANs have become powerful tools in the fight against problems, such as data scarcity, missing or damaged data, and data security. In contrast, full-length data sequences cannot be produced using conventional autoregressive models despite their effectiveness in forecasting singular values. This indicates a significant change in the methodology for time-series synthesis [5].

In this chapter, we begin a thorough investigation of the use of Generative Adversarial Networks for the creation of time-series data. We explore the fundamental ideas behind GANs, revealing their adversarial structures and the complex relationships between discriminator and generator networks. Expanding on this basis, we investigate the role of GANs in tackling important issues in the context of time-series data, ranging from denoising and data protection to augmentation and imputation.

In addition, we compare GANs to conventional autoregressive models, explaining the development of time-series synthesis and the revolutionary effect of GANs in this field. We review various generative techniques, such as GANs and autoencoders, highlighting the benefits of the latter in producing high-quality data. However, we also face problems that GANs face, such as assessment measures and model instability, which require coordinated research and development.

We aim to provide a comprehensive understanding of time-series GANs by examining their applications, architectures, and data synthesis advancements through rigorous analysis and classification. Our research also showcases the efficacy of various time-series GAN configurations through experimental results, thereby paving the way for continued progress in this developing field. As pioneers in the exploration of Generative Adversarial Networks and their implications for time-series data generation, we are on the cusp of unlocking the transformative potential of GANs to revolutionize artificial intelligence and usher in an era of unprecedented creativity and innovation.

2.2 Tale of Two Minds: Unveiling the GAN Mechanism

2.2.1 Origins

The notion of neural networks playing a zero-sum game was first presented by Schmidhuber in 1991, when Generative Adversarial Networks (GANs) originated. This ground-breaking concept establishes a framework for a completely new generative modeling method. Two neural networks, the discriminator and generator, play an adversarial game under Schmidhuber's paradigm, with the goal of outperforming the other.

The applications of GAN technology have expanded as it has developed, demonstrating its adaptability and influence in a variety of fields. GANs have consistently pushed the limits of generative modeling, from picture improvement to fine arts and even game reproduction. GANs are the result of a novel combination of neural networks and adversarial game theory, which produced a potent framework for generative modeling that continues to influence the field of artificial intelligence.

2.2.2 Foundational Concepts of Generative Adversarial Network

The origins of Generative Adversarial Networks (GANs) reveal the dynamic interaction between discriminator and generator neural network models. With learnable parameters θ_G, the generator function, represented as $G(z;\theta_G)$, receives input noise z from a previous distribution $p(z)$. The discriminator function $D(x;\theta_D)$ with parameters θ_D on the other hand, seeks to determine the likelihood that the input x is authentic or fraudulent as shown in Figure 2.1.

The genuine data distribution is represented by $p_{\text{data}}(x)$ in this case. While the discriminator tries to increase its ability to differentiate real from fake samples ($\log D(x)$), the generator tries to decrease the likelihood

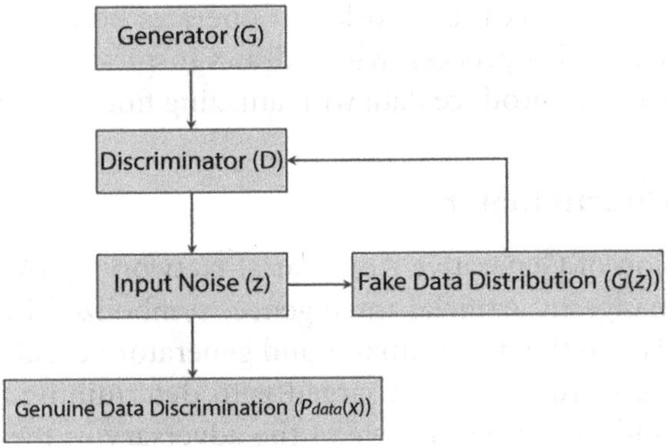

Figure 2.1 Flowchart of the foundational concept of GANs.

that the discriminator properly identifies produced samples as fake $\log(1 - D(G(z)))$.

In this adversarial game, the discriminator aims to correctly distinguish between produced and actual samples, while the generator attempts to convert input noise z from a previous distribution into realistic samples.

There are several alternative ways to formulate the cost function $J(G)$ for the generator and $J(D)$ for the discriminator. The negative log-likelihood of the discriminator's true vs. fake labels given the input is represented by $J(D)$ in the original formulation. The minimax GAN (M-GAN) method sets $J(G) = -J(D)$ for the generator, which results in a simple minimax game analysis [7].

The objective of the training procedure is to locate a local Nash equilibrium, where, under the assumption that the other player's parameters stay unchanged, neither player can further lower its cost. It is a common practice to use gradient-based optimization to repeatedly reduce the cost of each player in relation to its parameters.

Although the core concepts of GANs are simple, they generate remarkably lifelike samples without explicit density function approximations. The effectiveness of the framework is derived from its capacity to represent the underlying data distribution directly, thereby reducing the sources of approximation errors present in other generative modeling approaches.

Specific guidance for GANs is rapidly growing as a study subject, reflecting the ongoing growth and improvement of GAN approaches over time. The fundamental idea of GANs is to provide a dynamic adversarial process controlled by a minimax framework that operates between the generator and discriminator. This process, which draws inspiration from game theory, enables GANs to produce data with amazing fidelity and realism.

2.2.3 The Discriminator

The introduction of Generative Adversarial Networks (GANs) represents a paradigm change in artificial intelligence, symbolized by the complex interaction between the discriminator and generator neural networks. The discriminator, a sturdy sentinel charged with determining the validity of data samples and assuming the role of the adversary in the GAN ecosystem, is at the center of this revolutionary design. The discriminator acts as the watchful gatekeeper in the GAN architecture, carefully examining the data samples to ensure the accuracy of the outputs that are produced. Its mathematical foundations, as outlined by the minimax objective function, highlight its critical significance in propelling the adversarial learning process, which is at the heart of the creative power of GANs. Using theoretical analysis and empirical updating, the function of the discriminator clarifies the origins and development of GANs, shedding light on the complex dynamics underlying their mechanism. A dynamic equilibrium is produced by the generator and discriminator's adversarial interaction, which is characterized by mutual improvement and iterative refinement. The generator's ability to replicate the complexities of real-world data distributions improved as the discriminator improved [8].

2.2.3.1 Theoretical Understanding

The basic minimax objective function V(D,G), which coordinates the antagonistic dance between discriminator D and generator G, is essential to comprehending the role of the discriminator:

$$\min_{D}\max_{G} V(D,G) = \mathbb{E}_{x\sim p(x)}[\log D(x)] + \mathbb{E}_{z\sim p(z)}[\log (1 - D(G(z)))] \tag{2.1}$$

The goal of the discriminator is to minimize the possibility of misclassification while optimizing its ability to discriminate, as shown in Figure 2.2. Dissecting this formula reveals the discriminator's two goals and its unrelenting search for truth amid a sea of artificial fabrication.

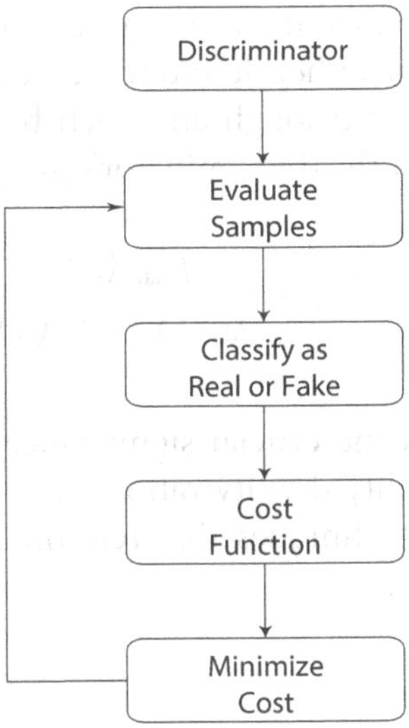

Figure 2.2 Flowchart of the discriminator.

2.2.3.2 *Objectives and Functionality*

Comparing actual data samples x to artificial samples $G(z)$, the discriminator functions as a binary classifier. Its main goal, which is represented by the minimax objective function, is to correctly categorize inputs by giving the produced data a low probability and genuine data a high likelihood.

$$V(D,G) = \mathbb{E}_{x\sim p(x)}[\log D(x)] + \mathbb{E}_{z\sim p(z)}[\log (1 - D(G(z)))] \quad (2.2)$$

The discriminator plays a crucial role in maximizing the logarithm of the probability allocated to the actual data and reducing the logarithm of the probability assigned to the created data, as demonstrated by this equation. The discriminator sharpens its discriminating skills through this antagonistic dialectic, edging closer to the illusive Nash equilibrium when neither player can unilaterally enhance their approach.

2.2.3.3 *Mathematical Formulation*

Mathematically speaking, the discriminator's training program develops like a tactical dance performed to hone its discriminating skills.

The discriminator was trained in one or more epochs to improve its capacity to distinguish between authentic and fraudulent samples. The generator then takes the lead, going through an epoch-based training program to produce samples that test the discriminator's judgment.

$$D^*(x) = \frac{p_{\text{data}}(x)}{p_{\text{data}}(x) + p_g(x)} \tag{2.3}$$

This formula clarifies the crucial significance of the discriminator in determining the probability density ratio, which is a fundamental divergence from traditional techniques that rely on Markov chains or lower bound techniques.

2.2.4 The Generator

With the Development of Generative Adversarial Networks (GANs), artificial intelligence (AI) has entered a new phase marked by a spectacular convergence of creativity and invention. A mysterious generator, a neural network with the ability to create artificial data samples that reflect the complexities of reality, is at the center of this ground-breaking design.

2.2.4.1 The Generator's Objective and Mathematical Formulation

The fundamental goal of the generator is to replicate the distribution of the underlying data as closely as possible to provide a smooth transition between the actual and artificial data domains. The function of the generator can be mathematically summarized using probability distributions. The Generator is designed to approximate the genuine data distribution $p_{\text{data}}(x)$, given a latent vector z taken from a predetermined prior distribution $p_z(z)$. This allows the generator to orchestrate the synthesis of data samples that blend with real-world observations [9].

This transformation process is contained in the domain of a minimax optimization framework, which is representative of the antagonistic interactions observed in GANs. The optimization goal of the generator is deeply entangled with the dynamics of adversarial competition (as shown in Figure 2.3), which requires it to traverse a complex terrain of creative ability.

The Generator's primary goal is to reduce the log chance that the Discriminator will properly identify the generated data as

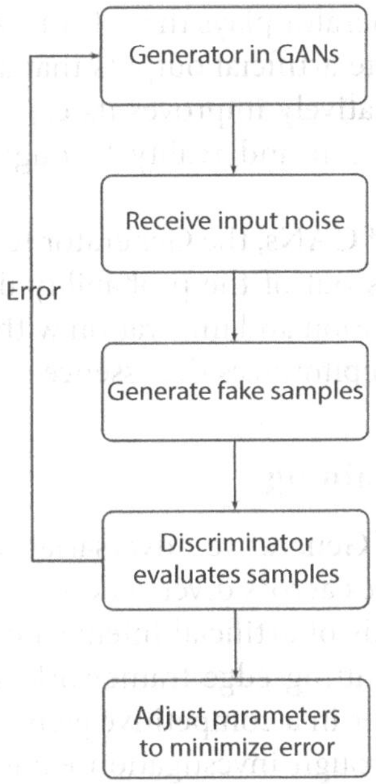

Figure 2.3 Flowchart of the generator.

fraudulent $(D(G(z)))$. The following optimization statement effectively captures this goal:

$$\min_{G}\max_{D} f(D,G) = \mathbb{E}_{z\sim p_z(z)}[\log(1 - D(G(z)))] \tag{2.4}$$

In this case, G stands for the Generator function, D for the Discriminator function, and $f(D,G)$ for the Generator's loss function, which is closely linked to the Discriminator's output. Drawn from the previous distribution $p_z(z)$, the latent vector z provides the creative energy that enables the Generator to weave complex data representations.

2.2.4.2 *Creative Dynamics of the Generator*

The fundamental ability of the generator to access the latent dynamics stored in the latent space and follow various paths to reveal new data representations is essential for its operation. Because of its intrinsic adaptability, the generator can investigate a wide range of data distribution modalities, which promotes the creation of rich and diverse synthetic samples.

Furthermore, the Generator plays the role of a skilled illusionist, always improving its art to create artificial outputs that are very similar to actual data. The Generator iteratively improves its capacity to produce artifacts that conflate the simulation and reality through the complex dance of adversarial learning.

Within the dialectic of GANs, the Generator functions as a prototypical artist, sculpting fantasies out of the probability distributions. It signals a new age of artificial invention and innovation with adversarial conflict and iterative refining, which epitomizes the essence of generative brilliance.

2.2.5 Adversarial Training

The Amazing capacity of Generative Adversarial Networks (GANs) to produce realistic data samples across diverse domains has attracted considerable attention in the fields of artificial intelligence and machine learning. Adversarial training, a cutting-edge framework that sets two neural networks against one another in a competitive game, is the fundamental idea behind GANs. This thorough investigation explored foundational ideas, training dynamics, applications, difficulties, and potential future developments of adversarial training in GANs.

2.2.5.1 Fundamental Principles of Adversarial Training

In GANs, adversarial training entails training a discriminator and generator neural network simultaneously. While the discriminator network learns to distinguish between actual and false samples, the generator network is charged by creating synthetic data samples that closely resemble the real data. A minimax game might be used to describe the training process, in which the discriminator's goal is to correctly distinguish between genuine and false data, whereas the generator's goal is to trick it by producing increasingly realistic examples. Both networks participate in an ongoing tug-of-war with the aim of surpassing the other through iterative training [10].

2.2.5.2 Training Dynamics in Adversarial Training

A fine balance between the discriminator and generator networks characterizes the training dynamics of GANs. First, the discriminator works easily because the generator generates random noise. However, as the training progresses, the generator picks up the ability to produce more realistic samples, which makes it harder for the discriminator to distinguish between genuine and false data, as shown in Figure 2.4. For GANs

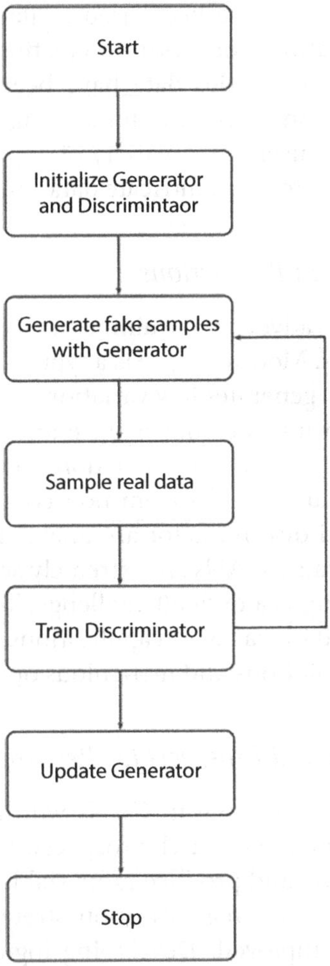

Figure 2.4 Flowchart of adversarial training.

to be successfully trained, a dynamic equilibrium must exist between the generator and discriminator networks. However, striking this balance is frequently difficult and can result in problems such as nonconvergence, training instability, and mode collapse.

2.2.5.3 Adversarial Training Application

Generative modeling has been revolutionized by the extensive use of adversarial training in several fields. GANs have been applied in image creation, style transfer, super-resolution, and picture inpainting applications in computer vision. GANs have been used in natural language processing for language translation, conversation creation, and text production. Additionally, artificial time-series data have been created via adversarial training for applications including forecasting, modeling, and anomaly detection. GANs are useful in a variety of applications owing to their adaptability and capacity to learn intricate data distributions.

2.2.5.4 Difficulties and Restrictions

Despite its effectiveness, adversarial training in GANs presents several difficulties and restrictions. Mode collapse is a typical problem in GAN training, when the generator generates low variations in the produced samples. Training instability can impede convergence and provide less than ideal outcomes. It often takes the form of oscillations in the training loss or gradients. Poor sample quality results from non-convergence, which occurs when the generator and discriminator are unable to reach stable equilibrium. Furthermore, because GANs are extremely sensitive to hyperparameters, optimizing training is a difficult challenge. To guarantee that GANs are trained and deployed in real-world applications, addressing these problems requires creative solutions and meticulous optimization.

2.2.5.5 Future Paths and Prospects for Research

In the future, adversarial training in GANs will have various intriguing avenues for advancement and research prospects. To reduce the difficulties involved in GAN training and produce more stable and dependable models, new training algorithms, regularization strategies, and architectural advancements can be employed. Developing logical answers to current problems requires investigating the theoretical foundations of adversarial training and comprehending the dynamics of GAN optimization. Furthermore, there is much promise for fostering creativity and solving pressing issues by expanding the use of GANs in new fields and multidisciplinary applications. As a fundamental method in Generative Adversarial Networks, adversarial training allows the creation of realistic data samples in various fields [11]. GANs have revolutionized generative modeling and produced substantial advancements in a number of domains, including computer vision, natural language processing, and time series analysis, by utilizing the strength of adversarial learning. Ongoing research is necessary to address issues such as mode collapse, training instability, and non-convergence; however, these problems still exist. By tackling these obstacles and venturing into uncharted territory in GAN research, we can fully realize the possibilities of adversarial training and open the door to creative uses and breakthroughs in artificial intelligence.

2.3 From Brushstrokes to Breakthroughs: Diverse Canvas of GAN Applications

Based on game theory, generative adversarial networks (GANs) have become a new paradigm in machine learning. A dynamic framework for producing data that emulates real-world distribution features without explicit density function representation is created by the interaction of two neural network models: discriminator and generator. This chapter delves into the diverse range of applications that GANs have across several disciplines, examining how they overcome conventional limitations and open up new possibilities. GANs redefine the limits of creativity and innovation in artificial intelligence, from the mastery of aesthetics to data augmentation and unsupervised learning.

2.3.1 Dreaming Up New Worlds: Aesthetic Mastery

A new age of artistic creativity has been brought about by Generative Adversarial Networks (GANs), which allow designers and artists to push the frontiers of aesthetic expertise and imagine new worlds. GANs are highly effective at recognizing complex patterns and styles found in real-world data through adversarial training, which makes it easier to create visually appealing materials for a variety of media.

2.3.1.1 Mastery of Aesthetics Using GANs

The fundamental function of GANs is to reproduce the intricate distribution of creative styles found in training data. Through training as a game between a discriminator and generator, GANs repeatedly improve their capacity to generate realistic results. The boundaries between fact and imagination are blurred by this antagonistic training process, which encourages the creation of artwork that ranges from abstract compositions to lifelike landscapes. From a mathematical perspective, GANs seek to reduce the difference between the generated and real data distributions, as indicated by the adversarial loss function.

$$\min_{G}\max_{D} V(D,G) = \mathbb{E}_{x\sim p_{\text{data}}(x)}[\log D(x)] + \mathbb{E}_{z\sim p_z(z)}[\log(1 - D(G(z)))] \tag{2.5}$$

2.3.1.2 Improving Realism

One-Sided Label Smoothing and Feature matching techniques such as feature matching and one-sided label smoothing are used to increase the realism of the resulting art. By reducing the discrepancy between the predicted properties of the produced and real data, feature matching encourages the generator to create outputs that are consistent with the statistical characteristics of the genuine samples. By substituting smoothed values for positive classification objectives, one-sided label smoothing reduces the susceptibility of neural networks to adversarial cases and encourages a more sophisticated discriminator training method.

$$|| E_{x\sim p_{\text{data}}} f(x) - E_{z\sim p_z(z)} f(G(z)) ||_2^2 \tag{2.6}$$

2.3.2 Data Augmentation

In machine learning, a large and varied pool of training data is essential to ensure the effectiveness of the model. Using the data augmentation approach, GANs provide a potent solution to the problem of data scarcity. GANs increase the size of the training dataset and improve the resilience and generalization abilities of machine-learning models by producing synthetic samples that closely mimic actual data [12].

2.3.2.1 GAN-Based Enrichment of Data

In GAN-based data augmentation, artificial samples are created using a generator network, which is taught to generate data that is consistent with the distribution of actual samples. The training data are enhanced by this supplemented dataset, which exposes the model to a wider variety of events and variations. To improve the model performance, GAN-based data augmentation mathematically seeks to reduce the difference between the distributions of the generated and real data [12].

$$\min_{G}\max_{D} V(D,G) = \mathbb{E}_{x\sim p_{\text{data}}(x)}[\log D(x)] + \mathbb{E}_{z\sim p_z(z)}[\log(1 - D(G(z)))] \tag{2.7}$$

2.3.2.2 *Cross-Domain Applications*

Applications of GAN-based data augmentation may be found in many different fields, including medical imaging, natural language processing, and image classification. GANs allow academics to create more precise and dependable models by combining a variety of actual data samples and advancing several academic subjects.

2.3.3 Unsupervised Learning

The training of a model on unlabeled data without explicit direction or supervision is known as unsupervised learning in machine learning. Unsupervised learning algorithms derive patterns and correlations directly from the input data, in contrast to supervised learning, which trains a model on labeled data with predetermined outputs. Clustering is a typical activity, where the algorithm clusters data points that are related based on a measure of similarity. Without prior knowledge of the labels, this can assist in revealing hidden structures or groups within the data. Dimensionality reduction is another activity that entails reducing the number of variables or characteristics in the data while maintaining critical information. Methods such as t-distributed Stochastic Neighbor Embedding (t-SNE) and Principal Component Analysis (PCA) are frequently employed for this purpose.

2.3.3.1 *GANs in Unsupervised Learning*

GANs automatically identify and extract underlying patterns from unannotated data using adversarial training. GANs learn to extract meaningful representations from unprocessed inputs through competitive interaction between the discriminator and the generator. This allows them to be used for tasks, such as data clustering, anomaly detection, and feature learning.

GANs are used in a wide range of unsupervised learning applications, which are advancing artificial intelligence and providing insights into intricate data structures. GANs enable academics and practitioners to push the limits of machine learning and beyond by revealing hidden insights from unlabeled data. GANs have shown themselves to be a revolutionary force in the area of artificial intelligence, capable of creating entirely new worlds and solving enigmas surrounding unsupervised learning. GANs have completely changed the way we view and work with data because of their unmatched capacity to produce synthetic data, reveal hidden patterns, and inspire innovation. We are on the cusp of a new age when artificial intelligence and human brilliance combine to generate discoveries that push the bounds of possibility, as we continue to explore the vast canvas of GAN applications.

Uses in Various Fields: Beyond data augmentation and aesthetics, GANs influence a multitude of fields and applications. In the medical field, GANs are used to synthesize physiological data for research on disease diagnosis and treatment. To aid financial decision making, they generate a financial time series. Because of their extreme adaptability, GANs can be used to forecast soil temperature to identify trends in the stock market.

Prospects for the Future: As we proceed to the next phase of GAN research, several interesting areas invite inquiry. Advances in GAN architectures might further enhance data analysis and synthesis skills when combined with auxiliary techniques such as meta-learning and reinforcement learning. Collaboration between researchers from other fields might result in new discoveries and encourage creativity in the realm of GAN applications [13].

Throughout the range of deep-learning uses, GANs have emerged as ground-breaking instruments for creating new worlds and solving data mysteries. Their unparalleled ability to produce synthetic data, uncover hidden patterns, and push the boundaries of creativity revolutionizes our knowledge of and interactions with information. As we explore the vast spectrum of applications of GANs, we are on the verge of a new age when human brilliance and artificial intelligence will come together to generate discoveries that will redefine possibilities in the area of artificial intelligence.

2.4 Challenges and Ethical Considerations

This clarifies the difficulties associated with training GANs and emphasizes the significance of resolving nonconvergence and instability issues. These difficulties open new avenues for investigation and creativity to improve the efficiency and dependability of GANs for a range of uses. Many difficulties and moral issues arise in the field of Generative Adversarial Networks (GANs), which have a significant influence on their use and implementation. To ensure diversity in the produced outputs, mode collapse—where GANs often create samples centered on only a few representative modes of the data distribution—poses a significant challenge. This problem is worsened by training instability, which is typified by fluctuating model parameters and an inability to reach a stable equilibrium, resulting in unexpected behaviors from the model. This problem is exacerbated by nonconvergence, which results from imbalanced training dynamics between the discriminator and generator, making it more difficult to achieve peak performance. These difficulties not only make GANs less successful, but also give rise to moral questions about the validity and equity of the outputs that are produced. This highlights the vital need for strong assessment metrics and moral frameworks to direct GAN creation and use. To fully realize the promise of GANs and ensure their ethical and responsible deployment across several domains, it is necessary to address these problems.

2.4.1 Mode Collapse

In the field of generative adversarial networks (GANs), mode collapse presents a major challenge: the generator fails to provide meaningful and varied samples, which causes a collapse in the diversity of the produced outputs. This issue occurs when the generator generates samples that are too similar for the discriminator to distinguish them, which leaves the generator unable to increase the coverage of its modes.

Applying batch normalization independently to actual and false minibatches, especially in the discriminator, is a critical tactic to solve mode collapse. Comparing this method to feeding mini-batches with an equal mixture of actual and false samples, significant gains were observed. To counteract mode collapse, batch normalization balances the distribution of instances within each mini-batch [14].

Imagine a situation in which fictitious and authentic batches do not achieve independent normalization. In this instance, mode collapse was visible, as shown in Figure 2.3. The discriminator finds it difficult to discern between several modes that are covered by the generator because every sample is assessed separately. The generator requires direction to improve its mode coverage because it is difficult to distinguish between authentic and fictitious samples.

Moreover, the problem is worsened by the discriminator's lack of batch normalization, which causes the generator to produce noisy instances. The discriminator evaluates each sample independently, making it difficult to identify and reduce this noise efficiently. To handle this problem, separate normalization of noisy actual and fake instances is necessary before feeding them into the discriminator.

This method is invaluable, particularly for models such as SNGAN, which do not have integrated batch normalization. The discriminator can distinguish between genuine and fake instances more successfully by applying independent normalization. This encourages the generator to generate higher quality samples with improved mode coverage.

In conclusion, mode collapse in GANs is greatly aided by the use of batch normalization, especially when combined with the independent normalization of genuine and fake minibatches. This method not only improves the discriminator's capacity to discern between authentic and fraudulent instances, but also offers a significant direction to the generator, promoting better mode coverage and producing a wider range of significant and varied outputs.

Equation for the Penalty Term in DRAGAN Algorithm:

$$\lambda \cdot \mathbb{E}_{x \sim P_{\text{real}}, \delta \sim \mathcal{N}(0, cI)} (\| \nabla_x D_\theta (x + \delta) \|_2 - k)^2 \tag{2.8}$$

Where:

- λ where denotes the penalty coefficient.
- x represents real data points sampled from the real data distribution P_{real}.
- δ represents noise sampled from a normal distribution with mean 0 and covariance cI.
- D_θ denotes the discriminator function parameterized by θ.
- k is a hyperparameter that controls the desired norm of the gradients around the real points.

By limiting the norm of discriminator gradients around actual points, this penalty term, which is used in the Differentiable Augmentation for GANs (DRAGAN) algorithm, helps mitigate the mode collapse issue in GAN training.

2.4.2 Instability During Training

One of the difficulties in training Generative Adversarial Networks (GANs) is the intrinsic instability of the optimization process. This instability results from the nonconvex character of the underlying goal functions, as well as the intricate interactions between the discriminator and generator networks. Here, we examine the main causes of training instability in GANs, and consider possible solutions to these problems [15].

1. **Complexity of the Optimization Landscape:** Navigating the optimization terrain of GANs is intrinsically difficult because of the abundance of saddle points and local minima.

GANs need to identify a saddle point to arrive at an optimal solution, in contrast to standard deep learning frameworks where optimizers seek to converge to a local minimum. The non-convexity of the goal functions adds to this complexity and causes unpredictable behavior during training.

2. **Sensitivity to Initialization:** GANs require a meticulous network parameter setup to converge to a saddle point. During training, random initialization may result in poor convergence or divergence. The necessity for techniques that enable efficient exploration of the optimization landscape has been underscored by recent research, which highlights the significance of starting procedures in achieving stable convergence.
3. **Existence of Equilibrium and Assessment Measures:** The presence of an equilibrium when both the generator and discriminator attain a stable state is a crucial difficulty in GAN training. GAN convergence is difficult to determine because the trained distribution may still differ significantly from the target distribution, even after training seems to have converged. Robust metrics that precisely measure the difference between the target and training distributions are necessary to evaluate convergence.

The Generator (G) in conventional Generative Adversarial Networks (GANs) uses two loss functions.

1. The first loss function, denoted as J_1, is defined as:

$$J_1 = -\Sigma_z\, w \cdot \log D_{LG}(W) \cdot N_z \tag{2.9}$$

This loss function may result in a gradient vanishing issue for the generator in cases where the discriminator (D) can easily discern between authentic and fraudulent samples. Reducing the generator loss for an optimum discriminator is equivalent to reducing the Jensen-Shannon divergence (JSD) between the produced and real picture distributions. In this case, the generator's loss gradient vanishes towards zero, a phenomenon known as vanishing gradients on G, as the JSD approaches $2 \cdot \log 2$. This enables the optimum discriminator to assign a probability of zero to fictitious samples and one to actual samples.

2. The Second loss Function, denoted as J_2, is given by:

$$J_2 = -\Sigma_z H \cdot \log(1 - D_{LG}(W)) \cdot N_{OP} \tag{2.10}$$

The goal of this loss function is to minimize the cross-entropy between the anticipated distribution of the discriminator and the target class. G seeks to enhance this cross-entropy in the GANs, whereas D seeks to limit it. The gradient of G's loss disappears when D rejects the samples generated by G while its confidence is high. One potential workaround for this problem is to use the "-log D" method described in the literature, or to flip the target used to build the cross-entropy cost.

Furthermore, the minimization of G's loss function, denoted as J, is equal to:

$$J = -\Sigma_h \; z \cdot H \cdot \log\,(1 - D_{LG}(W)) \cdot N_{OP} \tag{2.11}$$

During training, unstable gradients result from this formulation's simultaneous minimization of the Kullback-Leibler () divergence and maximization of the JSD. Consequently, the quality of the produced samples is affected when the gradients of G expand quickly, and their variance rises.

2.4.3 Absence of Convergence

Two loss functions are used in the conventional design of Generative Adversarial Networks (GANs), yet these can sometimes cause serious problems during training. A gradient vanishing problem might arise from the initial loss function, \(Ww \log DLG(W)Nz \), especially if the discriminator (D) can distinguish between actual and fictitious samples with ease. As D gets good at this, it basically gives a probability of 0 for bogus samples and a probability of 1 for true samples, which makes the generator's loss gradient go closer to zero. The training process is hampered by this occurrence, which is called vanishing gradients on G [16].

Furthermore, in GANs, the generator wants to enhance the same cross-entropy, while the discriminator aims to lower it. Nevertheless, if the discriminator overestimates its capacity for classification, it may reject the samples produced by the generator, which would cause the gradient of the generator to disappear. Reversing the target label used to build the cross-entropy cost is one possible way to deal with this issue and maybe aid with the gradient disappearing issue.

The paragraph also highlights the wider difficulties and possible problems related to training GANs, concentrating on non-convergence and instability concerns within the framework of the generator's loss function. Among these problems are:

1. **Gradient Vanishing Problem:** When the discriminator is very good at differentiating between real and false samples, gradient vanishing problems may arise due to the previous loss function that the generator utilized. The generator's training may be hampered by this early discriminator learning as the generator's loss function optimization resembles reducing the Jenson-Shannon Divergence (JSD).
2. **Cross-Entropy Optimization:** In GANs, the generator wants to increase the same cross-entropy, while the discriminator seeks to lower it. The discriminator only takes genuine samples when it performs well, which makes the gradient of the generator's loss disappear.

Several strategies have been put out to deal with these issues, such as using the "logD trick" and flipping the target label for the cross-entropy cost. Furthermore, as an important problem impacting sample quality, the instability of the generator's gradient updates—which arises from concurrently optimizing JSD and reducing the KL divergence—is emphasized.

2.5 A Glimpse into the Future: Where GANs Will Lead Us

In recent times, Generative Adversarial Networks (GANs) have become one of the most revolutionary technologies due to its exceptional ability to produce synthetic data and content in a wide range of fields. With their seemingly endless potential, GANs provide the promise of revolutionary advancements in tailored content production, targeted picture synthesis, better data manipulation, conditional generation, and overcoming implementation problems. In this thorough investigation, we examine each of these facets, imagining the future of GANs and the significant influence they will have on several domains as shown in Figure 2.5.

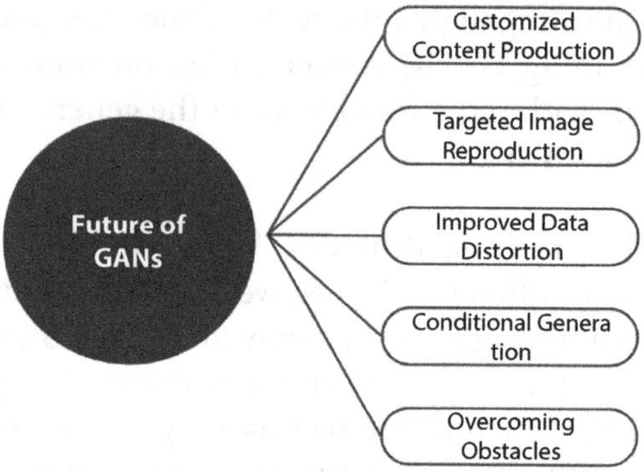

Figure 2.5 Future of GAN's.

2.5.1 Customized Content Production

The amazing potential of Generative Adversarial Networks (GANs) will propel customized content production in the future. These artificial intelligence (AI) driven systems have already shown promise in customizing material across a variety of media, from photos and videos to music and written text, to each user's tastes and preferences. We may anticipate an excess of specific material that speaks to users individually as GAN technology develops, enhancing user experiences and engagement.

Personalized creation of content has considerable promise in domains include healthcare. Healthcare professionals may create synthetic patient records with personalized medical histories, treatment plans, and prognoses by utilizing GANs. By using a more individualized approach to healthcare, physicians may provide more focused treatment options that enhance patient outcomes and maximize the use of available resources. Moreover, GANs can help create immersive virtual experiences, adaptive learning platforms, and individualized educational materials based on the preferences and learning styles of each individual student.

GANs have the potential to completely transform content generation in a variety of industries, including marketing and entertainment. Content producers may enhance user happiness and engagement by delivering tailored experiences that appeal to a variety of audience segments by utilizing the power of GANs [17]. With the help of GANs, content producers may engage with their audience more deeply and build enduring relationships and brand loyalty through customized news articles, product suggestions, and adverts.

2.5.2 Targeted Image Reproduction

Apart from producing customized information, Generative Adversarial Networks (GANs) have unparalleled potential for targeted picture synthesis. This allows users to produce images with certain attributes or traits according to user specifications or inputs. This focused synthesis creates new avenues for problem-solving and creative expression in a variety of fields, including design and manufacturing, healthcare, and entertainment.

GANs have the potential to transform medical imaging and diagnostics by producing synthetic pictures that faithfully depict certain diseases, physiological processes, and anatomical structures. Researchers may get high-fidelity pictures for diagnostic purposes, enabling early detection, precise diagnosis, and customized treatment planning, by training GAN models on big datasets of medical images. Targeted image synthesis can also save healthcare costs, enhance patient outcomes, and expedite medical imaging workflows [18].

GANs are revolutionizing the entertainment sector in ways that go beyond healthcare. One such application is Anime-to-Anime deepfakes, which allows the smooth replacement of one anime character's face with another. By enabling artists to tailor images to their own creative vision, this focused synthesis improves animation and filmmaking's visual effects and narrative. Additionally, GANs may be used for fast prototyping and product visualization in industries like design and manufacturing, allowing designers to effectively explore various design iterations and concepts.

2.5.3 Improved Data Distortion

Generative Adversarial Networks (GANs) have the potential to transform data augmentation and manipulation methods, enabling practitioners and academics to glean insightful information and arrive at well-informed conclusions in a variety of fields. Organizations may overcome the constraints of data scarcity by using GANs to generate synthetic data that closely resembles real-world distributions. This allows for the training of more robust models, which improves performance and generalization [19].

By producing synthetic data for anomaly detection and fraud prevention, GANs can improve data manipulation skills in industries like banking and cybersecurity. Organizations may improve the identification of fraudulent activity and security breaches by using GANs to train more accurate anomaly detection models, which are made possible by synthesizing different and representative datasets. Furthermore, GANs may be used for inventory management and demand forecasting in sectors like retail and e-commerce, helping businesses improve customer happiness and streamline supply chain processes.

2.5.4 Conditional Generation

Conditional generation, in which outputs are created based on user-specified restrictions or particular circumstances, is one of the most interesting potential applications of Generative Adversarial Networks (GANs). With this technique, content production may be done with never-before-seen flexibility and customization [20]. Users can define desired features or characteristics and have material created that precisely matches their needs.

Conditional GANs are revolutionizing picture synthesis by producing images depending on user-defined characteristics like composition, color, or style. This allows artists to realize their ideas with never-before-seen accuracy. Similar to this, conditional GANs in text generation enable the production of written material suited to certain subjects, genres, or target audiences, making it easier to create customized news stories, product descriptions, and advertising copy. Organizations may produce content that connects with their target audience and increases engagement and conversion rates by using conditional generating approaches.

2.5.5 Overcoming Obstacles

Although Generative Adversarial Networks (GANs) have enormous promise, a number of issues and barriers must be resolved before they can be fully utilized in a variety of fields. These difficulties can impair the functionality and performance of GAN models. They include training instability, mode collapse, and a lack of variety in produced samples. Furthermore, ethical issues including prejudice, fairness, and data privacy present serious difficulties that need for careful thought and mitigating measures.

Researchers and practitioners need to collaborate to create creative solutions and best practices for GAN deployment and training to overcome these obstacles. This entails creating strategies to guarantee fairness and transparency in AI-generated material, as well as creating rigorous assessment measures and benchmark datasets for evaluating the performance and generalization capabilities of GAN models.

Moreover, resolving ethical issues and guaranteeing the responsible and ethical application of GAN technology across several areas depend on multidisciplinary collaboration and stakeholder participation. We can fully utilize GANs to generate innovation and good social impact by cultivating an inclusive, transparent, and accountable culture. This will eventually improve results for people, businesses, and society at large [21].

There is a lot of potential for tailored content production, targeted picture synthesis, improved data manipulation, conditional generation, and overcoming implementation hurdles using Generative Adversarial Networks (GANs) in the future. We can open up new avenues for innovation, discovery, and advancement in a variety of fields and domains by fully utilizing GANs and addressing important ethical issues. In the end, this will help to shape a future in which AI-driven technologies will improve and enrich human experience.

2.6 Conclusion: The Revolutionary Impact of Generative Adversarial Networks (GANs)

Generative Adversarial Networks (GANs) are an incredible example of modern machine learning's inventiveness since they can provide realistic data in a wide range of fields like never before. GANs have transformed generative modeling through adversarial training, pushing the envelope of machine creativity and changing the artificial intelligence field. Producing data with exceptional authenticity and realism is made possible by the core concepts of GANs, which are based on a dynamic adversarial process governed by a minimax framework between the discriminator and generator [22]. This adversarial learning process, which draws inspiration from ideas in game theory, propels GANs ongoing development and enhancement, enabling them to more accurately mimic the intricacies of real-world data distributions. As a watchful gatekeeper inside the GAN architecture, the discriminator carefully reviews data samples to guarantee the correctness of the outputs that are produced. Its crucial importance—highlighted by the minimax objective function—drives the adversarial learning process and clarifies the complex dynamics that underpin GANs.

GANs have revolutionary potential, but they are not without problems. Problems like non-convergence, mode collapse, and training instability still exist, necessitating continued study to get past them and reach the full potential of adversarial training. We can create new avenues for creativity and artificial intelligence advancements by taking on these problems and exploring unexplored ground in GAN research.

In summary, GANs are a game-changing force in artificial intelligence, with hitherto unheard-of powers for producing synthetic data, exposing hidden patterns, and spurring creativity. We are at the start of a new era when human brilliance and artificial intelligence will come together to produce discoveries that will push the boundaries of what is possible as we continue to explore the huge canvas of GAN applications.

AI disclosure statement: The author acknowledges the use of AI-based tools for minor language editing or grammatical correction. However, all intellectual contributions, analyses, and conclusions presented in this chapter are entirely the author's own.

References

1. Goodfellow, I., Pouget-Abadie, J., Mirza, M., Xu, B., Warde-Farley, D., Ozair, S., Courville, A., Bengio, Y., Generative Adversarial Networks, 2014.
2. Saxena, D. and Cao, J., Generative Adversarial Networks (GANs): Challenges, Solutions, and Future Directions, 2015.
3. Salimans, T., Goodfellow, I., Zaremba, W., Cheung, V., Radford, A., Chen, X., Improved Techniques for Training GANs, 2016.
4. Chavdarova, T. and Fleuret, F., SGAN: An Alternative Training of Generative Adversarial Networks, 2017.
5. Wang, K., Gou, C., Duan, Y., Lin, Y., Zheng, X., Wang, F.-Y., Generative adversarial networks: introduction and outlook. *IEEE/CAA J. Autom. Sin.*, 4, 4, 588–598, 2017.
6. Kodali, N., Abernethy, J., Hays, J., Kira, Z., On convergence and stability of gans, 2017.
7. Creswell, A., White, T., Dumoulin, V., Arulkumaran, K., Sengupta, B., Bharath, A.A., Generative Adversarial Networks: An Overview, 2018.
8. Alqahtani, H., Kavakli-Thorne, M., Kumar, G., Applications of Generative Adversarial Networks (GANs): An Updated Review. *Int. J. Inf. Manag. Data Insights*, 100004, 2019.
9. Hong, Y., Hwang, U., Yoo, J., Yoon, S., How Generative Adversarial Networks and Their Variants Work: An Overview, 2019.
10. Jenni, S. and Favaro, P., On Stabilizing Generative Adversarial Training with Noise.
11. Kumar, S. and Dhawan, S., A Detailed Study on Generative Adversarial Network, 2020.
12. Chen, H., Challenges and Corresponding Solutions of Generative Adversarial Networks (GANs): A Survey Study. *J. Phys.: Conf. Ser.*, 1827, 1, 012066, 2021.

13. Jabbar, A., Li, X., Omar, B., A Survey on Generative Adversarial Networks: Variants, Applications, and Training. *ACM Comput. Surv. (CSUR)*, 54, 8, 1–49, 2021.
14. Gui, J., Sun, Z., Wen, Y., Tao, D., Ye, J., A Review on Generative Adversarial Networks: Algorithms, Theory, and Applications, 2021.
15. Liu, Z., Yuan, T., Lin, Y., Zeng, B., Recent Advances of Generative Adversarial Network, 2022.
16. Audichya, P., Gupta, D., Singh, A., Generative Adversarial Networks: Models and Techniques - A Review, 2022.
17. Singh, D. and Ahlawat, A., Generative Adversarial Networks, Their Various Types, A Comparative Analysis, and Applications in Different Areas, 2022.
18. Lin, H., Liu, Y., Li, S., Qu, X., How Generative Adversarial Networks Promote the Development of Intelligent Transportation Systems: A Survey. *IEEE/CAA J. Autom. Sin.*, 2023.
19. Krichen, M., Generative Adversarial Networks, 2023.
20. Brophy, E., Wang, Z., She, Q., Ward, T., Generative Adversarial Networks in Time Series: A Systematic Literature Review. *ACM Comput. Surv.*, 55, 10, 1–31, 2023.
21. Lim, W., Yong, K.S.C., Lau, B.T., Tan, C.C.L., Future of generative adversarial networks (GAN) for anomaly detection in network security: A review. *Comput. Secur.*, 13, 9, 103733, 2024.
22. Ghosheh, G.O., Li, J., Zhu, T., A Survey of Generative Adversarial Networks for Synthesizing Structured Electronic Health Records. *ACM Comput. Surv.*, 56, 6, Article 147, 1–34, 2024.

3

Reinforcement Learning in Generative AI

Kanthavel R.[1], Adline Freeda R.[2] and Dhaya R.[1*]

[1]*School of Electrical and Communication Engineering, PNG University of Technology, Lae, Papua New Guinea*
[2]*Dept. of Information Technology, KCG College of Technology, Chennai, India*

Abstract

For the recent generation, generative artificial intelligence (AI) has emerged as a potentially fascinating advancement in modern trends. In a similar period of time, reinforcement learning (RL) has evolved as a promising methodology across various machine learning applications. The machine learning community has long considered deep generative AI as a crucial topic in various applications such as computer vision and text generation. Maximum likelihood estimation (MLE) trains generative models to capture and approximate target data distributions by minimizing divergence between the model and target distributions. This formulation can effectively summarize the objective of generating tasks; however, it neglects some qualities that a generative model should possess according to an end user's expectations. Different aspects of reinforcement learning have contributed to its flexibility to incorporate human bias, such as adversarial learning, hand-designed rules, and learned reward models for building preferment models. Reinforcement learning has become a popular and competitive option in the world of AI. It allows us to inject new training signals and create fresh objectives that take advantage of novel signals. This opens up a whole new realm of possibilities for generative AI in terms of model development and usage. It's important to thoroughly evaluate these advancements and shed some light on the state of the art. This book chapter provides an in-depth exploration of the current state of the art, potential developments, and outstanding problems in generative AI with reinforcement learning. It also discusses different applications for generative AI,

**Corresponding author*: dhayavel2005@gmail.com; ORCID: https://orcid.org/0000-0002-3599-7272
Kanthavel R.: ORCID: https://orcid.org/0000-0001-5537-2571
Adline Freeda R.: ORCID: https://orcid.org/0009-0002-3335-0907

N. Gayathri, S. Rakesh Kumar, Ramesh Chandran, Pethuru Raj Chelliah and Danilo Pelusi (eds.) Generative AI: Disruptive Technologies for Innovative Applications, (57–72) © 2025 Scrivener Publishing LLC

including how to embed desired characteristics, the limitations of current models, and how we can push the boundaries of generative AI.

Keywords: Generative artificial intelligence, reinforcement learning, maximum likelihood estimation, data distribution

3.1 Introduction

Reinforcement learning (RL) is a potent paradigm in machine learning that allows agents to interact with their surroundings and acquire optimal behaviors. Developments in the creation of text, images, and other kinds of data have resulted from its application in generative AI, which has attracted a lot of interest recently. With a focus on its main ideas, approaches, applications, and difficulties, this abstract gives a broad overview of the integration of reinforcement learning in generative artificial intelligence [1].

Two examples of generative AI models that aim to generate fresh data samples similar to a given training dataset are Generative Adversarial Networks (GANs) and Variation Auto-Encoders (VAEs). By framing the generation process as a sequential decision-making problem, RL offers a unique approach to typical training approaches for these models, which rely on supervised learning. Here, an environment (which offers feedback in the form of rewards) interacts with an agent (the generative model) to teach it a policy that maximizes cumulative rewards.

The Markov Decision Process (MDP), a fundamental idea in reinforcement learning, offers a mathematical framework for simulating decision-making in situations with stochastic dynamics. States, actions, rewards, and state transitions make up the MDP. By experimenting with different actions and gathering feedback, which it then uses to adjust its policy, the agent gains experience navigating this environment. Actor-critical approaches, policy gradients, and Q-learning are important RL methodologies. These methods have different benefits with regard to efficiency, stability, and convergence [2].

In the field of text generation, reinforcement learning can optimize models to generate diverse, logical, and contextually relevant content. Reward signals that incorporate relevance and linguistic quality can help RL-trained models outperform conventional supervised models. For instance, OpenAI has refined its GPT models using RL to enhance their text production capabilities. In a similar vein, RL improves GAN performance in image generation. A GAN's discriminator directs the generator to create more realistic images by sending it a reward signal. This adversarial training process benefits from RL's ability to handle high-dimensional, intricate areas.

The uses of RL go beyond creating text and images; they also encompass robotics and gaming. Deep Mind's AlphaGo, which uses reinforcement learning (RL) to beat human go champions, is an example of how RL has shown impressive success in gaming. In robotics, reinforcement learning (RL) helps robots learn difficult tasks by making mistakes and then optimizing their movements to accomplish desired outcomes.

Despite its successes in generative AI, RL faces a number of obstacles. Since reinforcement learning (RL) frequently needs enormous amounts of data and interactions to learn successfully, sample efficiency is a crucial problem. It is also necessary to carefully adjust hyper parameters and algorithms to ensure stability and convergence throughout training. Furthermore, research on how well RL scales to more complicated and varied tasks are still ongoing. As generative models driven by reinforcement learning proliferate, ethical concerns, including guaranteeing equity, openness, and responsibility, become increasingly important [3].

Incorporating reinforcement learning into generative AI is a revolutionary method that expands the potential of generative models into new fields. By utilizing reinforcement learning concepts, generative models can achieve greater performance and inventiveness. However, the responsible and successful application of these cutting-edge AI systems depends on overcoming the inherent difficulties and moral dilemmas. More research into cutting-edge RL methods and their applications is probably in store for the future, opening the door for more advanced and potent generative AI systems.

3.2 Current State of the Art in Generative AI with Reinforcement Learning

Reinforcement learning (RL) and generative artificial intelligence (AI) have come together to create extremely realistic and contextually relevant data across a wide range of fields. This synergy takes advantage of generative models' ability to generate novel data samples and reinforcement learning's ability to optimize sequential decision-making processes. Here, we explore the most recent developments, approaches, and uses of RL-enhanced generative artificial intelligence. Figure 3.1 says about the significant models and methods.

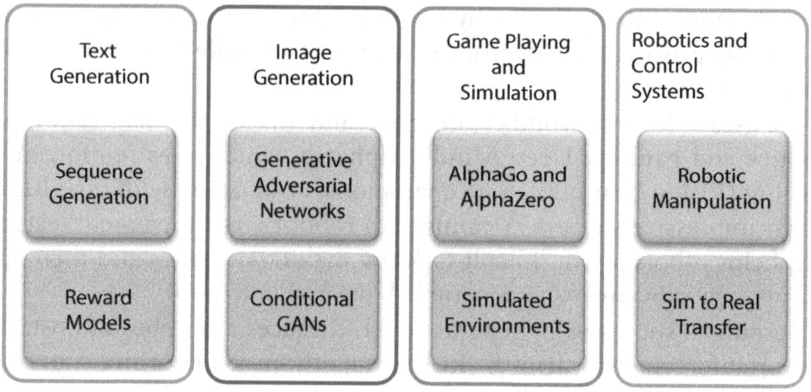

Figure 3.1 Significant models and methods.

Reinforcement Learning for Text Generation

- **Sequence Generation:** Among other applications, RL has optimized language models for conversational agents, machine translation, and text summarization. OpenAI's GPT-3 and its versions use reinforcement learning (RL) to enhance outputs through reward signals that measure coherence, relevance, and fluency [4].
- **Reward Schemas:** Two techniques, Proximal Policy Optimisation (PPO) and Reinforce, optimize reward models that aid in text production. These models evaluate the generated sequences and provide recommendations to improve future outcomes.

Reinforcement Learning for Image Generation

- **Generic Adversarial Networks (GANs):** We have combined RL with GANs to enhance the generator's performance. The discriminator functions as a reward signal in this configuration, assisting the generator in producing more lifelike images. Methods such as self-supervised GANs and Wasserstein GANs with Gradient Penalty (WGAN-GP) employ RL to enhance image quality and stabilize training.
- **Conditional GANs:** By conditioning GANs on specific attributes, RL optimizes the production of images with desired features. Applications such as picture painting, super-resolution, and style transfer widely use this method.

RL in Simulation and Game Playing

- **AlphaGo and AlphaZero:** These two AIs have revolutionized the gaming industry. These systems perform at a superhuman level in games like Go, Chess, and Shogi because they use reinforcement learning (RL) to learn game strategies from scratch. The combination of deep RL algorithms with Monte Carlo Tree Search (MCTS) enables efficient exploration and exploitation of game states.
- In simulated settings, reinforcement learning (RL) is commonly used to teach agents to do tasks that require long-term strategy and planning. These environments supply abundant, high-dimensional data that tests and improves the generative models [5].

Control Systems and Robotics

- Reinforcement learning has made significant progress in robotic manipulation tasks, training robots to interact with environments and objects through trial and error. Methods such as Soft Actor-Critic (SAC) and Deep Deterministic Policy Gradient (DDPG) train robots for complex tasks like assembly, navigation, and object grabbing.
- **Sim-to-Real Transfer:** One of the main areas of concentration should be on closing the gap between simulated and real-world surroundings. Research is currently underway to develop reinforcement learning (RL) algorithms that facilitate the seamless transfer of policies learned in simulations to practical implementations [13].
- Reinforcement learning integration with generative artificial intelligence is a dynamic, quickly developing field with a lot of promise. Recent developments show how RL can improve the efficiency and inventiveness of generative models, resulting in innovations in robotics, gaming, text and image production, and other fields. The combination of generative AI with reinforcement learning holds the potential to develop even more advanced and potent artificial intelligence systems in the future, provided that research keeps addressing current issues and breaking new ground.

3.3 Different Applications for Generative AI with Reinforcement Learning

Artificial intelligence is being pushed to new heights through the application of Reinforcement Learning (RL) in conjunction with Generative AI in a variety of domains. These applications include practical robotics, strategic gaming, and artistic pursuits. The following Figure 3.2 shows the important applications where this potent combination is having a big influence.

Text Generation

- **Conversational Agents:** By improving chatbots' and virtual assistants' responses for coherence, relevance, and user happiness, reinforcement learning (RL) makes them better. These agents utilize reinforcement learning (RL) to learn how to make their interactions better over time in response to user feedback.

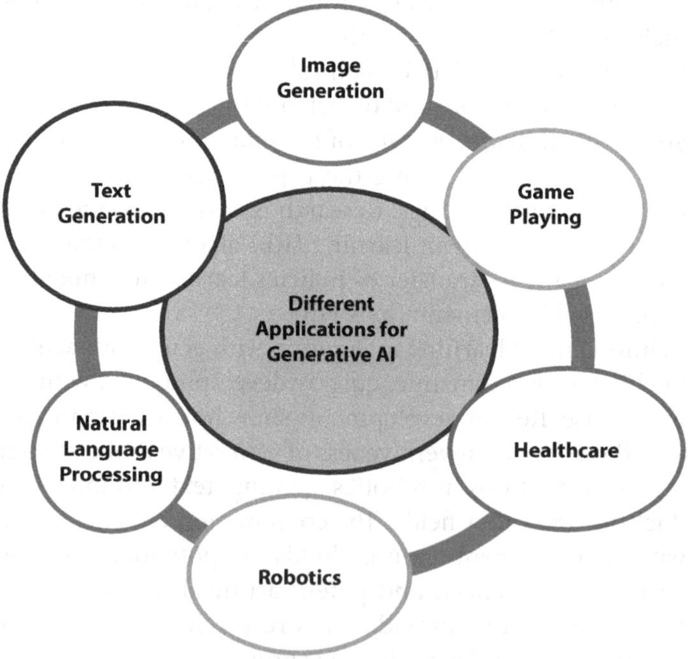

Figure 3.2 Different applications for generative AI.

- **Text summary:** Generative models, like GPT, can succinctly summarize extensive texts or articles. To ensure that summaries are both succinct and thorough, RL fine-tuning helps these models prioritize pertinent information.
- **Translation Systems:** RL enhances machine translation systems by maximizing translation accuracy and fluency. Since models receive rewards based on the quality of their translations, they can translate text more accurately and naturally [6].

Image Development

- **Art and Design:** By generating innovative artwork and designs, RL-powered GANs expand the boundaries of human creativity. These resources help artists experiment with new aesthetics and produce original works of art.
- **Style Transfer:** RL improves style transfer software so that users can apply the well-known painters' artistic styles to their images more consistently and in higher quality.
- **Super-quality:** RL enables the production of high-quality images from inputs with low resolution. Satellite photography, consumer applications, and medical imaging all employ this technology to improve photos.

Game Playing

- RL has transformed the use of AI in strategic gaming. Systems like AlphaGo and Alpha Zero have demonstrated superhuman powers in games such as Go, chess, and shogi. These models use RL to acquire sophisticated techniques and decision-making abilities.
- **Procedural Content Generation:** In video games, RL aids in the creation of levels, maps, and scenarios that make for an exciting and dynamic game play experience. This method creates huge, exposable environments in video games like No Man's Sky and Mine craft [7].

Robotics

- **Manipulation Tasks:** Repetitive loop training (RL) teaches robots to carry out complex tasks such as assembly, tool use, and object manipulation. Through trial and error, robots develop their abilities in settings that they encounter in the real world.
- **Autonomous Navigation:** Drones and self-driving cars are developed using reinforcement learning. These systems pick up the ability to maneuver over challenging terrain, steer clear of hazards, and plan routes for maximum effectiveness and security.
- **Sim-to-Real Transfer:** This crucial application involves training robots in simulations prior to their deployment in real-world tasks. Reinforcement learning (RL) facilitates the efficient transfer of policies learned in simulated settings to real-world [14].

Healthcare

- **Drug Discovery:** By maximizing the production of chemical compounds, RL helps in the search for novel medications. Rewarding the models based on the compounds' potential efficacy and safety accelerates drug development.
- **Medical Imaging:** RL improves medical imaging's precision and quality, which helps with diagnosis and therapy planning. We train models to produce sharper images and detect irregularities more accurately.

Natural Language Processing (NLP)

- **Proof Creation:** The combination of generative AI and reinforcement learning aids in article authoring, marketing material, and personalized recommendation generation. We train these algorithms to produce engaging, timely content that meets the specific needs of each user.
- **Sentiment Analysis:** Reinforcement learning (RL) fine-tunes models to better comprehend and interpret the subtleties of human emotions in text data, thereby improving the accuracy of sentiment predictions [8].

- Frontiers are being opened in a variety of fields by the combination of generative AI and reinforcement learning. AI's potential is being pushed to new heights by this potent combination, which is boosting creativity in the arts and design and optimizing strategic decision-making in robotics and games. Even more impactful and sophisticated applications that change industries and enhance people's lives in many ways should emerge as research and development continue.

3.4 Characteristics of Generative AI with Reinforcement Learning

Reinforcement learning (RL) in conjunction with generative AI displays special properties that augment its capabilities and set it apart from conventional generative models. These qualities make it possible to develop

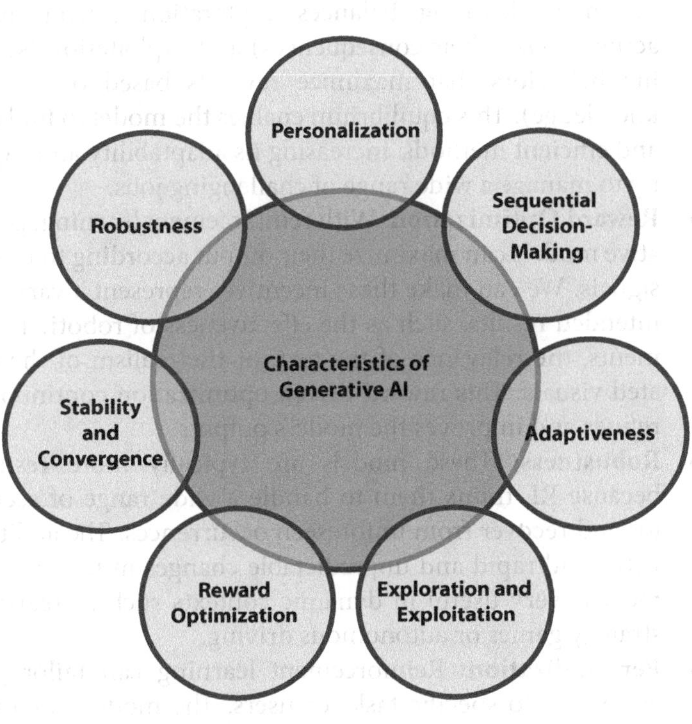

Figure 3.3 Salient features.

increasingly complex, flexible, and effective AI systems in a variety of fields. The following Figure 3.3 shows the salient features:

- **Adaptiveness:** Using reinforcement learning, generative AI is able to modify its actions in response to external input. This flexibility is necessary to guarantee that the outputs produced satisfy certain requirements or objectives and to continuously improve performance. For example, in text generation, the model can adjust in response to user interactions and feedback to generate more logical and contextually appropriate sentences [15].
- **Sequential Decision-Making:** RL allows for sequential decision-making, in contrast to classic generative models, which frequently make decisions in a single step. This implies that the model can organize and carry out a sequence of steps to accomplish a long-term goal. This feature is especially helpful in applications where strategic planning across several steps is necessary, such as gaming [9].
- **Exploration and Exploitation:** Generative AI with reinforcement learning balances exploration (trying novel actions to see their consequences) and exploitation (selecting behaviors that maximize rewards based on current knowledge). This equilibrium enables the model to find new and efficient methods, increasing its adaptability and capacity to manage a wide range of challenging jobs.
- **Reward Optimization:** With reinforcement learning, generative models can maximize their output according to reward signals. We can make these incentives represent a variety of intended results, such as the effectiveness of robotic movements, the relevance of the text, or the realism of the created visuals. This reward-driven optimization continuously refines and improves the model's outputs.
- **Robustness:** These models are typically more resilient because RL trains them to handle a wide range of scenarios and recover from unforeseen occurrences. The ability to withstand rapid and unpredictable changes in the environment is very useful in dynamic contexts such as real-time strategy games or autonomous driving.
- **Personalization:** Reinforcement learning can tailor generative AI to specific tasks or users. The model's ability to customize its outputs to match individual preferences and

needs by including user-relevant feedback can increase user happiness and engagement.

- **Stability and Convergence:** The stability and convergence of training processes have been the main goals of recent advances in reinforcement learning. The goal of methods like Trust Region Policy Optimization (TRPO) and Proximal Policy Optimization (PPO) is to guarantee more consistent and dependable training results, which is essential for implementing reinforcement learning in real-world settings.

Machine learning with reinforcement Learning builds highly adaptive, effective, and sophisticated models by fusing the best aspects of both paradigms. These models perform exceptionally well on tasks requiring long-term planning, sequential decision-making, and feedback-driven continuous improvement. These models' features will develop further with study, broadening their applicability in different domains and augmenting their capabilities.

3.5 Outstanding Problems in Generative AI with Reinforcement Learning

Significant obstacles and unsolved issues still exist despite the impressive progress that generative AI has made in a number of fields. For the responsible and efficient creation of generative models, these problems, which have technological, ethical, and practical aspects, call for targeted research and innovation. Given that those generative models especially those that use reinforcement learning demand enormous amounts of data and processing power, sample economy is a crucial concern. Problems such as mode collapse in GANs and instability in RL training make it harder to improve stability and guarantee dependable convergence. Models' ability to manage more datasets and more complicated tasks without sacrificing efficiency and generalizability presents another formidable challenge: scalability [18].

Gaining trust and understanding the often opaque decision-making processes of generative models depend on their interpretability and explainability. We must develop techniques for bias detection, mitigation, and fairness assurance, taking into account ethical issues and bias in generative AI that arise from training data. Moreover, since models frequently perform poorly outside of their training data, it is crucial to guarantee robustness and generalization to new, unforeseen contexts. There are serious concerns about data security and privacy, particularly when models trained on sensitive data unintentionally disclose personal information. Computational limitations make real-time and interactive generation difficult, necessitating effective techniques without sacrificing quality. Evaluating model performance also requires developing strong assessment measures that are in line with human judgment [12].

Current models struggle to capture and retain long-term relationships in data, which are essential for tasks like coherent story production and long-horizon planning in robots. Furthermore, multimodal generation remains a difficult problem. It entails integrating and producing data across several modalities, including text, image, and audio. Addressing these outstanding problems is essential for advancing generative AI, and requires collaborative efforts and innovative solutions to unlock the full potential of these powerful technologies.

3.6 Limitations of Generative AI with Reinforcement Learning

Although generative AI enhanced with reinforcement learning (RL) has shown great promise in a variety of applications, a number of obstacles hinder its wider use and reduced effectiveness. Comprehending these constraints is essential for directing upcoming investigations and advancements [10].

Inefficiency of Samples

- To learn efficiently, generative models trained with reinforcement learning (RL) frequently need large volumes of data and interactions. Sample inefficiency makes these models computationally expensive and time-consuming to train, which limits their use in situations where data is scarce.

Unpredictability in Training

- Using RL to train generative models can lead to instability. Methods like GANs are especially vulnerable to problems like mode collapse, in which the generator generates a finite range of outputs. Instability in RL algorithms can also occur during training, resulting in oscillations or policy divergencies.

Scalability Difficulties

- Scaling generative models and RL algorithms to handle larger datasets and more demanding tasks gets difficult as they become more complex. Not all scholars or organizations may have access to the substantial computational resources and sophisticated infrastructure needed for this [11].

The Exploration-Exploitation Balance

- A key problem in reinforcement learning (RL) is striking a balance between exploitation—using previously proven actions—and exploration—trying new ones. A model's performance can be unsatisfactory due to poorly balanced strategies, which either prevents models from discovering new and potentially superior methods or waste resources on ineffective actions [17].

Exorbitant Cost of Computation

- Integrating RL with generative models often results in high computing requirements. The lengthy training timeframes and sophisticated hardware, such as GPUs or TPUs, typically required for training may hinder the widespread adoption of these models.
- Though there is much promise for generative AI with reinforcement learning, its growth and wider application depend on resolving its limitations. Key issues for continued research include improving interpretability, fairness, robustness, privacy, and stability, as well as scalability, processing costs, and sample efficiency. To overcome these obstacles, generative AI with reinforcement learning can reach its full potential and produce AI systems that are more potent, dependable, and morally sound.

Boundaries of Generative AI

- Generative artificial intelligence functions within specific bounds that determine its potential, moral issues, and real-world restrictions.

- **Data Dependency:** The caliber, variety, and volume of training data used by generative AI determine how much it can produce. Beyond the connections and patterns found in its training dataset, it is unable to produce new content [16].

Generalization vs. Specificity: While generative AI may excel at tasks it has learned, it may struggle to understand context outside of its training domain or to demonstrate true creativity. It performs well within prescribed bounds but is not as cognitively sophisticated as others.

- **Ethical and Legal Frameworks:** Deep fakes and other unethical outcomes of using generative AI call for legal frameworks to control its application and reduce associated hazards.
- **Technological Restrictions:** The ability of current generative AI to create cohesive long-term narratives, comprehend complicated emotions, or seamlessly integrate many knowledge domains is limited. These technological limitations affect its applicability in different settings.
- **Security and privacy:** Generating AI raises two concerns: creating false information or violating someone's privacy by creating personal data. To stop abuse and safeguard user privacy, strong security measures are required.
- **Resource Intensity:** The development and implementation of generative AI models necessitate substantial computational resources, which restricts their scalability and accessibility in situations with limited resources.

To harness generative AI ethically, we must manage risks, ensure ethical and successful application across a range of areas, and navigate these boundaries.

3.7 Conclusion

Finally, processes like reinforcement learning, which provide goal-directed optimization and iterative learning to enhance model capabilities, can advance generative AI. Recent successes have shown that reinforcement learning (RL) is effective for tasks like game playing and self-directed decision-making, indicating that RL has the potential to enhance the performance and adaptability of generative models. In the future, it will still be crucial to overcome obstacles like computational needs and inefficient samples. The main goal of future work should be to create more effective RL algorithms that can be easily integrated with deep learning frameworks. This integration may increase the ability of generative AI to process complex data and generate more advanced results in a variety of fields. Furthermore, the resolution of ethical issues such as privacy protection, openness, and justice will determine the general adoption and social acceptance of RL-driven generative AI. RL in generative AI has the potential to revolutionize a variety of industries, including healthcare and entertainment, as well as usher in a new era of intelligent and adaptive systems by promoting interdisciplinary collaborations and algorithmic advances. Realizing RL's full potential to influence the direction of generative AI will require seizing these opportunities while overcoming the related obstacles.

AI disclosure statement: The author acknowledges the use of AI-based tools for minor language editing or grammatical correction. However, all intellectual contributions, analyses, and conclusions presented in this chapter are entirely the author's own.

References

1. Aghakhani, H. *et al.*, Detecting deceptive reviews using generative adversarial networks, in: *2018 IEEE Security and Privacy Workshops (SPW)*, pp. 89–95, IEEE, 2018.
2. Akizuki, Y. *et al.*, Generative Modelling with Design Constraints–Reinforcement Learning for Object Generation, in: *RE: Anthropocene, Design in the Age of Humans–Proceedings of the 25th CAADRIA Conference*, vol. 1, pp. 445–454, Association for Computer Aided Architectural Design Researchin Asia, Chulalongkorn University Bangkok, Thailand, 2020.
3. Akyürek, A.F. *et al.*, RL4F: Generating Natural Language Feedback with Reinforcement Learning for Repairing Model Outputs, 2023, preprint arXiv:2305.08844.
4. Anuchitanukul, A. *et al.*, SURF: Semantic-level Unsupervised Reward Function for Machine Translation, in: *Proceedings of the 2022 Conference of the North American Chapter of the Association for Computational Linguistics: Human Language Technologies*, Association for Computational Linguistics, Seattle, United States, pp. 4508–4522, 2022, https://doi.org/10.18653/v1/2022.naacl-main.334.
5. Atance, S.R. *et al.*, De novo drug design using reinforcement learning with graph-based deep generative models. *J. Chem. Inf. Model.*, 62, 20, 4863–4872, 2022.

6. Baek, M. *et al.*, Accurate prediction of protein structures and interactions using a three-track neural network. *Science*, 373, 6557, 871–876, 2021.
7. Bai, Y. *et al.*, Training a helpful and harmless assistant with reinforcement learning from human feedback, 2022, arXiv preprint arXiv:2204.05862.
8. Bellman, R. *et al.*, The theory of dynamic programming. *Bull. Amer. Math. Soc.*, 60, 6, 503–515, 1954.
9. Bilodeau, C. *et al.*, Generative models for molecular discovery: Recent advances and challenges. *Wiley Interdiscip. Rev.: Comput. Mol. Sci.*, 12, 5, e1608, 2022.
10. Dhaya, R., Kanthavel, R., Venusamy, K., AI Based Learning Model Management Framework for Private Cloud Computing. *J. Internet Technol.*, 23, 7, 1633–1642, Dec. 2022.
11. Blaschke, T. *et al.*, Memory-assisted reinforcement learning for diverse molecular de novo design. *J. Cheminf.*, 12, 1, 1–17, 2020.
12. Brown, N. *et al.*, GuacaMol: benchmarking models for de novo molecular design. *J. Chem. Inf. Model.*, 59, 3, 1096–1108, 2019.
13. Carreira-Perpinan, M.A. *et al.*, On contrastive divergence learning, in: *International workshop on artificial intelligence and statistics*, PMLR, pp. 33–40, 2005.
14. Chen, H. *et al.*, A survey on dialogue systems: Recent advances and new frontiers. *ACM SIGKDD Explor. Newslett.*, 19, 2, 25–35, 2017.
15. Chen, X. *et al.*, Catch: Context-based meta reinforcement learning for transferrable architecture search, in: *Computer Vision–ECCV 2020: 16th European Conference, Glasgow, UK, August 23–28, 2020, Proceedings, Part XIX 16*, pp. 185–2022, Springer, Glasgow, UK, 2020.
16. Sangeetha, S.K.B. *et al.*, An empirical analysis of machine learning frameworks for digital pathology in medical science. *J. Phys.: Conf. Ser.*, 1767, 012031, 2021, DOI: 10.1088/1742-6596/1767/1/012031.
17. Freeda, A.R., A., A., Venket, K., R., D., Kanthavel, R., Role of ChatGPT in Smart Cities, in: *Applications, Challenges, and the Future of ChatGPT*, pp. 189–201, 2024, DOI: 10.4018/979-8-3693-6824-4.ch010.
18. Sangeetha, S.K.B. and Dhaya, R., Deep Learning Era for Future 6G Wireless Communications—Theory, Applications, and Challenges, in: *Artificial Intelligent Techniques for Wireless Communication and Networking*, p. 105, 2022.

4

Pix2pix GAN for Image-to-Image Translation: A Comparative Study with Diverse Datasets

Lakshmipriya B.[1]*, Pankaj Kumar Singh[2] and Jayalakshmy S.[3]

[1]School of Engineering, Jawaharlal Nehru University, New Delhi, India
[2]School of Computer Science and Engineering, Vellore Institute of Technology, Chennai Campus, Chennai, India
[3]Department of Electronics and Communication Engineering, IFET College of Engineering, Villuppuram, India

Abstract

Image-to-image translation (I2IT) is a complex task involving the transformation of images from one domain to another while retaining their essential content. With the onset of generative adversarial networks (GANs), image translation has attracted interest recently as it can synthetically generate images belonging to a new domain or scene from the images available in another domain. I2IT essentially learns the mapping of patterns from images in one domain to another domain and finds a wider application ranging from satellite images to medical image enhancement and autonomous driving simulations. Pix2pix GAN is a groundbreaking I2IT architecture that has completely changed how realistic images are produced from input data. This chapter examines the effectiveness of pix2pix GAN in producing high-quality output images from a variety of datasets, including urban planning, medical imaging, and underwater image enhancement. Through an analysis of pix2pix GAN's performance on these datasets, the project aims to offer important insights into the technology's advantages, disadvantages, and possible uses in a variety of fields. In addition, the project will investigate ways to improve the scalability and performance of pix2pix GAN, increasing its usefulness for I2IT tasks in the real world. Pix2pix GAN employs a generator to translate input images into realistic outputs and a discriminator to contradistinguish the synthetic images from the actual and utilize the paired image datasets

**Corresponding author*: lakshmipriya@mail.jnu.ac.in

N. Gayathri, S. Rakesh Kumar, Ramesh Chandran, Pethuru Raj Chelliah and Danilo Pelusi (eds.) Generative AI: Disruptive Technologies for Innovative Applications, (73–90) © 2025 Scrivener Publishing LLC

for training employing adversarial and L1 loss functions to optimize generator and discriminator networks iteratively, ensuring high-quality image translation. A comparative study for the performance of pix2pix GAN architecture on three datasets are as follows: (i) satellite aerial images to map generation from Kaggle pix2pix dataset and (ii) underwater image enhancement using large-scale underwater image (LSUI) dataset and magnetic resonance imaging (MRI) to synthetic computed tomography (CT) image generation.

Keywords**:** Conditional GAN, domain adaptation, generative adversarial networks, image-to-image translation, pix2pix

4.1 Introduction

Image-to-image translation (I2IT) is a generative artificial intelligence (AI) task wherein an image is translated to another image retaining its core content with an alternative style or appearance [1, 2]. I2IT finds extensive applications in various fields such as style transfer, medical imaging, image enhancement, and satellite imagery. The translation is implemented using machine learning models by learning the mapping patterns from images belonging to two domains. Examples include removing the rain streaks from rainy images [3–5], generating high-contrast magnetic resonance imaging (MRI) from MRI images acquired using low-contrast dosage [6], and enhancing underwater images [7] and day-to-night image translation [8]. A generative adversarial network (GAN) is a robust deep learning architecture developed to generate realistic synthetic images that closely resemble the actual images belonging to a latent space [9]. GAN architecture essentially consists of two convolutional neural networks (CNN)—a generator and a discriminator. A generator network in the GAN is a CNN architecture that generates images from the training dataset bearing a resemblance to original images, whereas the discriminator tends to identify the real and the generated images by providing a probability score as an illustration of whether the images are real or generated. GAN is basically an adversarial network where the generator is trained in such a way that the discriminator cannot discriminate between the real and generated images and the discriminator learns to maximize the accuracy of binary classification between the real and the generated images. Adversarial learning is a thriving force in GAN enabling a competitive learning environment between the generator and discriminator resulting in the generation of highly realistic synthetic images. GANs are initially deployed in image classification for image augmentation to inflate the quantity of training dataset and to scale down the class imbalance resulting in a robust model for image classification [10, 11]. A diverse set of GAN architectures has been deployed for image augmentation, which includes the variants of deep convolution GAN (DCGAN) [12] and conditional GAN (cGAN) [13]. These GAN architectures for image generation consist of two supervised learning models—generative and discriminative models with a prime motive of learning the probability distribution of the images from the training dataset. Upon successful training, new images are generated following the training dataset distribution. The advent of GAN architectures further made possible the translation of images from one domain to another, resulting in the evolution of I2IT. Translation typically involves the transformation of styles or inherent traits of the image from one domain to another. GAN architecture for I2IT consists of one or more sets of generators and discriminators and can either be supervised or unsupervised. The dataset used to train the GAN architecture for I2IT consists of paired images, i.e., for every image in one domain, the corresponding image in the other domain forms a pair. The popular baseline architectures for I2IT are pix2pix [1], cycleGAN [14], and unsupervised I2IT (UNIT) [2]. Pix2pix GAN is a supervised cGAN architecture with a single generator and discriminator specialized in learning the I2IT mapping under a conditional learning environment. This chapter demonstrates the functionality of generative AI with the help of I2IT using pix2pix GAN for three distinct use cases belonging to different applications. The three use cases deliberated in this study include map image generation from satellite imagery, underwater image enhancement, and generation of computed tomography (CT) from MRI scans.

4.1.1 Significance of Generative AI in the Three Use Cases

The significance and challenges of the aforementioned use cases in everyday routine as well as the need for generative AI to address the challenges faced in these use cases are presented in this section.

Map images are of considerable significance in daily routine activities encompassing navigation, city planning, geographical understanding of landscapes, estimating demographic data of the population in a locality, tracking epidemics, disaster management, tourism, and boundary tracking. Map images are generated from high-resolution images captured by satellite sensors, aircraft, drones, and global positioning system (GPS) devices. Generating map images from these modalities includes geo-referencing; correcting terrain-related distortions; making atmospheric corrections to compensate for scattering and light absorption; conducting supervised and unsupervised classification of geographic terrains like water, urban, and vegetation areas; detecting objects to identify structures like roads, streets, buildings, and agricultural lands; and enhancing images through color balancing and contrast adjustments [15]. It is evident that map image generation involves multiple processes that may be user-guided or automated. Nevertheless, generative AI can result in an alternative method of generating map images without the need for multiple processing techniques.

Underwater image enhancement plays a pivotal role in many day-to-day practical applications including marine life exploration, underwater archeological investigation to identify shipwrecks and geological structures, underwater pollution monitoring, facilitating human safety and rescue operations, and so on. However, scattering and light absorption, water turbidity, lack of natural lights in the deep sea, and color distortion due to selection wavelength absorption by deep sea water cause visibility problems in the images captured inside the sea or ocean [16]. These challenges demand for enhancement of low-contrast underwater images to improve the contrast, lucidity, and color accuracy of these images in the aforementioned real-time underwater image processing applications. However, one single enhancement algorithm cannot address all these challenges and can handle only one or a few challenges at a time. Hence, multiple algorithms are required to effectively handle underwater image enhancement, and generative AI can provide a handshake addressing all constraints single-handedly.

CT and MRI are the two popular imaging modalities used for the diagnosis, prognosis, and treatment planning of a variety of diseases. Both modalities provide a comprehensive view of human anatomy with CT a better choice for visualization of bones and hard structures of the body, whereas MRI is effective in soft tissue picturization. Although MRI scans involve no radiation, their acquisition is not patient-friendly, owing to high noise and motion artifacts due to breathing [17]. Conversely, CT acquisition is comparatively easy but is prone to radiation exposure [18]. For some diseases like brain, neurological, spinal, oncological, and musculoskeletal disorders, both CT and MRI are crucial for diagnosis. However, there are a few exceptions wherein a patient cannot undergo either MRI or CT. For example, patients with kidney diseases cannot undergo contrast-enhanced CT for cancer diagnosis, and for patients with metallic implants like cardiac pacemakers and cochlear implants, MRI is not possible. For these patients, and in general, to avoid additional radiation exposure, technological assistance by virtue of generative AI can be offered as an attempt to generate CT images from the MRI scans.

4.2 Related Works

I2IT involves the task of translating the image from one domain to another by learning the necessary mapping between the images in both domains. The implementation of image generation has been realized with the help of GAN architectures. Learning a translation can be done either in paired or unpaired training data by performing joint training of the generator and discriminator. Multiple variants of GANs are being proposed for this task. The functionality of cGANs in a conditional environment has been explored as a versatile generative model for I2IT for a variety of translation tasks in [1] to learn the mapping between images as well as the loss function. Recognizing connections between different data domains without supervision can be challenging. DiscoGAN, a GAN architecture that learns the mapping between domains without the need for paired data, enables style transfer while preserving important attributes like orientation and identity [19]. Authors of [20] created avatars in an unsupervised manner using GAN architecture. This GAN exploited domain adaptation and cross domain transition to map an input image to a pair composed of a vector of parameters and an image. TextureGAN, a conditional network proposed by Xian *et al.*, learns to map textural features to the object boundaries with multiple losses—feature loss, adversarial loss, style loss, pixel loss, and color loss to propagate texture into representative objects [21]. Dynamic multi-domain translation (DMTNet) with deep unfolding network for image reconstruction powered with proximal gradient descent learning leverages in identifying the rain streaks and demonstrates efficient deraining [22]. Domain translation network with contrastive learning for the translation of blurred images to sharpened counterparts trained with unpaired datasets resulted in deblurred images that are almost sharp [23]. Image-to-image translation also finds applications in medical education by translating a diseased scan image onto a scanned image of a healthy person. Similar work was demonstrated for cardiovascular diseases using cycleGAN to generate either diseased or healthy image datasets to achieve better training of deep learning models with the augmented dataset [24]. GAN architectures are also used in the medical domain to generate high-contrast images equivalent to full-dose contrast-enhanced MR images from MR images acquired with low-contrast dosage. This enables scan acquisition with less contrast dosage and avoids side effects of contrast agents on patients but with a diagnostic accuracy near to full-dose contrast MR [6]. Similarly, virtual translation between two modalities—frozen section and paraffin section—in histopathology analysis for swift and accurate intra-surgical decision is made possible through GAN with ResNet generator and PatchGAN discriminator [25]. GAN with deformable skip connections with an associated nearest neighbor loss in place of traditional L_1 and L_2 losses (PoseGAN) was employed to generate human images with different hand poses [26]. Despite the availability of multiple GAN architectures for image translation belonging to different applications, the images generated lack consistency of semantic information present in the images in both domains. This might be due to insufficient mapping toward intricate features, mode collapse, lack of paired dataset, generalization issues on unseen data, mode dropping, and so on. The inability to learn intricate features can be overcome by the integration of explainable latent space manipulations with a structured GAN architecture [27]. Mode collapse in GAN results in generating very few images repeatedly without apprehending the entire distribution of the dataset, which is addressed using a variational autoencoder in the GAN module [28]. The generalization issue in I2IT is handled by self-supervised learning, ensemble learning, and through regularization techniques. Contrastive learning, when applied at I2IT, enhanced the diagnostic workflow for pathologists by maximizing the mutual information between unstained and stained skin tissue images [29]. Ensemble learning, in combination with image translations and self-supervised learning, enhanced the generalization by virtue of the model's exposure to diverse training data in domain adaptation tasks, alleviating the source domain bias [30].

This chapter delves into analyzing the performance of pix2pix GAN, a prominent I2IT architecture generating images belonging to one domain from another.

4.3 Methodology

This section deals with the methodology considered for image translation in this chapter. This chapter explores the functionalities of pix2pix GAN architecture for image translation tasks belonging to diverse sets of data. The framework adopted in this is presented in Figure 4.1. Three different tasks, *viz.*, translation of satellite images to maps, underwater image enhancement, and MR to CT image translation and vice versa, are considered in this chapter and the potential of pix2pix architecture in these tasks is assessed in this section.

Pix2pix is a cGAN with a conditional conversion of an image from one domain to another by virtue of supervised learning using one generator

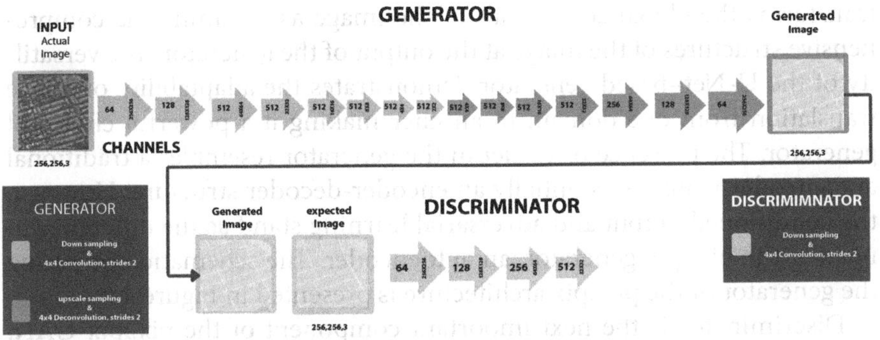

Figure 4.1 The architecture of pix2pix GAN.

and one discriminator. The realm of pix2pix architecture is that it is an enhancement of U-Net, a semantic segmentation architecture, as the generator and the discriminator are realized using a patchGAN architecture. The architecture of the pix2pix GAN architecture examined in this chapter is presented in Figure 4.1.

The generator network generally starts from a random vector and projects it to a higher dimensional space with the help of deconvolution operations. In contrast, the U-Net employed as the generator is equipped with an encoder and a decoder together with skip connections between the encoder and decoder. The encoder consists of multiple stages of convolutional and batch normalization layers activated by leaky ReLU to downsample the input image sequentially. Successive downsampling greatly assists the network in learning the image representation precisely by apprehending the crucial features of the image. At the lower end of the encoder, a bottleneck layer is present with the most compressed image representation and this acts as a bridge between the encoder and decoder. The decoder part of the generator is constructed using stages of deconvolution to reconstruct the image from the downsampled version of image representations. The number of stages of transposed convolution layers is the same as the count of convolutional layers in the encoder of the generator. Similar to the encoder, the decoder blocks are also activated by leaky ReLU functions. Skip connections linking the synonymous layers of the encoder-decoder module serve the purpose of perpetuating the spatial information lost during the compressive action in the encoder. The upsampling process in the decoder block generates the output image. The U-Net–based generator plays a critical role in handling complex morphology as well as intricate structures of the image and assists in the generation of high-resolution images with close-grained details. Additionally, the encoder-decoder architecture transforms the global contextuals of the image ascertaining the comprehensive structures of the image at the output of the generator. The versatility of the U-Net–based generator demonstrates the adaptability of image translation from one domain to another making it a powerful choice of generator. The presence of U-Net in the generator resembles a traditional autoencoder which is essentially an encoder-decoder structure. However, the conditioned output and adversarial learning stand as the difference in making the pix2pix generator, an autoencoder. The schematic of training the generator of the pix2pix architecture is presented in Figure 4.2.

Discriminator is the next important component of the pix2pix GAN. Discriminator does the conventional task of discriminating the generated from the ground truth images, however, in a different method. Unlike the discriminator in other GAN architectures, the discriminator in pix2pix assesses the generator performance in a patch-by-patch manner instead

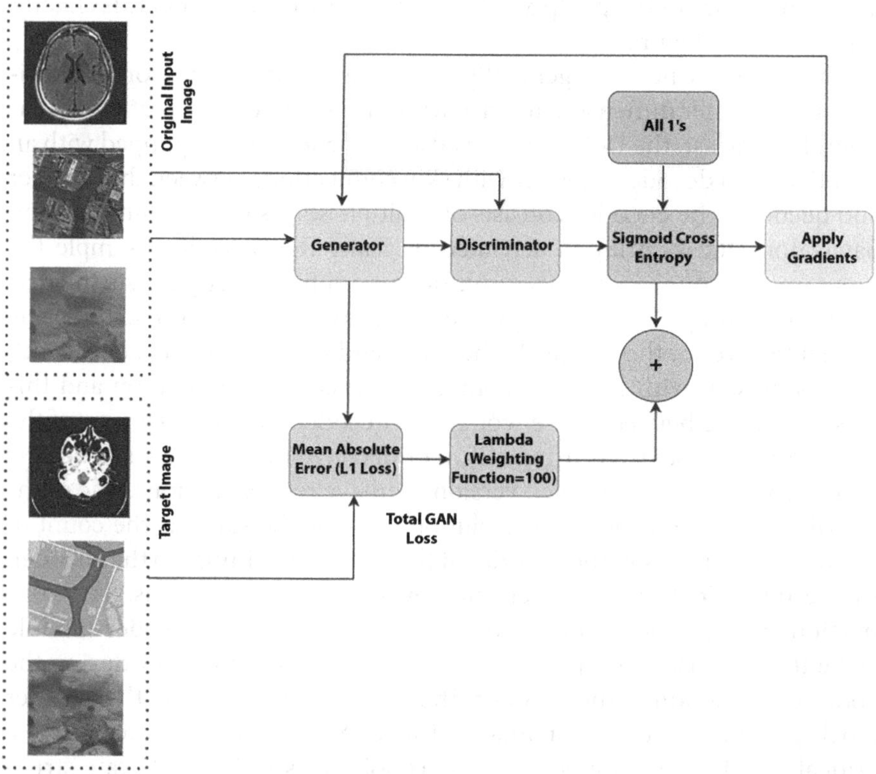

Figure 4.2 Training the generator of pix2pix GAN.

of classifying the entire image. Pix2pix uses patchGAN as a discriminator which divides the entire image into several patches and performs classification on every smaller patch. By doing so, the discriminator focuses on a local patch of the image instead of the entire image and learns the high-frequency components from the local patch more efficiently. This makes the discriminator more plausible to local textural patterns and structures of the image with relatively fewer parameters. Unlike the traditional GAN architectures, the discriminator makes use of two loss functions—adversarial loss and conditional loss. Adversarial loss serves to assess the potential of the discriminator to differentiate the ground truth and the generated images, and conditional loss quantifies how well the generated image resembles the ground truth image and corresponds to the input image in another domain.

4.4 Results and Discussions

4.4.1 Dataset

This chapter explores the functionality of pix2pix GAN in image translation tasks belonging to three different applications, *viz.*, i) generating map images from satellite imagery, ii) underwater image enhancement, and iii) generating CT images from MRI. Kaggle pix2pix dataset for I2IT corresponding to maps [31], CT and MRI brain scans of brain cross sections taken from Kaggle [32], and LSUI dataset consisting of 5,004 pairs of images taken under different lighting and water conditions [33] were considered for experimentation in this chapter. Accordingly, three different datasets were used in this study. All the implementations were carried out using the torchvision library in NVIDIA 3070 GPU. The satellite-map image dataset has paired images of dimensions 600 × 1,200 × 3 which are first cropped to separate the satellite and map images of dimensions 600 × 600 × 3. The images are then resized to 256 × 256 × 3 for further processing by the pix2pix architecture. The MRI-CT dataset [33] consists of a total of 2,486 pairs of CT and MR images and 5,004 underwater image pairs available in the LSUI dataset with an image dimension of 256 × 256 × 3. The dimension of the images in the MRI-CT dataset is 630 × 630 × 3 which is then resized to 256 × 256 × 3. The number of image pairs considered for training and testing for the three datasets is presented in Table 4.1. Four sample image pairs for every dataset are presented in Figure 4.3 for better understanding.

Table 4.1 Dataset distribution.

Dataset	Number of image pairs	
	Training	**Testing**
Satellite-map dataset	1,536	658
LSUI	3,503	1,501
MRI-CT	1,744	744

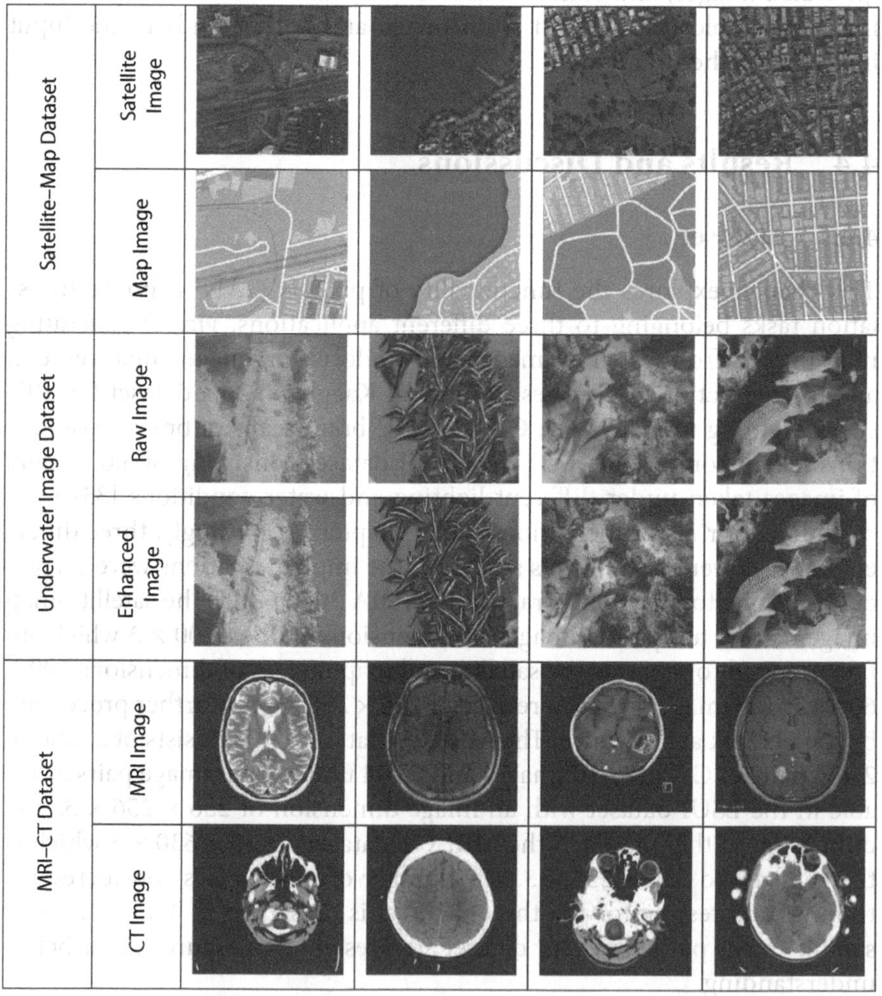

Figure 4.3 Source and target images for the three datasets.

4.4.2 Experimental Assessment

The pix2pix GAN architecture is trained with the abovementioned three dataset images separately and their outcomes are assessed visually as well as quantitatively. The hypermeter setting maintained for training is tabulated in Table 4.2. The generated images are presented in Figures 4.4 to 4.6 for satellite-map, underwater, and MRI-CT datasets, respectively.

From the visual outcomes presented in Figure 4.4 for the satellite-map image dataset, it is seen that the generated images precisely look like the ground truth map images. Different terrains like vegetation areas, bodies of water, street view, and roads are clearly identified from the aerial images in the generated map images closer to reality. The major edges and boundaries in the generated images have sharp clarity, whereas the minute high-frequency components within a structure like street view are not very sharp and are slightly blurred in some images. For the case of underwater image enhancement, the generated images upon visual examination appear to be of good quality equally to that of the ground truths. There is no need for color compensation for the generated images as they seem to be a replica of the ground truth images. The visual examination of generated CT images for the MRI-CT dataset reveals that the boundary delineation is sharp and the bony structures are replicated as that in the ground truth CT images. However, the texture information within the soft tissues of the brain seems to be lost and appear homogenous.

In addition to the qualitative assessment of the generated images through visual inspection, the performance of the pix2pix GAN architecture is quantified by virtue of image processing–based metrics. The performance quantification is performed by the comparison of generated images with

Table 4.2 Hyperparameter settings.

Parameter	**Value**
No. of epochs	100
Image dimensions	$256 \times 256 \times 3$
Batch size	32
Solver	Adam
Momentum $\beta 1$	5×10^{-1}
Momentum $\beta 2$	9×10^{-3}
L1 regularization λ	100

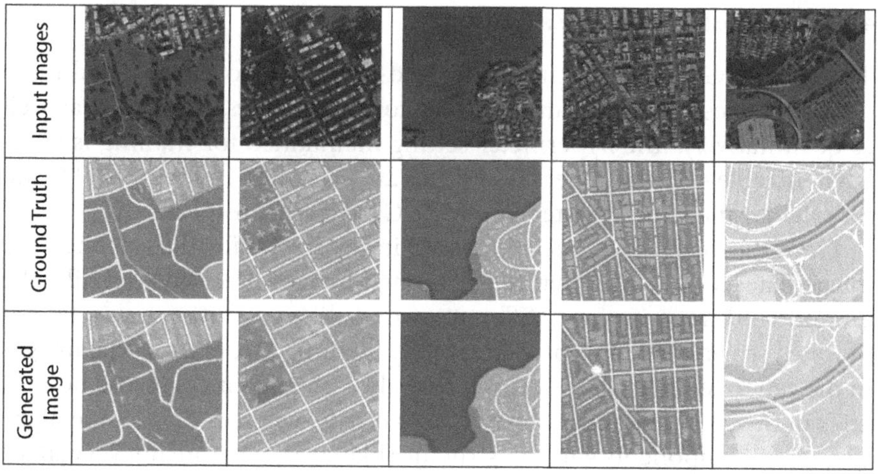

Figure 4.4 Visual outcomes of pix2pix GAN trained with satellite-map images.

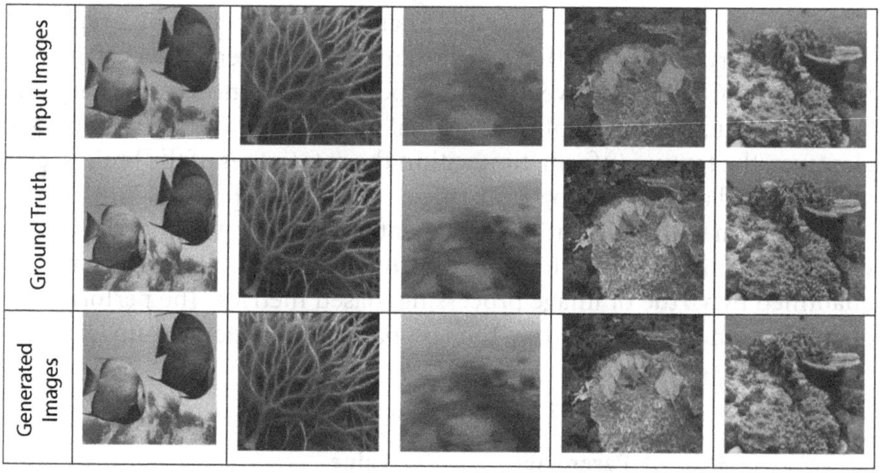

Figure 4.5 Visual outcomes of pix2pix GAN trained with underwater image dataset.

the ground truths in terms of similarity. The similarity assessment is done with the help of structural similarity index measure (SSIM), correlation measure (CORR), and MI between the generated and the ground truth images. SSIM is a statistical measure popularly used in computer vision applications to assess the degree of resemblance between the images. This measure compares the two images with the help of local binary patterns of pixel distribution in terms of luminance and contrast information. SSIM measure takes a value in the rage [0, 1] with a value closer to one indicating

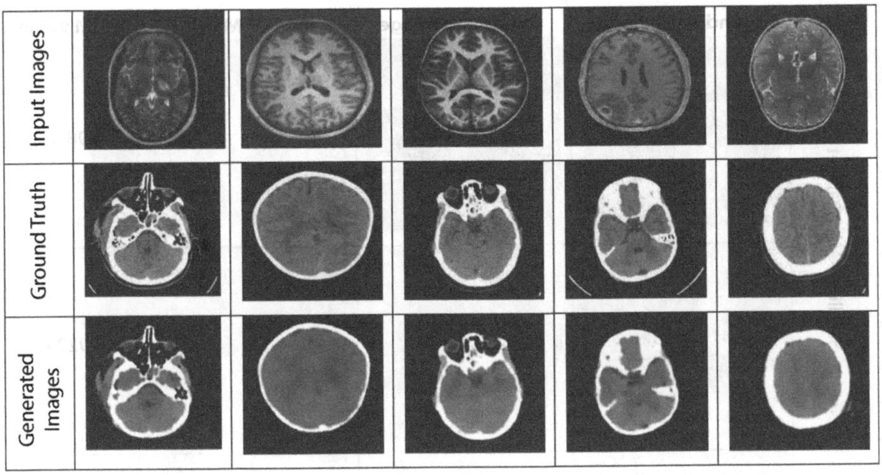

Figure 4.6 Visual outcomes of pix2pix GAN trained with MRI CT image dataset.

better similarity between the images being compared. In addition to providing a numerical value, this measure also provides a visualization map indicating the similarity relationship between the two images. SSIM map is essentially a grayscale image representation with dimensions the same as that of the images being compared. The map provides a visual intuition with brighter pixels in the areas within the image that are highly similar. In the areas where the similarity between the local patterns is less, darker patterns will be seen. SSIM map is presented in Figure 4.7 for a sample of two cases in all three datasets considered in this study.

It is observed from Figure 4.7 that among all three datasets, for the case of underwater images, the perceptual quality of the generated images has a very close resemblance to that of the ground truth images. Accordingly, the SSIM map between the ground truth and the generated images of the underwater image dataset has brighter areas and only the pixels corresponding to edges or high-frequency components have slight dark values in the SSIM map with a value of SSIM closer to one. The SSIM map corresponding to the underwater dataset stands as evidence that even the minute texture details are replicated closer to the original in the images generated by pix2pix architecture. For the case of map image generation from aerial images, the homogenous as well as prominent edge and high-frequency structures are reproduced with a high degree of accuracy in the generated images. However, minute texture details appear to be blurred and the same is witnessed in the SSIM map. In the event of CT image generation from the MRI dataset, the bone structures are reproduced as original, whereas

Dataset	Ground Truth Image	Generated Image	SSIM Map	SSIM value
Satellite – Map Dataset		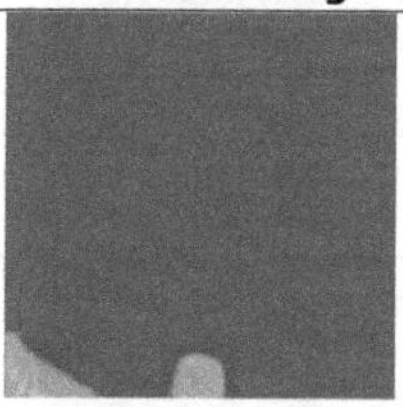		0.9820
	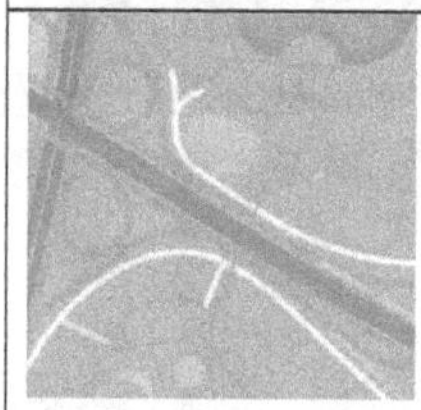	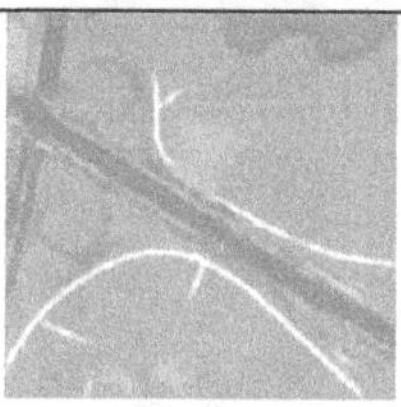	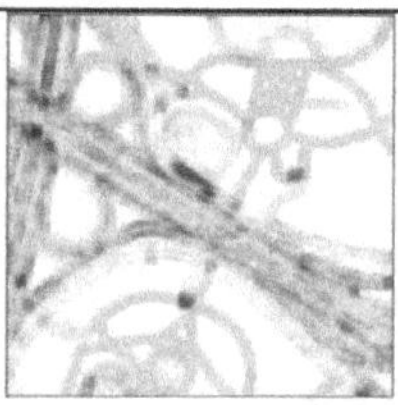	0.9225
Underwater Image Dataset	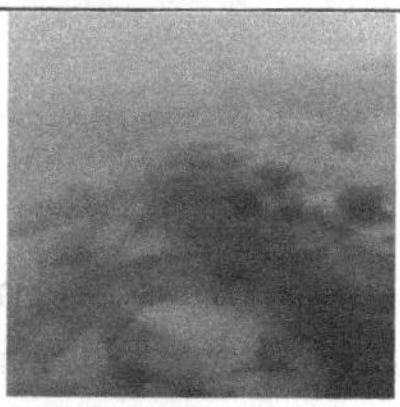			0.9876
	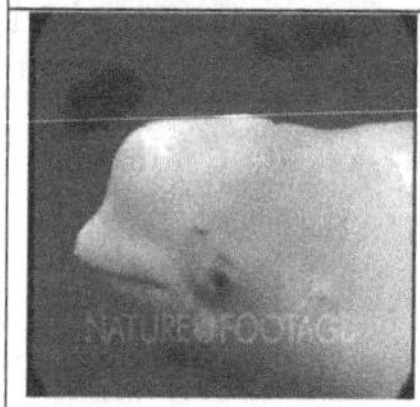	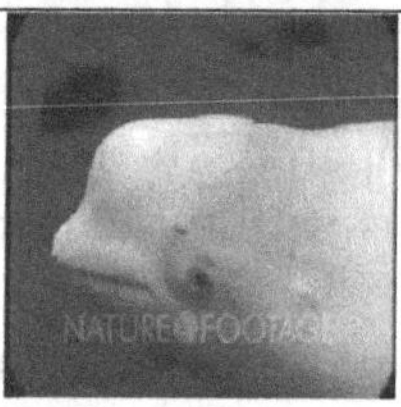		0.9924
MRI – CT Dataset	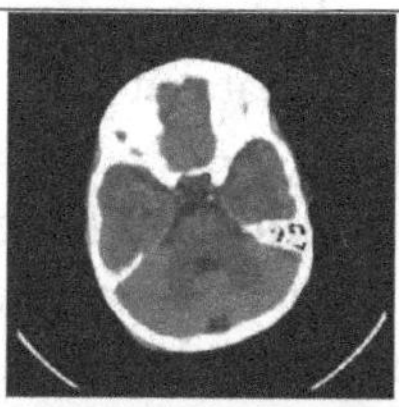	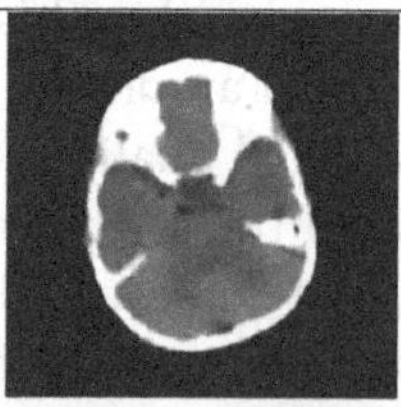	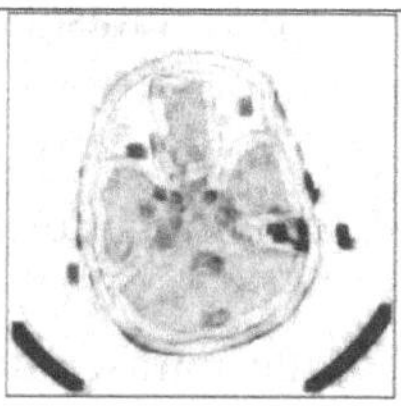	0.9056
	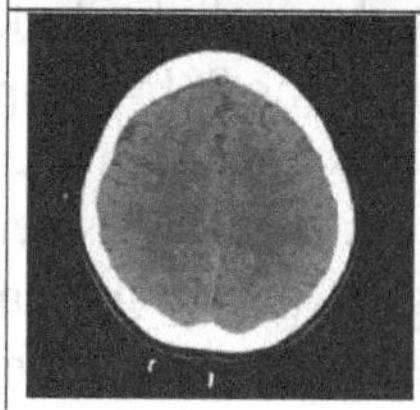	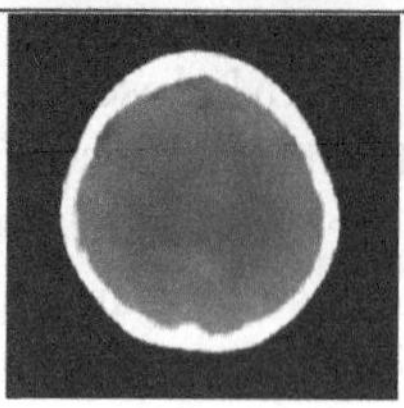	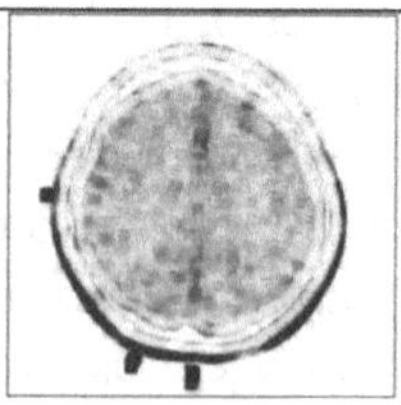	0.8791

Figure 4.7 Illustration of SSIM map between generated and ground truth images.

the finer texture details of the soft tissues appear homogeneous in the generated images. The same is perceived in the SSIM map with darker areas corresponding to the soft tissues in the CT image. Also, the SSIM value corresponding to the generated and the ground truth images is comparatively low. CORR is a statistical measure of Pearson's correlation coefficient between the generated image and the ground truth image. CORR takes the value in the range [−1, +1] with a value closer to +1 indicating a perfect correlation between two images, 0 indicating no correlation, and −1 implying an inverse correlation. The performance of the pix2pix architecture in this work is also quantified by means of MI, which is a measure of the extent of information about an image through another image. The quantitative assessment of the performance of pix2pix GAN architecture in terms of SSIM, CORR, and MI is presented in Table 4.3. The values presented in the table are obtained by calculating the average of the values of the metric computed for every image in the test dataset.

The evaluation metrics presented in the table ascertain the performance of pix2pix GAN architecture in the task of I2IT on three different datasets. For all three datasets considered in this study, the generated images closely resemble the target images, and the same is quantified in the table. However, among the three datasets considered, comparatively high-quality images are generated for the underwater image dataset. For the case of map image generation from aerial images, the performance is close to actual in the regions of homogenous structures in the map images and finer texture details are found to experience a slight blur which is seen sharp in the target images in the dataset. The same is reflected in the metrics presented in the table with values slightly less than that of the underwater dataset. However, for the MRI-CT dataset, though the hard tissue delineation is good in the generated images, the soft tissues appear homogeneous and no details on the finer texture contents are visually appreciated. Accordingly, the metrics show lesser values compared to the other two datasets.

Table 4.3 Performance evaluation of pix2pix GAN.

Dataset	SSIM	CORR	MI
Satellite-map dataset	0.9626	0.9518	0.9607
Underwater image dataset	0.9889	0.9813	0.9734
MRI-CT dataset	0.9145	0.8997	0.8801

4.5 Conclusion

The potential of pix2pix GAN architecture in the I2IT work belonging to three different applications, *viz.*, generating maps from aerial images, enhancing underwater images, and generating CT images from MRI scans, is explored. Leveraging the training dataset with paired images belonging to two domains, the pix2pix GAN by virtue of end-to-end training derives the mappings between the images ensuring the generation of realistic images with a high degree of fidelity compared to ground truths. The results presented in this chapter stand as a testament to robust image-to-image translation in diverse applications.

AI disclosure statement: The author acknowledges the use of AI-based tools for minor language editing or grammatical correction. However, all intellectual contributions, analyses, and conclusions presented in this chapter are entirely the author's own.

References

1. Isola, P., Zhu, J.Y., Zhou, T., Efros, A.A., Image-to-image translation with conditional adversarial networks, in: *Proceedings of the IEEE conference on computer vision and pattern recognition*, pp. 1125–1134, 2017.
2. Liu, M.Y., Breuel, T., Kautz, J., Unsupervised image-to-image translation networks, in: *Advances in neural information processing systems*, vol. *30*, 2017.
3. Jin, X., Chen, Z., Li, W., AI-GAN: Asynchronous interactive generative adversarial network for single image rain removal. *Pattern Recognit.*, *100*, 107143, 2020.
4. Pu, J., Chen, X., Zhang, L., Zhou, Q., Zhao, Y., Removing rain based on a cycle generative adversarial network, in: *2018 13th IEEE Conference on Industrial Electronics and Applications (ICIEA)*, 2018, May, IEEE, pp. 621–626.
5. Cao, P., Zhang, J., Zou, P., Li, D., Li, W., Zhong, C., Cui, H., Removal of Rain Streaks in Air Using GAN, in: *2021 4th International Conference on Artificial Intelligence and Big Data (ICAIBD)*, 2021, May, IEEE, pp. 589–593.
6. Gong, E., Pauly, J.M., Wintermark, M., Zaharchuk, G., Deep learning enables reduced gadolinium dose for contrast-enhanced brain MRI. *J. Magn. Reson. Imaging*, *48*, 2, 330–340, 2018.
7. Chaurasia, D. and Chhikara, P., Sea-Pix-GAN: Underwater image enhancement using adversarial neural network. *J. Visual Commun. Image Represent.*, *98*, 104021, 2024.

8. Lin, C.T., Huang, S.W., Wu, Y.Y., Lai, S.H., GAN-based day-to-night image style transfer for nighttime vehicle detection. *IEEE Trans. Intell. Transp. Syst.*, *22*, 2, 951–963, 2020.
9. Goodfellow, I., Pouget-Abadie, J., Mirza, M., Xu, B., Warde-Farley, D., Ozair, S., Bengio, Y., Generative adversarial networks. *Commun. ACM*, *63*, 11, 139–144, 2020.
10. Motamed, S., Rogalla, P., Khalvati, F., Data augmentation using Generative Adversarial Networks (GANs) for GAN-based detection of Pneumonia and COVID-19 in chest X-ray images. *Inf. Med. Unlocked*, *27*, 100779, 2021.
11. Jayalakshmy, S., Priya, L., Sudha, G.F., Synthesis of respiratory signals using conditional generative adversarial networks from scalogram representation, in: *Generative adversarial networks for image-to-image translation*, pp. 161–183, Academic Press, San Diego, California, 2021.
12. Dong, G.S., Wan, H.P., Luo, Y., Todd, M.D., A fast sparsity-free compressive sensing approach for vibration data reconstruction using deep convolutional GAN. *Mech. Syst. Signal Process.*, *188*, 109937, 2023.
13. Kang, M. and Park, J., Contragan: Contrastive learning for conditional image generation, in: *Advances in Neural Information Processing Systems*, vol. *33*, pp. 21357–21369, 2020.
14. Zhu, J.Y., Park, T., Isola, P., Efros, A.A., Unpaired image-to-image translation using cycle-consistent adversarial networks, in: *Proceedings of the IEEE international conference on computer vision*, pp. 2223–2232, 2017.
15. Hughes, L.H., Marcos, D., Lobry, S., Tuia, D., Schmitt, M., A deep learning framework for matching of SAR and optical imagery. *ISPRS J. Photogramm. Remote Sens.*, *169*, 166–179, 2020.
16. Raveendran, S., Patil, M.D., Birajdar, G.K., Underwater image enhancement: a comprehensive review, recent trends, challenges and applications. *Artif. Intell. Rev.*, *54*, 5413–5467, 2021.
17. Summers, P., Saia, G., Colombo, A., Pricolo, P., Zugni, F., Alessi, S., Petralia, G., Whole-body magnetic resonance imaging: technique, guidelines and key applications. *Ecancermedicalscience*, *15*, 1–16, 2021.
18. Power, S.P., Moloney, F., Twomey, M., James, K., O'Connor, O.J., Maher, M.M., Computed tomography and patient risk: Facts, perceptions and uncertainties. *World J. Radiol.*, *8*, 12, 902, 2016.
19. Kim, T., Cha, M., Kim, H., Lee, J.K., Kim, J., Learning to discover cross-domain relations with generative adversarial networks, in: *International conference on machine learning*, 2017, July, PMLR, pp. 1857–1865.
20. Wolf, L., Taigman, Y., Polyak, A., Unsupervised creation of parameterized avatars, in: *Proceedings of the IEEE International Conference on Computer Vision*, pp. 1530–1538, 2017.
21. Xian, W., Sangkloy, P., Agrawal, V., Raj, A., Lu, J., Fang, C., Hays, J., Texturegan: Controlling deep image synthesis with texture patches, in: *Proceedings of the IEEE conference on computer vision and pattern recognition*, pp. 8456–8465, 2018.

22. Huang, Z. and Zhang, J., Dynamic Multi-Domain Translation Network for Single Image Deraining, in: *2021 IEEE International Conference on Image Processing (ICIP)*, 2021, September, IEEE, pp. 1754–1758.
23. Zhao, B. and Li, W., A domain translation network with contrastive constraint for unpaired motion image deblurring. *IET Image Proc.*, *17*, 10, 2866–2880, 2023.
24. Ali, H., Nyman, E., Näslund, U., Grönlund, C., Translation of atherosclerotic disease features onto healthy carotid ultrasound images using domain-to-domain translation. *Biomed. Signal Process. Control*, *85*, 104886, 2023.
25. Gadermayr, M., Tschuchnig, M., Stangassinger, L.M., Kreutzer, C., Couillard-Despres, S., Oostingh, G.J., Hittmair, A., Improving automated thyroid cancer classification of frozen sections by the aid of virtual image translation and stain normalization. *Comput. Methods Programs Biomed. Update*, *3*, 100092, 2023.
26. Siarohin, A., Sangineto, E., Lathuiliere, S., Sebe, N., Deformable gans for pose-based human image generation, in: *Proceedings of the IEEE conference on computer vision and pattern recognition*, pp. 3408–3416, 2018.
27. Ko, K., Yeom, T., Lee, M., Superstargan: Generative adversarial networks for image-to-image translation in large-scale domains. *Neural Networks*, *162*, 330–339, 2023.
28. Srivastava, A., Valkov, L., Russell, C., Gutmann, M.U., Sutton, C., Veegan: Reducing mode collapse in gans using implicit variational learning, in: *Advances in neural information processing systems*, vol. *30*, 2017.
29. Asaf, M.Z., Rao, B., Akram, M.U., Khawaja, S.G., Khan, S., Truong, T.M., Abbasi, M.S., Dual contrastive learning-based image-to-image translation of unstained skin tissue into virtually stained H&E images. *Sci. Rep.*, *14*, 1, 2335, 2024.
30. Piva, F.J. and Dubbelman, G., Exploiting image translations via ensemble self-supervised learning for unsupervised domain adaptation. *Comput. Vis. Image Underst.*, *234*, 103745, 2023.
31. https://www.kaggle.com/datasets/vikramtiwari/pix2pix-dataset?select=maps
32. https://www.kaggle.com/datasets/darren2020/ct-to-mri-cgan?resource=download
33. https://www.v7labs.com/open-datasets/lsui

5

Study of State-of-the-Art Performance Metrics in NLP: Specifically for Text Summarization in the Medical Domain Using the SumPubMed Dataset

M. Sridhar[1], Mohammad Irfan[2*] and Sukumar Kathirmani[3]

[1]NSB Academy, Business School, Bangalore, India
[2]Christ University, Bangalore, India
[3]Quelit Innovations Pvt Ltd., Chennai, India

Abstract
Text summarization is becoming very important given the number of documents produced each year across domains. In this paper we explore the various traditional metrics for text summarization, such as ROUGE, BLEU, METEOR, etc., and look at improving the performance of the existing metric by taking the state-of-the-art untrained metric SUPERT, and clubbing it with a readability score and a penalty for long summaries. The SUMPUBMED dataset was used for this research and a BERT extractive summarizer was used for generating the summaries. It was found that using a readability score with an unsupervised metric such as SUPERT helped in assessing the quality of the summary more accurately than earlier metrics. We compared the metrics such as SUPERT scores and BERT scores with and without involving the human annotated summaries in the SUMPUBMED dataset and found that untrained metrics perform better than when involving a reference annotated summary.

Keywords: NLP, text summarization, metrics, BERT scores, SUPERT

**Corresponding author*: drmohdirfan31@gmail.com

N. Gayathri, S. Rakesh Kumar, Ramesh Chandran, Pethuru Raj Chelliah and Danilo Pelusi (eds.) Generative AI: Disruptive Technologies for Innovative Applications, (91–106) © 2025 Scrivener Publishing LLC

5.1 Introduction

Text summarization is becoming very important given the number of documents produced each year across domains. Given the volumes of text being produced, text summarization has become an important application since humans find it difficult to read long passages with limited attention spans. Also, with more and more algorithms producing summaries, it is becoming important to evaluate these metrics and understand the reliability and accuracy of such summaries before the models are used for decision making.

5.2 Literature Review

A paper on the factors affecting automatic text summarization [1] in the medical domain classified metrics into extrinsic and intrinsic depending on how they are used. Extrinsic metrics emphasize the process in which we get summaries and look at time to summarization and decision-making accuracy. Intrinsic metrics on the other hand, look at the quality of the summaries themselves--the accuracy, the readability, the conciseness, etc.

In a paper titled "Text summarization and its evaluation technique" [2], the authors showed that text summarization measures are to be performed in 3 phases:

- Co-selection (requiring a reference summary)
- Content evaluation (using reference free metrics)
- Original document review

The intrinsic metrics to evaluate text summaries can be classified as:

Trained or supervised metrics: These need reference values or human annotated summaries to assess the accuracy, and these are slower to generalize.

a) n gram-based metrics: e.g., Rouge score [3], BLEU score [4]
b) edit distance-based metrics: e.g., WMD, moverscore [5]
c) embedding based metrics: e.g., BERTSCORE [6]

Untrained or unsupervised metrics: These metrics do not need human annotation or reference summaries and can generalize better and capture meanings better than the trained metrics: for example, SUPERT [7], InfoLM [8].

In a paper on the BARYSCORE [9], the authors note that untrained metrics are further split into string based, edit based, and embedding based metrics. They also note that the metrics for NLG focus mainly on fluency and fidelity, while text summarization focus more on conciseness and readability and coherence.

The advantages and disadvantages of various metrics are summarized in the Table 5.1.

One of the challenges that researchers face when working with metrics is to compare them across. Since different metrics are defined differently, comparability is a big challenge.

Repositories such as SacreROUGE [10] and SummEval can be used to compare different metrics easily during implementation with multiple datasets.

Table 5.1 Summary of various metrics used in text summarizations.

Metric	Advantage	Disadvantages
ROUGE and other n gram metrics	Easy to use	1. Do not take position and meanings of words into account 2. Correlate poorly with human annotated summaries
BERTSCORE, WMD and embedding based metric	1. Correlate well with human annotated summaries 2. Take the sentence meanings and positions of words into account.	1. Quality of human annotated summaries vary widely between humans; and hence, difficult to scale and generalize.
Reference free metrics- SUPERT, InfoLM, Shannon score	Do not require a reference summary explicitly and model the scores better than embedding based metrics	Do not take brevity and redundancy into account directly as part of the metric. (Also, SUPERT builds a pseudo reference metric internally to compare)

5.3 Research Methodology

Overview on the SumPubMed dataset

In a paper on re-evaluating text summarization [11], the authors speak about the text summarization metrics and benchmark datasets not being current.

Most of the summarizing models are trained on datasets from 2007/08 and the most popular metric is still the Rouge metric from 2004. This brings up the need for more recent datasets with clearly annotated summaries to train summaries and achieve state of the art performance.

For the text summarization tasks, two of the biggest challenges are:

1) to find a dataset with a human annotated summary, and
2) coverage, since most of the summarized information in the news datasets is present in the first few lines.

In this context, the SumPubMed [12] dataset contains human annotated summaries which are based on the whole document, not necessarily in the first few lines. To verify the quality of summaries, they looked at aspects such as coverage of important content without repetition, readability, coherence, and informativeness.

They observed that the Rouge scores did not correlate well with the human annotated summaries, and they noted that the Rouge scores worked with news datasets only because of the placement of the summaries in the first few words.

We found that untrained metrics have generally fallen into 2 categories: Those that operate using BERT embeddings to find a reference summary (e.g., SUPERT, BLANC), and those that are based on probability distributions (Shannon scores, for instance).

In a paper on evaluation of text summaries by contrastive learning [13], the authors found that the evaluation can be divided along 3 areas of document quality:

1. Semantic quality
2. Linguistic quality
3. Others which we cannot classify.

Based on our study, we see the metrics in the unsupervised categories following one of 2 main approaches:

1. There are metrics such as SUPERT, BLANC, etc. which use BERT embeddings or even NER and fact extraction to prepare a pseudo reference internally.

2. Then there are metrics which use probabilistic methods: InfoLM, Shannon scores, etc.- these look at information difference or other ways of identifying the information captured in a summary.

Irrespective of how the summaries are generated, almost all these metrics evaluate their summaries using conciseness, consistency, coherence, readability, fluency, relevance, etc.

In this project, the author studied the metrics used in text summarization.

a) how compression ratio of the summaries affects the BERT scores and other metrics.
b) how we can take the BERTscores and SUPERTscores and add a readability metric to it; we choose the readability scores in python.

We started with the Rouge score and used the SumPubMed [14] dataset and a BERT extractive summarizer to generate summaries, calculate the rouge 1 scores between the generated and the reference summaries for the first 100 records at different compression ratios. Figure 5.1 shows the negative correlation between the compression ratio and Rouge score-the more the compression, the poorer the word matching.

I then took the BERTscores and SUPERTscores and compared these to the rouge scores.

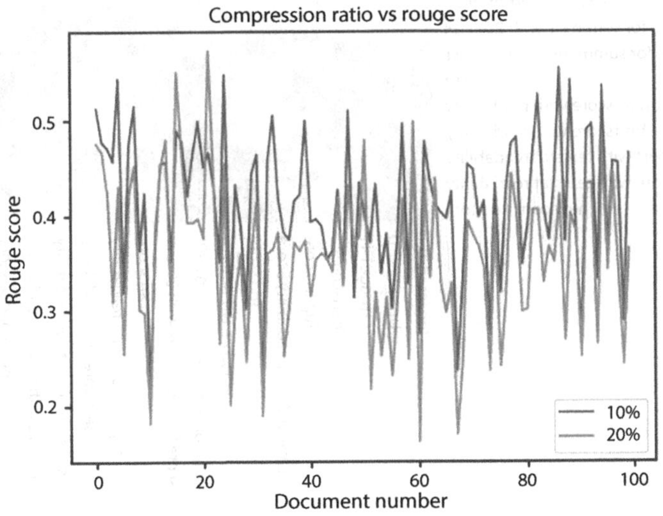

Figure 5.1 Compression ratio vs rouge score.

To assess the readability, we used the Linsear Write readability score [15] since this is meant for assessing the readability of technical documents.

The harmonic mean of the SUPERTscore and a readability score was used along with a penalty for large summaries to assess the texts.

These were compared with similar metrics by replacing the SUPERTscore with the BERTscores taken between the original document to the summarized one.

5.4 Results

1. The quality of matching between the abstract and the summary does not depend on the compression ratio.

For the compression ratio, we find that even on reducing the compression ratio, the rouge score is not necessarily going up. This means that as we reduce the compression we may have less overlap because the overlapping words may not always increase in the same proportion.

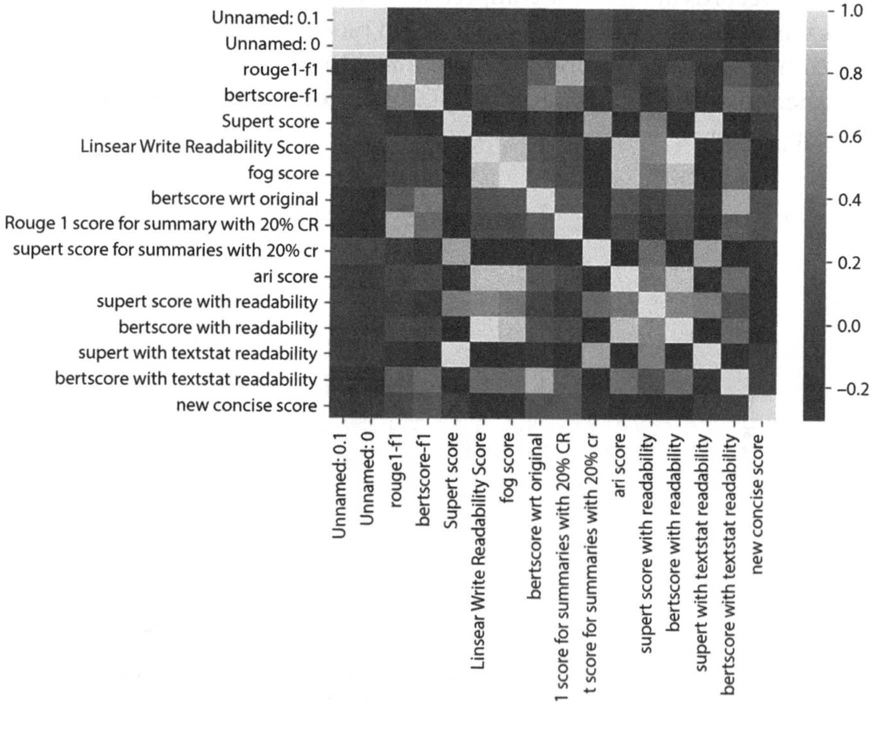

Figure 5.2 Correlation between different text summarization scores.

2. The BERTscore tallies very well with the human annotated summaries for the CNN news summarization dataset.
3. There appears to be very little correlation between metrics such as BERTscore and rouge on the one hand, and metrics like SUPERT on the other hand, which means the best summaries which are meaningful do not necessarily score high on relevance. Figure 5.2 shows that the new state of the art metrics do not correlate well with the older metrics, they do however correlate extremely well with visual judgement.

The correlation between different metrics used for summarization is given below.

Visual correlation with SUPERTscores

At a maximum SUPERTscore, the author found the grammatical construction of the sentence to be very good, with sentences clearly relating and flowing from the previous ones. Figure 5.3a shows the generated summaries at high SUPERTscore which correlate well with visual judgement. In the figure below, we see the generated summary follows a coherent sentence construction with each sentence logically related to the previous sentence.

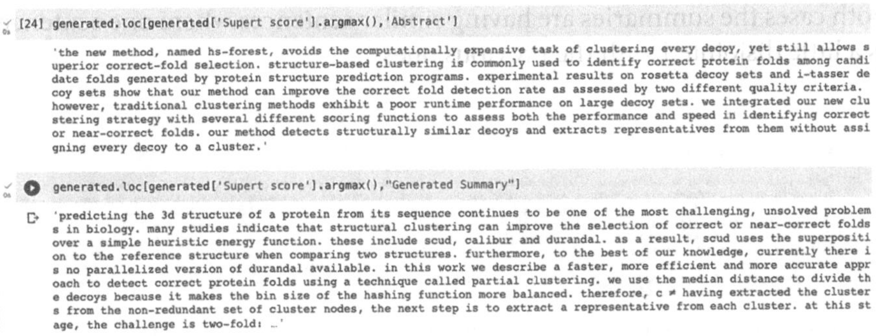

```
[24] generated.loc[generated['Supert score'].argmax(),'Abstract']

'the new method, named hs-forest, avoids the computationally expensive task of clustering every decoy, yet still allows s
uperior correct-fold selection. structure-based clustering is commonly used to identify correct protein folds among candi
date folds generated by protein structure prediction programs. experimental results on rosetta decoy sets and i-tasser de
coy sets show that our method can improve the correct fold detection rate as assessed by two different quality criteria.
however, traditional clustering methods exhibit a poor runtime performance on large decoy sets. we integrated our new clu
stering strategy with several different scoring functions to assess both the performance and speed in identifying correct
or near-correct folds. our method detects structurally similar decoys and extracts representatives from them without assi
gning every decoy to a cluster.'

generated.loc[generated['Supert score'].argmax(),"Generated Summary"]

'predicting the 3d structure of a protein from its sequence continues to be one of the most challenging, unsolved problem
s in biology. many studies indicate that structural clustering can improve the selection of correct or near-correct folds
over a simple heuristic energy function. these include scud, calibur and durandal. as a result, scud uses the superpositi
on to the reference structure when comparing two structures. furthermore, to the best of our knowledge, currently there i
s no parallelized version of durandal available. in this work we describe a faster, more efficient and more accurate appr
oach to detect correct protein folds using a technique called partial clustering. we use the median distance to divide th
e decoys because it makes the bin size of the hashing function more balanced. therefore, c ≠ having extracted the cluster
s from the non-redundant set of cluster nodes, the next step is to extract a representative from each cluster. at this st
age, the challenge is two-fold: …'
```

(a)

Figure 5.3a Generated summaries at high SUPERTscore.

Where the SUPERTscore is minimum, we find that the sentence construction and the relation between consecutive pairs of sentences appears a little off. Here we see the generated summary does not have a clear coherence, where sentences are not following each other logically. Figure 5.3b shows generated summaries with low SUPERTscore, which correlate well with visual judgement.

```
'most producers appeared to be familiar with the broad concept of the term biosecurity, although risks due to indirect co
ntacts, rather than direct contacts, were more frequently highlighted. in agreement with other studies conducted in the u
k, farmers most preferred to obtain information and advice on biosecurity from private veterinarians, but also highlighte
d defra as a source. further understanding of these issues is needed in order to more effectively communicate information
in regards to herd health and disease prevention. the limited use of biosecurity practices by many in the farming communi
ty is likely to be due to a range of factors; further understanding of this issue is required. in this study, attitudes a
nd behaviours of producers relating to selected biosecurity practices and the farming industry were studied by interviewi
ng cattle farmers within a 100\xa0km study area in north-west england using an interview-based questionnaire. most produc
ers felt the nominated biosecuri…'

[30] generated.loc[generated['Supert score'].argmin(),'Generated Summary']

'there are a range of benefits proposed to arise from implementation of biosecurity practices to assist in the prevention
and control of disease on cattle farms. other practices where more than 20% of farmers thought practices were useful but
stated they did not carry them out were; isolating animals moving onto the farm, buying stock from known health status fa
rms and ensuring that visitors clean and disinfect themselves after a farm visit. don't know' and 'not applicable' respon
ses were removed resulting in not all rows adding up to responses. discussion there appears to be an overall understandin
g of the term 'biosecurity' in the majority of the farming community in this area, with producers having wide and varied
attitudes towards the usefulness of particular biosecurity practices that have been recommended in the literature. simila
rly, in a study by hernandez et al., if producers don't perceive something is within their capabilities, this will result
in inaction. it is interesting …'
```

(b)

Figure 5.3b Generated summaries with low SUPERTscore.

Visual correlation with BERTscores

We tried using the BERTscore between the generated summary and the original article, not just the human annotated summary. Figure 5.4a shows generated summaries with high BERTscore, and these do not correlate well with Supert scores or human judgement.

For the best and worst scores of the BERTscores, it was found that in both cases the summaries are having similar sentences where one sentence is a little disjointed with the previous ones.

```
generated.loc[15,'Generated Summary']

'genetical genomics as a new approach which combines gene-expression data and marker genotypes in a segregating populatio
n, offers great perspectives to make a major contribution to the dissection of complex traits. the detected eqtl can repr
esent a locus that lies close to the gene that is being controlled or one or more loci that are unlinked to the gene that
is being controlled. taking into account own observations on the reliability of eqtl mapping we highlight eqtl located on
the same chromosome as the corresponding genes themselves. the eqtl were distributed over all autosomes with some regions
harboring particularly many eqtl with high significance. such correlations were reported by many studies. the level of ex
pression of and probe-sets, respectively, were correlated with the new composite traits that were generated by principal
component analysis pc and pc. the detection of eqtl provides information about the positional aspects of gene expression
regulation. we demonstrate tha…'

[43] generated.loc[15,'Abstract']

'accordingly, expression levels obtained by microarray analysis were taken as phenotypes in a linkage analysis to map eqt
l. linkage analysis of expression levels of these probe-sets provided eqtl at the suggestive significance threshold of lo
d > we mapped eqtl on the same chromosome as the corresponding gene and these were designated as'putative cis-eqtl'. corr
elations between transcript abundance and meat quality traits, combined with genetic positional information of eqtl allow
ed us to prioritise candidate genes for further study. by using an up-to-date annotation and localization of the respecti
ve probe-sets, the integration of eqtl mapping data and information of trait correlated expression finally served to poin
t to candidate genes for meat quality traits. in order to link eqtl to the traits of interest, probe-sets were addressed
with relative transcript abundances that showed correlation with meat quality traits at p ≤. furthermore, association of
expression levels with composite …'

[44] generated.loc[15,'Article']

' genetical genomics as a new approach which combines gene-expression data and marker genotypes in a segregating populati
on, offers great perspectives to make a major contribution to the dissection of complex traits. genetical genomics aims a
t detecting genomic loci that control variation in gene expression, so-called expression qtl ). the detected eqtl can rep
resent a locus that lies close to the gene that is being controlled or one or more loci that are unlinked to the gene tha
t is being controlled. expression-qtl for genes showing high correlation with the phenotype may provide the necessary inf
ormation required for identifying genes that control quantitative phenotypes. those cis-eqtls resulting from the correlat
ion of expression profiles with phenotypic measurements represent candidate genes for the genetic regulation underlying t
he variation of the physiological traits. we have previously reported on the identification of eqtl of genes showing expr
```

(a)

Figure 5.4a Summaries with high BERTscore.

For example, in the case below, the second sentence in the summary starts with "the detected eqtl", which has been introduced only later in the article.

Similarly in the article below, where the BERTscore is lower, we can clearly see the sentences are not coherent or readable. Figure 5.4b shows generated scores with low BERTscore, these do not correlate well with the Supert score.

For example, we find sentences like:

"the experimental protocol of this study was approved by the ethics committee of the university of insubria isolation and amplification of genomic dna genomic dna was extracted from mg of liver with dneasy blood & tissue kit according to the manufacturer\'s procedure".

```
In [93]:  data['supert score with readability'].argmin()
Out[93]:  60

In [130]: data.loc[60,['Supert score','supert score with readability']]
Out[130]: Supert score                     0.172772
          supert score with readability    0.071082
          Name: 60, dtype: object

In [101]: data.loc[60,'Generated Summary']
Out[101]: 'small molecules are of increasing interest for bioinformatics in areas such as metabolomics and drug discovery. bo
          th are commercially well established but closed source products with a large variety of different functionality. im
          plementation the here introduced cdk-taverna plugin takes advantage of the plug-in detection manager of taverna for
          its installation. uses cdk revision like taverna itself the cdk-taverna plug-in uses maven as a build system. for t
          he integration of these different resource types taverna provides various interfaces and protocols for its extensio
          n. a larger list of workflows is available from myexperiment.org. the non-matching structures are converted into th
          e chemical markup language file format. the property vectors may then be used for statistical analysis, clustering
          or machine learning purposes. the last database worker checks whether the set of loaded molecules is the last of th
          is query or if further molecules must be loaded. a last but essential worker is fail_if_true. the workflow creates
          two text files, one containing the identifier of all molecules with unknown atom types, created by the iterative_fi
          le_writer, and a second one containing information about which atom of which molecule is unknown to the cdk. cs and
          az conceived the project, and lead the further development. all co-authors contributed to the manuscript.'
```

(b)

Figure 5.4b Generated scores with low BERTscore.

Impact of combining readability scores

When the readability scores were combined with the SUPERTscores and Bertscores, the picture was found to be more accurate, as follows.

I found the Linear Write readability scores for my documents varied between 12 and 30, which categorized them in the "difficult to read" category as expected. I therefore created a new formula by normalizing the readability score and taking its harmonic mean with the SUPERTscore.

SUPERTscore with readability=(Readability score * SUPERT score) /(100 * ((Readability score/100) + SUPERTscore)))

Table 5.2 shows the ranges of the various metrics that we have used in our study. The ranges of the metrics are given below.

Table 5.2 Ranges of different metrics.

Measure	Type of measurement	Range
BERTscore	Cosine Similarity	0 to 1
SUPERT	Cosine Similarity	-1 to +1
Linsear Write Readability Scores		-inf to +inf (70+ considered easy to read)
Bert scores with readability		0 to 1
Supert scores with readability		0 to 1
New concise supert score		0 to 1

On adding the Linsear. Write readability score to the SUPERT metric, the new score was found to correlate even better to reflect the quality of the summaries.

It was found on adding the readability score that the documents having the maximum and minimum scores were the same with the SUPERTscore or the BERTscore when readability was added. Figure 5.5 shows the impact of combining BERT score with readability, it correlates very well with visual judgement.

```
In [181]: data['bertscore with readability'].argmax()
Out[181]: 71

In [184]: data.loc[71,['bertscore with readability', 'supert score with readability']]
Out[184]: bertscore with readability        0.223917
          supert score with readability      0.12919
          Name: 71, dtype: object

In [182]: data['bertscore with readability'].argmin()
Out[182]: 60

In [185]: data.loc[60,['bertscore with readability', 'supert score with readability']]
Out[185]: bertscore with readability        0.105462
          supert score with readability     0.071082
          Name: 60, dtype: object
```

Figure 5.5 Combining BERT score with readability.

For example, in this case shown below, the maximum value of our new score shows that the summary is actually less readable than the SUPERTscore. Figure 5.6a shows the effect of combining SUPERTscore with readability: where the new score is maximum, again it correlates very well with visual judgement.

In the case where the new score is less, the gaps in the sentence construction show up clearly, and the summary shows clearly disjointed sentences. Figure 5.6b shows the effect of combining SUPERTscore with readability: where the new score is maximum, again it correlates very well with visual judgement.

```
In [92]:  data['supert score with readability'].argmax()
Out[92]:  71

In [129]: data.loc[71,['Supert score','supert score with readability']]
Out[129]: Supert score                      0.224615
          supert score with readability     0.12919
          Name: 71, dtype: object

In [99]:  data.loc[71,'Generated Summary']
Out[99]:  'the monophyly of the supraordinal placental mammalian clade afrotheria, whose living members include the endemic af
          ro-arabian aardvarks, elephant-shrews or sengis, golden moles, tenrecs, sea cows, hyraxes, and elephants, is now str
          ongly supported by diverse forms of genomic data, including indels, sines, "protein sequence signatures", chromosoma
          l syntenies, and nuclear and mitochondrial dna sequences. extinct taxa should play a critical role in efforts to res
          olve placental supraordinal phylogeny because fossils exhibit unique combinations of primitive and derived character
          s that help to break up long branches that otherwise might attract due to homoplasy rather than homology. the only r
          ecent phylogenetic analysis to have scored members of all extant afrotherian orders included only two undoubted foss
          il afrotherians, however, both of which were extinct paenungulates. deletion of basal eocene taxa, such as the herod
          otiines chambius and herodotius, the hyracoids microhyrax and seggeurius, the proboscidean phosphatherium, and the s
          irenian prorastomus did not alter the optimal interordinal topology, but afrotherian interordinal phylogeny did prov
          e to be sensitive to placement of the root of the placental tree: if exafroplacentalia was constrained to be monophy
          letic, afroinsectivora again broke down and macroscelidea was placed as the sister taxon of other afrotherians. cons
          istency index excludes uninformative characters. results followed by an asterisk are those that occur in the adams c
          onsensus of all equally parsimonious trees. os = ordered and scaled analysis; u = unordered analysis. the results of
          the current analysis are more consistent with the stratigraphic succession of early proboscideans in placing the old
          est taxa as the most basal forms, slightly younger numidotherium koholense as the sister group of middle eocene-to-r
          ecent proboscideans, and moeritherium in a more nested position. in contrast to previous studies that positioned gen
          iohyus as the sister taxon of other hyracoid genera, in this study the small-bodied paleogene forms thyrohyrax and s
          aghatherium are consecutive sister taxa of large-bodied forms including geniohyus. considerable ambiguity is introdu
          ced by missing data and different methods for optimizing character states onto slightly different afrotherian phylog
          enies, but it remains distinctly possible that there are a number of morphological synapomorphies of crown afrotheri
          a, and that the ancestral crown afrotherian more closely resembled a "proto-ungulate" than an "insectivore". of inte
          rest in this regard is the phylogenetic placement of the alleged stem macroscelidean herodotius, from the late eocen
```

(a)

Figure 5.6a Combining SUPERTscore with readability: where the new score is maximum.

```
In [93]:  data['supert score with readability'].argmin()
Out[93]:  60

In [130]: data.loc[60,['Supert score','supert score with readability']]
Out[130]: Supert score                      0.172772
          supert score with readability     0.071082
          Name: 60, dtype: object

In [101]: data.loc[60,'Generated Summary']
Out[101]: 'small molecules are of increasing interest for bioinformatics in areas such as metabolomics and drug discovery. bo
          th are commercially well established but closed source products with a large variety of different functionality. im
          plementation the here introduced cdk-taverna plugin takes advantage of the plug-in detection manager of taverna for
          its installation. uses cdk revision like taverna itself the cdk-taverna plug-in uses maven as a build system. for t
          he integration of these different resource types taverna provides various interfaces and protocols for its extensio
          n. a larger list of workflows is available from myexperiment.org. the non-matching structures are converted into th
          e chemical markup language file format. the property vectors may then be used for statistical analysis, clustering
          or machine learning purposes. the last database worker checks whether the set of loaded molecules is the last of th
          is query or if further molecules must be loaded. a last but essential worker is fail_if_true. the workflow creates
          two text files, one containing the identifier of all molecules with unknown atom types, created by the iterative_fi
          le_writer, and a second one containing information about which atom of which molecule is unknown to the cdk. cs and
          az conceived the project, and lead the further development. all co-authors contributed to the manuscript.'
```

(b)

Figure 5.6b Combining SUPERTscore with readability: where the new score is maximum.

Impact of conciseness of summaries on the SUPERTscore

One of the important attributes of any summary is that it should be "concise" or that its length should be brief.

This is depicted in other metrics such as BLEU which impose a brevity penalty.

A penalty factor of 10000/length of the summary on top of the SUPERTscore was used to check for conciseness.

Therefore, the new score used is:

$$\textbf{New concise score} = \textbf{SUPERTscore with readability}$$
$$\textbf{*10000/Length of the generated summary}$$

With the new score the results from the SUPERTscore was found to have improved.

In the above example, the summary was found to be better and shorter than just using SUPERTscore alone. Figure 5.7a shows the generated summary where the new concise SUPERTscore is maximum.

```
In [17]: data['new concise score'].argmax()
Out[17]: 95

In [23]: data.loc[95,['new concise score','supert score with readability']]
Out[23]: new concise score               0.918107
         supert score with readability   0.088414
         Name: 95, dtype: object

In [24]: data.loc[95,'Generated Summary']
Out[24]: 'transcription factors regulate the expression of genes by interacting with cis-regulatory elements in dna sequenc
         es in response to internal and external stimuli. the method takes the advantage that the ability to detect tf bind
         ing sites improves with both the number of comparison species and the evolution distance between species. the modi
         fied program was implemented in c under linux. however, the methods may also eliminate the true tf binding sites a
         s the number of species required to have the same base as human in a multiple alignment column, t, approaches we u
         sed the muscle data set to assess the effect of masking methods on the size of searching space and on the percenta
         ge of true binding sites retained. when wbmm was applied and t was set at the same four tf dna binding motifs were
         detected with combined sensitivity equal to and ppr. these gene clusters with similar expression patterns are like
         ly to be regulated by common transcription factors.'
```

(a)

Figure 5.7a Generated summary where the new concise SUPERTscore is maximum.

Similarly in this case, the summary using the new score is better than when using the SUPERTscore alone. Figure 5.7b shows the generated summary where the new concise SUPERTscore is minimum.

```
In [26]: data.loc[data['new concise score'].argmin(),['new concise score','supert score with readability']]

Out[26]: new concise score              0.178884
         supert score with readability  0.088977
         Name: 79, dtype: object

In [27]: data.loc[79,'Generated Summary']

Out[27]: 'due to the continued growth of biomedical publications, it has become very difficult for scientists to keep up wi
         th the new findings reported in the literature. however, they do require domain experts to be closely involved in
         the design and implementation of the system to capture the patterns used for extracting the necessary information.
         others use deep parsers with hand-crafted patterns. to improve the applicability of the generated patterns, we inc
         orporate two additional design features. with this method, two phrases referring to the same entity or in a partic
         ular relation are detected in text, and links are established between them. some of these relations were later con
         sidered in biomedical information extraction systems in order to improve their performance. thus, this pattern con
         tains information described in two places: lexical trigger that specifies the arguments, the selection restriction
         s on the argument, and the role they play, and the syntactic constraints corresponding to different constructs. th
         is step enables the system to find relations between more appropriate entities than the ones referred by textual e
         xpressions in the argument position. to make it easier to specify triggers, we ask users to provide the trigger's
         root, which is the primary lexical unit of a word. in a few cases, we ask the users for this confirmation. it spec
         ifies the arguments of the trigger. furthermore, in combination with the constraints expressed within the trigger
         specification, the use of template will succeed only if np is ggp, whereas the use of template will succeed even i
         f np is a protein part. nominal triggers in addition to the standard pattern templates that are based on verbal fo
         rms of the trigger, we also consider cases where the trigger verb is nominalized. for example, one constraint in e
         nglish is that only transitive verbs can be passivized. following are some examples of elliptical constructions, a
         nd how they would be written if the trigger-argument association would be required. therefore, we get <phosphoryla
         testrigger, nfat4theme >. but even with a large number of patterns automatically generated in the proposed manner,
         the recall of the resulting system is still low because sentence constructions and writing styles vary considerabl
         y in actual text, and the number of variations to be considered is overwhelmingly high. complex constructs, e.g.,
         coordinations and relative clauses, pose a challenge for state-of-the-art full parsers. our primary concerns are c
         oordinations of nouns, noun phrases, verbs, and verb phrases. full relative clauses are introduced by relative pro
         nouns, such as "which", "who", and "that". appositions can be simplified into two sentences: one with the referred
         noun phrase and the other with the appositive. sometimes, the referred entity is mentioned somewhere else in the t
         ext. then we use the patterns to get instances for a trigger. furthermore, the data set should include trigger ann
         otations needed to automatically generate patterns. among these, we focused on events with simple entities as them
         es. in the ge corpora, we consider the same events as well. additionally, we eliminated verb triggers like "find"
         and "form" because they are not specific to particular biomedical events.table selected triggers see above see abo
         ve see above this predication is always used together with "mrna". to extract the predicate in a consecutive verb
         group,, we looked at the verb phrase subtree and searched for its rightmost children. = events with selected trigg
         ers/all events. evaluation results on the whole, abstract, and full paper collections from the development set of
         bionlp-st ge task whole set \u2003total subset with selected triggers \u2003total performance is reported in terms
```

(b)

Figure 5.7b Generated summary where the new concise SUPERTscore is minimum.

Observations and results are summarized in the Table 5.3.

5.5 Conclusions

- The compression ratio does not affect the text summarization metric.
- SUPERTscores clearly reflect the quality of the text summary better than other scores in terms of both relevance and readability. Addition of a readability metric does not significantly affect the quality of the SUPERTscore.
- BERTscores correlate very well with the human annotated summaries and do not correlate very well with SUPERTscores.

Table 5.3 Results of visual inspection vs scores for 10% of the documents (Documents having min and max of each score).

Document number	Bertscore with readability	SUPERT score	SUPERT with readability	SUPERT with conciseness & readability	Document length	Visual judgement (on a scale of 5)
10	.1336	0.289	.1026	.2409	4259	4
71	.2213	.2246	.1291	.4490	2877	4.2
15	.1534	.1976	.0957	.7701	1243	3.9
60	.1054	.1727	.0710	.5184	1371	3.5
95	.1495	.1722	.0884	.9181	963	4.2
79	.1231	.2322	.0889	.1788	4974	3.5
28	.1609	.1677	.0914	.2324	3933	3.5
47	.1655	.1186	.0752	.5312	1416	3.4
33	.1388	.2301	.0964	.5694	1694	3.5
55	.1388	.1744	.0853	.3760	2270	3.4

- Adding a Linsear. By writing the score clearly, it will improve() the ability of the SUPERTmetric to score summaries accurately. Moreover, adding a penalty for longer summaries improved the ability of the SUPERTscore r to give shorter summaries a better score, with other aspects to quality remaining relatively unchanged.

5.6 Future Score of Work

In this project, the author focused on embedding based metrics such as the BERTSCORE and the SUPERT scores.

The following items can still be addressed to find a better metric:

1. We can examine models using probability distribution based metrics like the InfoLM score or Shannon score on medical documents and compare them to embedding based metrics.
2. One of the drawbacks with SUPERTscores identified in a paper [16] is that it cannot identify redundancies in the summary. In this context, there is a scope for improving the SUPERTscores to ensure that redundancy in summaries is penalized.
3. In a paper [17] on generating summaries using reinforcement learning, the authors highlight how using even a rouge score as a reward function can help generate better summaries. Therefore, using SUPEERT as a reward function and then using that as a reference summary can help improve the score.

AI disclosure statement: The author acknowledges the use of AI-based tools for minor language editing or grammatical correction. However, all intellectual contributions, analyses, and conclusions presented in this chapter are entirely the author's own.

References

1. Chaves, A., Kesiku, C., Garcia-Zapirain, B., Automatic Text Summarization of Biomedical Text Data: A Systematic Review. *Information*, *13*, 8, 393, 2022.
2. Rani, R. and Kaur, B., The text summarization and its evaluation technique. *Turk. J. of Comput. Math. Educ. (TURCOMAT)*, *12*, 745–752, 2021.

3. Lin, C.Y., Rouge: A package for automatic evaluation of summaries. *Text summarization branches out*, pp. 74–81, 2004, July.
4. Papineni, K., Roukos, S., Ward, T., Zhu, W.J., Bleu: a method for automatic evaluation of machine translation, in: *Proceedings of the 40th annual meeting of the Association for Computational Linguistics*, pp. 311–318, 2002, July.
5. Zhao, W., Peyrard, M., Liu, F., Gao, Y., Meyer, C.M., Eger, S., MoverScore: Text generation evaluating with contextualized embeddings and earth mover distance, 2019, arXiv preprint arXiv:1909.02622.
6. Zhang, T., Kishore, V., Wu, F., Weinberger, K.Q., Artzi, Y., Bertscore: Evaluating text generation with bert, 2019, arXiv preprint arXiv:1904.09675.
7. Gao, Y., Zhao, W., Eger, S., SUPERT: Towards new frontiers in unsupervised evaluation metrics for multi-document summarization, 2020, arXiv preprint arXiv:2005.03724.
8. Colombo, P.J.A., Clavel, C., Piantanida, P., Infolm: A new metric to evaluate summarization & data2text generation, in: *Proceedings of the AAAI Conference on Artificial Intelligence*, vol. 36, pp. 10554–10562, 2022, June.
9. Colombo, P., Staerman, G., Clavel, C., Piantanida, P., Automatic text evaluation through the lens of Wasserstein barycenters, 2021, arXiv preprint arXiv:2108.12463.
10. Deutsch, D. and Roth, D., SacreROUGE: An open-source library for using and developing summarization evaluation metrics, 2020, arXiv preprint arXiv:2007.05374.
11. Bhandari, M., Gour, P., Ashfaq, A., Liu, P., Neubig, G., Re-evaluating evaluation in text summarization, 2020, arXiv preprint arXiv:2010.07100.
12. Gupta, V., *et al.*, SumPubMed: Summarization dataset of PubMed scientific articles. *Proceedings of the 59th Annual Meeting of the Association for Computational Linguistics and the 11th International Joint Conference on Natural Language Processing: Student Research Workshop*, 2021.
13. Wu, H., Ma, T., Wu, L., Manyumwa, T., Ji, S., Unsupervised reference-free summary quality evaluation via contrastive learning, 2020, arXiv preprint arXiv:2010.01781.
14. Gupta, V., Bharti, P., Nokhiz, P., Karnick, H., SumPubMed: Summarization dataset of PubMed scientific articles, in: *Proceedings of the 59th Annual Meeting of the Association for Computational Linguistics and the 11th International Joint Conference on Natural Language Processing: Student Research Workshop*, pp. 292–303, 2021, August.
15. https://readable.com/readability/lensear-write-readability-formula/.
16. Chen, W., Li, P., King, I., A training-free and reference-free summarization evaluation metric via centrality-weighted relevance and self-referenced redundancy, 2021, arXiv preprint arXiv:2106.13945.
17. Böhm, F., Gao, Y., Meyer, C.M., Shapira, O., Dagan, I., Gurevych, I., Better rewards yield better summaries: Learning to summarise without references, 2019, arXiv preprint arXiv:1909.01214.

6

The Impact of Generative AI in Gaming: Exploring Immersive Experiences

Nalli Vinaya Kumari[1], G.S. Pradeep Ghantasala[2*], U. Ananthanagu[3], Pellakuri Vidyullatha[4] and Mudassir Khan[5]

[1]*Department of Computer Science and Engineering, Malla Reddy Engineering College for Women, Jawaharlal Nehru Technological University, Hyderabad, India*
[2]*Department of Computer Science and Engineering, Alliance College of Engineering and Design, Alliance University, Bengaluru, India*
[3]*Center of Excellence in Immersive Technologies, Alliance University, Bengaluru, India*
[4]*Department of Computer Science and Engineering, Koneru Lakshmaiah Education Foundation, Guntur, Andhra Pradesh, India*
[5]*Department of Computer Science, King Khalid University, Abha, Saudi Arabia*

Abstract

The integration of generative AI into video games and digital environments is ushering in a generation of transformation in virtual interactions, growing realism, creativity, and engagement in digital worlds. In this chapter, we discover the various packages of generative AI in video games and display how those superior technologies are revolutionizing sports design, individual development, and immersive storytelling. Generative AI algorithms along with generative adversarial networks (GANs) and variational autoencoders (VAEs) are used to create enormously practical textures, landscapes, and dynamic environments that evolve in reaction to participant actions, supplying an extra-immersive and customized gaming experience. One of the important things to focus on is procedural content material generation, wherein AI-pushed structures autonomously generate full-sized and sundry game worlds, lowering the need for guide content material advent and permitting builders to provide rich, expansive universes at scale. This now not only best hurries up the improvement method but also allows for countless replay ability, as no gaming studies are identical. Moreover, generative AI is instrumental in growing wise, non-playable characters (NPCs) that show off realistic behaviors and adapt

**Corresponding author*: ggspradeep@gmail.com

N. Gayathri, S. Rakesh Kumar, Ramesh Chandran, Pethuru Raj Chelliah and Danilo Pelusi (eds.) Generative AI: Disruptive Technologies for Innovative Applications, (107–130) © 2025 Scrivener Publishing LLC

to players' strategies, improving the complexity and intensity of interactions inside the game. The chapter additionally explores the capability of generative AI in digital environments past conventional gaming. Applications in education simulations, academic platforms, and digital reality (VR) stories are examined, highlighting how AI-generated content material can create practical and pleasant situations to familiarize and explore. The integration of generative AI in VR allows the advent of dynamic and interactive digital areas that respond to personal inputs, fostering a more immersive and interactive experience.

Keywords: Virtual environments, immersive experiences, generative AI, augmented reality, gaming

6.1 Introduction

Generative AI refers to a category of synthetic intelligence that makes use of system-studying strategies to create new content material. In gaming, this encompasses producing textures, landscapes, characters, narratives, and whole worlds, which have been historically created by human designers. The number one strategy in generative AI consists of generative adversarial networks (GANs) and variational autoencoders (VAEs). GANs paint by means of pitting neural networks toward each other—a generator and a discriminator—to create exceedingly sensible content material. VAEs, on the other hand, are aware of studying the underlying shape of information to generate new, comparable information points [1]. The utility of generative AI in gaming spans numerous factors: procedural content generation (PCG)—automatically growing large-scale sports environments, levels, and property; character and NPC development—crafting dynamic, realistic characters that can adapt and respond to participant interactions; storytelling and narrative design—generating complicated, branching storylines that evolve primarily based totally on participant decisions; texture and asset creation—generating high-decision textures and distinctive properties that exhibit visible fidelity; significance of AI technologies in transforming game experiences—generative AI technology is drastically reworking sports reviews by means of enhancing realism and immersion AI-generated environments and characters can acquire a degree of element and complexity that guide layouts frequently cannot match [2]. This results in more immersive and realistic sports worlds: increasing creativity and innovation—by automating recurring tasks, AI frees up human designers' awareness of more innovative factors of sports improvement. This can cause revolutionary gameplay mechanics and precise participant reviews: personalization and dynamic content—AI can tailor sports reviews to character gamers by means of studying their conduct and preferences. This ends in dynamic content material that evolves primarily based totally on participant moves, making every playthrough precise; scalability and efficiency—AI allows the introduction of vast, complicated sports worlds that are speedy and efficient, decreasing the time and costs. This scalability lets indie builders and smaller studios compete with large corporations by means of generating tremendous content material; replay ability—procedural content material technology guarantees that no playthrough is the same, improving the replay fee of video games. Players can discover new environments, come upon unique challenges, and enjoy numerous narratives every time they play. Intelligent AI-pushed NPCs can show off sensible behaviors, study from participant interactions, and adapt their strategies, making video games more attractive and challenging [16]. No Man's Sky—this sport makes use of procedural technology to create a whole universe with 18 quintillion planets, each with precise landscapes, ecosystems, and life forms. The vastness and range are made viable by means of generative algorithms. Minecraft—the procedural technology in Minecraft creates limitless terrain and structures, supplying gamers with limitless exploration and creativity. The sport's achievement showcases the attraction of AI-pushed world-building. The Sims—using AI in The Sims franchise allows for the simulation of sensible human conduct and lifestyle scenarios. NPCs in The Sims have dynamic personalities and react to participant moves in complicated ways. AI Dungeon is an interactive, primarily text-based sport that makes use of GPT-3, a language model, to generate limitless narrative possibilities, demonstrating how AI can create attractive and unpredictable storytelling reviews [17]. By leveraging generative AI, the gaming enterprise is poised to provide richer, more enticing stories that constantly push the limits of what is feasible in digital environments. This bankruptcy will discover those improvements in element, imparting a complete expertise of the contemporary country and destiny as an ability of generative AI in gaming [3].

6.2 Realistic Textures and Landscapes

Generative AI has notably improved the realism of textures and landscapes in video games, developing more immersive and plausible environments. At the leading edge of this development are GANs and VAEs. GANs include neural networks, with the generator and the discriminator operating in tandem. The generator creates images, while the discriminator evaluates them toward actual images, iteratively enhancing the quality of the generated textures. This technique permits the advent of quite special and reasonable textures for numerous recreation elements, along with terrain, foliage, and concrete environments. For example, GANs can generate complicated rock formations, lush forests, and intricately designed cityscapes that upload intensity and realism to recreation worlds. This method now not only complements visible constancy but also reduces the time and assets necessary for guide texture advent [4]. Variational autoencoders study the underlying distribution of entering records and generate new record factors which are comparable; however, they are no longer the same as the original. In recreation layout, VAEs are used to create various and sensible textures by mastering a dataset of actual setting images. They can generate seamless textures that may be implemented to one-of-a-kind surfaces inside a recreation, thus improving visible consistency. For instance, VAEs can produce various bark textures for bushes or one-of-a-kind styles for stone walls, including the intensity and range for recreation environments. The utility of VAEs in the texture era permits for non-stop version and diversity, which is critical for the development of expansive and sundry recreation worlds [18]. The historical context and the evolution of texture and panorama era in gaming have been significant. Initially, textures have been hand-drawn pixel art, requiring vast attempts and proscribing the dimensions of games [19]. With improvements in PC graphics, procedural texturing strategies emerged, automating a few components; nevertheless, they require a good-sized guide entry. The creation of generative AI marks a brand-new era, wherein AI can autonomously create quite sensible textures and landscapes, pushing the limits of what is feasible in recreation layout [5].

Enhancing Visual Authenticity

The utility of GANs and VAEs in recreation layout notably complements visible authenticity. AI-generated textures and landscapes contribute to the general immersion of a recreation, making the digital worlds seem more reasonable and plausible [20].

Natural landscapes: AI can generate sensible mountains, forests, rivers, and deserts with every complex info that mimics actual-setting geography. The use of GANs permits the advent of assorted and special terrain features, along with snow-capped peaks, dense forests, and flowing rivers, which beautify the player's experience of exploration and discovery. This degree of element facilitates the creation of environments that are not only visually beautiful but also actual and alive. For example, in a recreation set in a mountainous region, GANs can generate sensible rock formations, vegetation, and climate effects, making the digital panorama indistinguishable from actual life [6].

Urban environments: GANs can create detailed textures for buildings, roads, and other urban elements, making cities in games look more lifelike. The potential to generate numerous architectural patterns and materials, consisting of brick, concrete, and glass, provides the realism of city settings. AI-generated graffiti is put on and torn, and different small pieces of information similarly contribute to the authenticity of the environment [21]. For instance, a cityscape in a sport can function realistically with weathered buildings, numerous avenue textures, and dynamic light conditions, all generated through AI to exhibit the visible experience.

Character textures: AI can generate sensible pores and skin textures, apparel patterns, and facial features, including intensity to individual models. This stage of element facilitates the creation of more relatable and visually compelling characters, improving the emotional connection among gamers and the recreation. For example, GANs may be used to create reasonable facial features, pores and skin tones, and apparel textures, making characters appear more human and expressive. This generation is mainly treasured in growing numerous and inclusive individual designs, reflecting an extensive variety of ethnicities and cultures. By automating the introduction of those specified textures, AI reduces the workload on artists, letting them recognize more innovative factors of recreation design. This performance now not only hurries up the improvement technique but also guarantees a better stage of visible exceptionality throughout the recreation. The capacity to generate first-rate textures on call additionally opens up new opportunities for dynamic content material generation, wherein textures can extrude and evolve in reaction to in-recreation activities and participant actions [7].

AI-driven environment evolution: Dynamic environments are important for growing attractive and immersive gaming experiences. The AI-pushed surroundings' evolution lets recreation worlds extrude and adapt in real time primarily based totally on participant movements and different variables, making the gameplay more interactive and unpredictable [22].

Responsive environments: AI algorithms can create environments that respond to participant movements in real time. For example, if a participant destroys a construction inside the game, the encircling surroundings would possibly extrude to mirror the impact, along with rubble scattering or close-by systems displaying signs of damage. This responsiveness provides a layer of realism and interactivity, as gamers can see the on-the-spot effects in their movements [23]. Such dynamic responses may be vital in video games in which environmental interplay is a central gameplay element, improving the participant's immersion and engagement.

Seasonal changes: AI can simulate seasonal modifications in a sport setting. Trees may shed their leaves in autumn, and snow may cover the floor in wintry weather, presenting a dynamic and immersive enjoyment that evolves. These seasonal versions now not only simply exhibit visible range but also introduce new gameplay mechanics, along with slippery surfaces in wintry weather or multiplied visibility in spring. For example, a sport set in a delusion setting may function as dynamic climate structures and seasonal modifications that affect gameplay, along with changing the provision of sources or the conduct of NPCs [24].

Historical context and evolution: Dynamic environments have developed drastically from static, unchanging settings. Early video games featured steady environments with a confined interaction. The creation of physics' engines allowed for more dynamic interactions, but these ones have been often pre-scripted and confined in scope. AI-driven environment evolution represents a tremendous jump forward, allowing interactive and responsive game worlds that may extrude and adapt in real time [25].

Customized gaming experiences: AI-driven environments can be tailored to individual game enthusiasts, enhancing personalization and ensuring that each player's experience is precise and attractive. Adaptive difficulty—the recreation environment can adapt its hassle based completely on the player's potential level. For example, if a player is struggling, AI can also additionally reduce the sort of enemies or provide more resources. Conversely, for professional game enthusiasts, AI can introduce harder obstacles and more difficult adversaries. This adaptive technique ensures that the game remains thrilling and hard for game enthusiasts of all potential levels. For instance, a first-individual shooter recreation can also additionally modify an enemy AI and spawn expenses based completely on the player's performance, ensuring a balanced and attractive experience. Tailored content—AI can observe player behavior and opportunities to generate content material fabric that suits their play style. For instance, a player who prefers exploration can also find more hidden areas and secrets; at the same time, a combat-focused player can also additionally come upon harder enemies. This personalization complements participant engagement by means of catering to character possibilities and playstyles, making the sport more exciting and immersive. For example, an open-global RPG may use AI to generate quests and activities tailor-made to the participant's movements and choices, making sure of a unique and customized adventure. Historical context and evolution personalization in video games has developed from easy trouble settings to more state-of-the-art adaptive structures. Early video games supplied simple trouble levels; however, those had been static and no longer adapted to the participant's converting ability level. Modern AI-pushed structures can dynamically alter the sports enjoyed in real time, presenting a more customized and pleasant enjoyment for every participant [8].

Procedural world generation—autonomous generation of game worlds: Procedural content material era allows for the advent of sizeable, various recreation worlds with minimum guide input. This approach is vital for growing large-scale video games that provide infinite exploration and replay ability. Terrain generation—AI algorithms can generate various terrains, such as mountains, valleys, lakes, and forests. This technique entails growing peak maps, which dictate the elevation of the terrain, after which textures and flowers are used to create a sensible landscape. For example, procedural era can create a sprawling mountain variety with various slopes, elevations, and flower types, supplying wealthy and sundry surroundings for gamers to explore. The generated terrain can also encompass dynamic capabilities consisting of rivers that float realistically and ecosystems that respond to participant actions. Structure placement procedural era can locate systems consisting of villages, cities, dungeons, and landmarks in the course of the sport setting [26]. AI guarantees that those systems are logically located and accessible, supplying coherent and navigable surroundings. For instance, a procedural set of rules would possibly generate a medieval village with an imperative marketplace, residential areas, and surrounding farmland, all related through a community of roads and pathways. This logical placement allows the creation of plausible and immersive worlds that seem herbal and lived-in. Historical context and evolution—the idea of the procedural era dates returned to early PC video games that used easy algorithms to create basic, repetitive content material. Over time, those strategies have advanced to supply more and more complicated and various recreation worlds. The modern AI-pushed procedural era represents the top of this evolution, permitting the advent of tremendously particular and sundry environments that rival the ones crafted by human designers. Reducing manual content creation—by automating the advent of recreation worlds, AI reduces the want for guide content material advent, permitting builders to recognize more innovative elements of recreation layout. Efficiency and scalability—the

AI-driven procedural era lets builders create expansive recreation worlds quickly and efficiently. This scalability is critical for large-scale video games that require sizeable environments for gamers to explore. By lowering the time and sources wanted for guide content material advent, builders can recognize refining gameplay mechanics, narrative, and different vital elements. For example, a recreation set in a post-apocalyptic setting would possibly use procedural era to create a sizeable, ruined cityscape, permitting builders to recognize crafting enticing storylines and compelling characters. Consistency and quality—the procedural era guarantees consistency inside the highly satisfactory fashion of the sport setting. AI algorithms can generate content material that clings to precise layout hints and aesthetic principles, preserving a cohesive appearance and sense in the course of the sport. This consistency is essential for growing immersive and plausible environments. For instance, a myth recreation would possibly use procedural era to create a constant and visually cohesive setting, with every location providing specific but thematically constant landscapes and systems. Historical context and evolution—manual content material advent has usually been a labor-in-depth and time-eating technique. Early video games relied closely on homemade ranges and assets, restricting their scope and scale [9]. The procedural era gives an approach to those limitations, allowing the introduction of huge and numerous sports worlds with minimum guide input. Modern AI-pushed strategies take this a step in addition, making an allowance for the introduction of especially precise and regular environments that beautify the general best of the sport [27].

Enhancing replay ability: The procedural era considerably complements replay ability by making sure that no playthroughs are the same. Each new sport can be characteristic of exclusive global layouts, structures, and demanding situations, providing a sparkling and attractive enjoyment each time.

Varied world layouts: Procedural algorithms can generate exclusive global layouts for every playthrough, making sure that gamers have a unique enjoyment each time they begin a brand-new sport. This variability maintains the sport to be sparkling and exciting, encouraging gamers to discover and find out new factors of the sport globally. For example, a rogue-like sport may generate a brand new dungeon format every time the participant enters, making sure that no runs are the same and retaining the gameplay to be dynamic and attractive [28].

Dynamic quest generation: AI can generate dynamic quests and targets that adapt to the participant's location, movements, and progress. This guarantees a steady circulation of the latest and sundry demanding situations, improving replayability and retaining the sport as enticing over a couple of playthroughs. For instance, an open-global RPG may use AI to generate quests primarily based totally on the participant's movements and selections, growing a customized and evolving narrative enjoyment that encourages a couple of playthroughs.

Historical context and evolution: Replayability has constantly been an essential issue of sports layout. Early video games did this through excessive issue ranges and constrained content material. The procedural era gives a more state-of-the-art solution, imparting countless ranges and new demanding situations with every playthrough. Modern AI-pushed strategies take this in addition, allowing the introduction of dynamic and customized content material that complements replayability and keeps gamers engaged for longer periods [10].

Prospects and challenges advances in AI technology: The destiny of generative AI in gaming is promising, with ongoing improvements in AI generation poised to additionally beautify sports layouts and participant enjoyment. As AI algorithms emerge as more state-of-the-art, they may be capable of generating even more precise and practical content material, pushing the bounds of what is viable in a digital world. Future traits in gadget mastering, especially in regions that include deep mastering and reinforcement mastering, will allow AI to create even more complicated and dynamic sports environments. Neural networks and beyond the subsequent era of neural networks, consisting of more superior GANs and VAEs, might be able to produce even more practical textures, landscapes, and person models [29]. These improvements will permit the introduction of hyper-practical sports worlds that rival actual lifestyles in phrases of visible constancy and detail. Additionally, the combination of AI with different rising technologies, which include virtual reality (VR) and augmented reality (AR), will, in addition, beautify the immersive ability of generative AI in gaming [30]. AI-driven narrative and storytelling destiny—AI structures might be able to produce dynamic and adaptive narratives that respond to participant movements and selections in actual time. This will permit the advent of customized and evolving storylines that provide, without a doubt, a particular and attractive reveal for every participant. The AI-pushed narrative era will permit for more complicated and nuanced storytelling, with characters and occasions that adapt and evolve primarily based totally on the participant's interactions.

Ethical considerations: The combination of AI in gaming additionally increases critical moral considerations. As AI structures end up more superior and more capable, it is way important to cope with troubles associated with facts privacy, algorithmic bias, and the capability effect on employment inside the gaming enterprise. Data privacy—AI structures regularly require massive quantities of facts to feature effectively. Ensuring that participant facts are gathered and utilized in an accountable and obvious way is important for retaining acceptance as true and safeguarding privacy [31]. Developers ought to put in force sturdy facts and safety measures and make sure that gamers are knowledgeable on approximately how their facts are being used. Algorithmic bias—AI algorithms can unintentionally reinforce biases present in educational data. It is critical for builders to cautiously curate and audit education facts to make sure that AI structures are honest and unbiased. This consists of taking steps to do away with bias in person layout, narrative elements, and gameplay mechanics. Impact on employment—the growing use of AI in recreation improvement might also additionally result in adjustments inside the workforce, with certain roles doubtlessly turning obsolete. It is critical to keep in mind the effect on employment and make sure that employees are furnished with possibilities for retraining and upskilling. The gaming enterprise ought to adapt to those adjustments with the aid of fostering a way of life of non-stop getting-to-know and innovation. Generative AI is revolutionizing recreation layout with the aid of automating the advent of sensible textures, dynamic environments, and procedurally generated worlds. Techniques inclusive of GANs and VAEs exhibit visible authenticity, making digital worlds more immersive and believable. The evolution and personalization of AI-pushed surroundings create enticing and particular studies for every participant, even as the procedural content material era permits the advent of vast, numerous recreation worlds that provide infinite exploration and replayability. These improvements now not only best lessen the workload on builders but also open up new opportunities for creativity and innovation in recreation layout. As the AI generation keeps evolving, its effect on the gaming enterprise will grow, pushing the limits of what is viable in digital environments and imparting gamers richer, more immersive studies than ever before as shown in Figure 6.1.

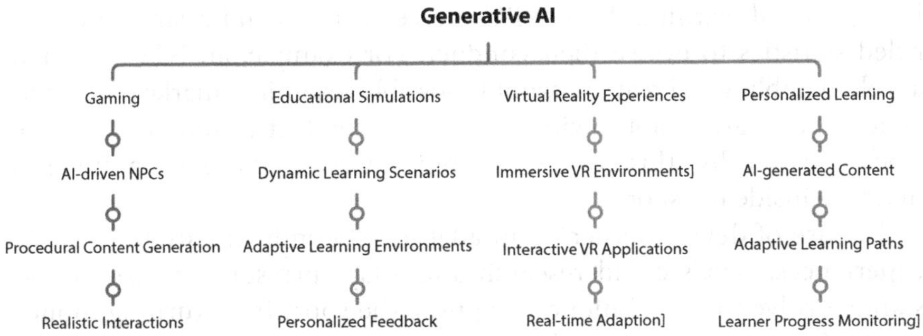

Figure 6.1 Generative AI.

6.3 Intelligent NPCS and Adaptive Behaviors

Machine learning for behavior adaptation: One of the maximum innovative programs of generative AI in gaming is the advent of smart non-playable characters (NPCs) that adapt their behaviors primarily based totally on participant movements and environmental changes. Adaptive AI makes use of device-mastering algorithms to permit NPCs to research from participant interactions and regulate their conduct accordingly. This makes NPCs more unpredictable, presenting a harder and more attractive gameplay revel [32].

Reinforcement learning: This approach includes educating AI sellers through trial and error. NPCs discover ways to maximize their rewards through appearing movements that yield fine results and warding off those who bring about terrible consequences. For instance, in a stealth recreation, NPC guards can discover ways to enhance their patrol routes and detection techniques primarily based totally on preceding encounters with the participant. Over time, those NPCs turn out to be more adept at watching for participant actions and putting in place ambushes, making the sport harder.

Supervised learning: In this method, NPCs are skilled in categorized datasets containing examples of favored behaviors. For example, an NPC warrior might be skilled in fight techniques by studying the recorded gameplay of professional gamers. This education allows the NPC to appoint superior tactics, including flanking maneuver coordinated attacks, making fight encounters more dynamic and practical [11].

Unsupervised learning: Here NPCs perceive styles and systems in unlabeled statistics to evolve their conduct. For example, an NPC dealer in a role-gambling recreation would possibly examine marketplace tendencies and participant buying and selling conduct to modify costs and stock dynamically. This creates a more immersive and practical financial machine inside the sport.

The use of device mastering in adaptive AI ends in harder gameplay experiences. NPCs could research and adapt pressure gamers to constantly evolve their techniques, stopping the sport from turning monotonous. This dynamic interplay keeps gamers engaged, as they should continuously stay on their toes and adapt to the converting behaviors of their adversaries.

Challenging gameplay experiences: Adaptive AI now not only best complements the mission of a recreation but also personalizes the problem stage to shape the participant's talent. This guarantees that each amateur and skilled gamer can revel in the sport at their very own pace.

Dynamic difficulty adjustment (DDA): AI can screen a participant's overall performance and modify the sport's problem in real time. For instance, if a participant is suffering in a fight, the AI would possibly lessen the wide variety of talent stages of enemies. Conversely, if a participant is breezing through the sport, the AI can introduce more difficult and demanding situations. This dynamic adjustment keeps a top-of-the-line stage of the problem, presenting a fulfilling revel for gamers of all talent levels.

Personalized challenges: Beyond adjusting problems, AI can tailor unique annoying conditions to personal game enthusiasts based mostly on their play style. For example, if a player prefers stealth over direct fighting, the AI can generate conditions that emphasize sneaking and evasion. This personalization enhances player engagement by catering to their favored techniques of play in Table 6.1.

Historical context and evolution: The concept of adaptive AI has advanced extensively over the years. Early video games featured static AI with pre-scripted behaviors, which are important to predictable and repetitive gameplay. The introduction of machine learning techniques has revolutionized NPC conduct, making them more adaptable and responsive. This evolution has delivered approximately more complex and harder gameplay research that keeps game enthusiasts engaged for longer periods [12].

Table 6.1 Generative AI in gaming, educational simulations, virtual reality experiences, and personalized learning.

The impact of generative AI in gaming and beyond	Element	Details
Generative AI in gaming	Realistic textures and landscapes	Use of GANs and VAEs Enhancing visual authenticity
	Dynamic environments	AI-driven environment evolution Personalized gaming experiences
	Procedural world generation	Autonomous generation of game worlds Reducing manual content creation Enhancing replayability
Intelligent NPCs and adaptive behaviors	Adaptive AI	Machine learning for behavior adaptation Challenging gameplay experiences
	Realistic interactions	Natural and meaningful NPC–player interactions Enhancing narrative and emotional depth
	Behavioral diversity	Variety in NPC behaviors and personalities Contributing to a rich gaming environment
	Educational simulations	Dynamic and interactive learning scenarios Enhancing educational experiences

(*Continued*)

Table 6.1 Generative AI in gaming, educational simulations, virtual reality experiences, and personalized learning. (*Continued*)

The impact of generative AI in gaming and beyond	Element	Details
Expanding Beyond Traditional Gaming	Virtual reality experiences	Creating responsive and immersive virtual spaces Interactive VR environments
	Personalized learning	Tailoring AI-generated content to individual learners Adapting to learner progress and preferences
	Technological advancement	Innovations in AI algorithms Cross-industry applications
Integration and Impacts	User experience	Improved immersion Increased engagement
	Future prospects	Emerging trends Potential ethical considerations

Realistic Interactions: Natural and Meaningful NPC–Player Interactions
One of the crucial element's desires of generative AI in gaming is to create NPCs that engage with game enthusiasts in natural and huge ways. This consists of using AI to simulate sensible conversations, feelings, and behaviors, enhancing the narrative depth and emotional impact of the game.

Natural language processing (NLP): NLP algorithms allow NPCs to understand and respond to player inputs in natural language. This allows for added fluid and dynamic conversations, in which NPCs can respond contextually to the player's speech selections. For instance, in a role-playing game, game enthusiasts can engage in deep, branching conversations with NPCs, in which their selections affect the tale's outcome [33]. NLP, moreover, allows NPCs to provide relevant information, offer quests, and react emotionally to the player's moves, providing a more immersive and interactive experience.

Emotion recognition: AI can take a look at player behavior and communicate selections to infer their emotional state and respond appropriately. For example, if a player often chooses aggressive communication options, NPCs might, in all likelihood, react with fear or hostility [34]. Conversely, if a participant suggests kindness and empathy, NPCs would possibly end up as more pleasant and supportive. This emotional responsiveness provides a layer of realism to NPC interactions, making them seem more human and relatable.

Historical context and evolution: Early NPC interactions have been confined to easy types primarily based on total dialogues with constant responses. The evolution of AI has enabled more state-of-the-art interactions, wherein NPCs can interact in significant conversations and show off quite some feelings. This development has notably improved the narrative and emotional intensity of games, permitting gamers to shape more potent connections with NPCs and end up more invested in the tale.

Enhancing narrative and emotional depth: Realistic NPC interactions contribute to the general narrative and emotional intensity of a game [34]. By developing characters that seem alive and responsive, builders can craft more enticing and emotionally resonant memories.

Dynamic storytelling: AI-pushed NPCs can adapt their conduct and talk primarily based totally on the participant's picks, main to dynamic and branching narratives. This allows for more than one storyline and ending, giving gamers a feel of business enterprise and affecting the game's outcome. For example, an NPC who will become a near best friend or a sour enemy primarily based totally on the participant's moves can notably modify the path of the tale, developing a more personalized and immersive experience.

Emotional engagement: NPCs that show off practical feelings and reactions can evoke more potent emotional responses from gamers. This is mainly crucial in narrative-pushed games, wherein the participant's connection to the characters and tale is crucial. By developing plausible and emotionally complicated NPCs, builders can craft memories that resonate with gamers on a deeper level. For instance, an NPC's tragic backstory or heartfelt talk can elicit empathy and emotional investment, making the participant's selections more significant and impactful [13].

Behavioral Diversity

Variety in NPC behaviors and personalities: Generative AI allows the introduction of NPCs with various behaviors and personalities, contributing to wealthy and sundry gaming surroundings. By simulating an extensive variety of manly or womanly developments and moves, AI can create NPCs that seem precise and lifelike.

Personality traits: AI can assign one-of-a-kind persona developments to NPCs, influencing their conduct and interactions with the participant. For example, an NPC with a careful persona is probably more hesitant to interact in a combat, while a formidable NPC would possibly advance into warfare fearlessly. These persona developments can also affect how NPCs respond to the participant's moves and decisions, developing a more dynamic and sundry gameplay revel.

Behavioral patterns: NPCs can showcase an extensive variety of behaviors primarily based totally on their roles and personalities. For instance, a service provider NPC would possibly observe an everyday habit of beginning their shop, interacting with customers, and staying up at night. Meanwhile, a defender NPC would possibly patrol an area, respond to threats, and inspect suspicious sports. By simulating sensible and sundry behaviors, AI can create a more immersive and plausible recreation setting.

Historical context and evolution: The idea of NPC behaviors and personalities has developed substantially over time. Early video games featured NPCs with restricted and repetitive behaviors, frequently appearing as static quest-givers or enemies. The advent of AI strategies has enabled the introduction of more complicated and sundry NPC behaviors, making recreation worlds seem more alive and dynamic. This evolution has improved the richness and variety of the gaming surroundings, contributing to a more immersive experience to revel in.

Contributing to a rich gaming environment: The variety of NPC behaviors and personalities enriches the gaming surroundings, making these seem more dynamic and alive. By populating the sport setting with precise and sundry characters, builders can create a more immersive and attractive revel for gamers [15].

Living worlds: AI-pushed NPCs contribute to the introduction of living, breathing worlds in which characters cross approximately in their everyday lives and engage with every different participant. These dynamic surroundings provide intensity and realism to the sport, making it seem like a colorful and evolving place. For example, in an open-setting RPG, NPCs would possibly interact in numerous sports inclusive of farming, trading, and socializing, developing an experience of network and lifestyles inside the sport setting.

Enhanced interactivity: The presence of various and dynamic NPCs complements interactivity inside the sport. Players can interact with NPCs in significant ways, forming relationships, making alliances, and influencing the sector around them. This interactivity makes the sport setting seem more responsive and immersive, encouraging gamers to discover and interact with the surroundings. For instance, in a Sandbox game, players might be able to build relationships with NPCs, unlock new quests and opportunities, and see the impact of their actions on the world and its inhabitants.

6.4 Expanding Beyond Traditional Gaming

Educational simulations' dynamic and interactive learning scenarios: Generative AI is not restrained to improving leisure in gaming; it additionally holds a sizeable capacity for revolutionizing instructional simulations. By developing dynamic and interactive knowledge of eventualities, AI could make instructional content material more enticing and powerful. Adaptive learning environments—AI-pushed instructional simulations can adapt in real time to the learner's movements and responses, developing a customized knowledge of enjoyment. For example, in a scientific school simulation, AI can modify the complexity of eventualities primarily based totally on the learners' progress, making sure that they may be always challenged and gaining knowledge at the most fulfilling pace. This adaptability facilitates catering to distinctive knowledge of patterns and paces, making schooling more inclusive and powerful.

Interactive problem-solving: AI can create eventualities wherein freshmen need to practice their expertise to resolve issues in real time. For instance, in a records simulation, freshmen are probably positioned in an ancient occasion wherein they need to make choices primarily based totally on the context and information to be had. These interactive problem-fixing eventualities foster vital wondering and deepen the learner's expertise in the problem matter [15].

Feedback and assessment: AI can offer instantaneous comments and assessments, assisting freshmen in apprehending their strengths and regions for improvement. For example, in a language gaining knowledge of simulation, AI can examine pronunciation, grammar, and vocabulary use, supplying optimistic comments to assist freshmen's enhancement. These instantaneous comment loop complements the manner of gaining knowledge and maintains the engagement of freshmen.

Historical context and evolution: Traditional instructional techniques regularly depend upon static and passive styles of gaining knowledge, which include lectures and textbooks. The integration of AI in educational simulations represents a giant evolution, offering dynamic and interactive studying reviews that actively interact with freshmen. This shift from passive to lively studying allows for beautifying knowledge retention and application, making education more effective and enjoyable. Enhancing educational experiences—generative AI enhances educational reviews by making studying more immersive, enticing, and interactive. By simulating real-world scenarios and presenting custom-designed comments, AI-driven educational gadgets can drastically beautify the quality and effectiveness of education.

Immersive learning: AI can create immersive mastering environments that mimic real settings, presenting learners with hands-on revel without the associated risks. For example, in a flight simulator, AI can reflect diverse climate situations and emergency eventualities, permitting trainee pilots to exercise and expand their abilities in a secure environment. This immersive knowledge of technique facilitates freshmen to benefit with sensible enjoyment and confidence. Engaging content—AI can generate enticing and interactive content material that captures the learner's interest. For instance, in a technological know-how simulation, AI can create interactive experiments wherein freshmen can manage variables and have a look at the outcomes. This hands-on technique makes gaining knowledge more enticing and facilitates freshmen to apprehend complicated principles better. Personalized learning paths—AI can create customized knowledge of paths primarily based totally on the learner's progress, interests, and needs. For example, in math when gaining knowledge of application, AI can perceive regions wherein the learner is suffering and offer focused sporting events to assist them in enhancement. This customized technique guarantees that freshmen obtain the aid they need to succeed [9].

Virtual Reality Experiences Creating Responsive and Immersive Virtual Spaces

Virtual reality (VR) is every other region wherein generative AI is creating a sizeable impact. By developing responsive and immersive digital areas, AI complements VR enjoyment, making it more enticing and interactive.

AI-driven environments: AI can generate sensible and dynamic digital environments that respond to personal moves in real time. For example, in a VR game, AI can create a digital town that evolves primarily based totally on the player's decisions, with NPCs and environments reacting dynamically. This responsiveness creates a more immersive and plausible digital world, improving the general VR enjoyment.

Interactive objects and characters: AI could make digital items and characters more interactive and lifelike. For instance, in a VR school simulation, AI-pushed digital characters can engage with the person in herbal and significant ways, imparting steering and feedback. This interactivity makes VR enjoy more enticing and sensible, supporting customers to expand their talents more effectively [14].

Enhanced immersion: AI can exhibit the immersion of VR studies by simulating sensible physics, lighting, and sound effects. For example, in a VR nature simulation, AI can mirror the sounds of wildlife, the motion of bushes inside the wind, and the play of mild and shadows, developing a surprisingly immersive environment. This degree of element complements the person's experience of presence, making the digital experience more convincing and enjoyable.

Historical context and evolution: Traditional VR studies frequently depend on pre-scripted environments and interactions, restricting their responsiveness and realism. The integration of AI represents a sizeable advancement, permitting the introduction of dynamic and interactive digital areas that respond to personal moves in real time [1]. This evolution complements the immersive capacity of VR, presenting customers with more enticing and sensible studies. Interactive VR environments—AI-pushed interactive VR environments provide more than a few programs past gaming, such as schooling, remedy, and education. By developing sensible and responsive digital areas, AI can rework how we engage with and enjoy digital reality. Training simulations—AI-pushed VR environments may be used for schooling in diverse fields, including medicine, aviation, and military.

For example, a VR scientific school simulation can mirror complicated surgical processes, permitting trainees to exercise and expand their talents in a managed and secure environment. AI can modify the problem of the processes primarily based totally on the trainee's progress, imparting customized and powerful schooling. Therapeutic applications—VR environments pushed through AI can also be used for healing purposes, consisting of publicity remedies for tension and phobias. For instance, a VR simulation can regularly reveal sufferers to their fears in a managed and secure environment, supporting them to conquer their tension. AI can adapt the publicity degrees primarily based totally on the patient's progress, imparting a customized and powerful remedy. Educational experiences—AI-pushed VR environments can create immersive instructional studies that make mastering more enticing and interactive. For example, a VR record simulation can deliver rookies to historic events, permitting them to discover and engage with the environment. This immersive technique enables rookies to take advantage of deeper expertise of records and their context.

Personalized Learning Tailoring AI-Generated Content to Individual Learners

Generative AI has the potential to revolutionize personalized learning by tailoring content to individual learners' needs, preferences, and progress. This personalized method complements the mastering level and allows freshmen to acquire their complete potential. Adaptive content generation—AI can generate personalized mastering content material primarily based totally on the learner's development, interests, and desires. For example, in a language-mastering application, AI can create custom-designed sports that concentrate on regions in which the learner desires improvement. This adaptive content material technology guarantees that freshmen obtain the aid they need to succeed, making mastering more powerful and enjoyable. Learning analytics—AI can examine learner information to pick out styles and trends, imparting insights into the learner's strengths and weaknesses. For instance, in a web mastering platform, AI can assess the learner's overall performance and offer suggestions for similar studies. This information-pushed method allows freshmen to apprehend their development and regions for improvement, improving their mastering revel. Personalized learning paths—AI can create personalized mastering paths primarily based totally on the learner's development and goals. For example, in a math mastering application, AI can pick out the learner's talent degree and create a custom-designed curriculum that demands them appropriately. This personalized method guarantees that freshmen obtain a tailor-made mastering revel that meets their character's desires and preferences. Historical context and evolution—Traditional training frequently is predicated on a one-size-fits-all approach, failing to deal with the numerous desires of novices. The integration of AI in personalized getting-to-know represents a huge shift in the direction of individualized and adaptive training, supplying tailor-made stories that cater to every learner's specific desires. This evolution facilitates to make trainings more powerful and accessible, empowering novices to obtain their complete potential. Adapting to learner progress and preferences—generative AI can adapt to a learner's development and options, imparting a customized and attractive getting-to-know reveal that evolves with the learner [7]. Real-time adaptation—AI can reveal the learner's development in real time and modify the content material and problem accordingly. For example, in an academic game, AI can solve the problem of demanding situations because the learner improves, making sure that they are always challenged and engaged. This real-time version facilitates holding the foremost stage of the problem, stopping boredom and frustration. Preference-based customization—AI can tailor the getting-to-know to reveal primarily based totally on the learner's options and interests. For example, in records familiarizing the application, AI can refer to precise ancient durations or activities that interest the learner. This preference primarily based totally on customization makes familiarizing more exciting and attractive, assisting novices to live encouraged and invested in their training. Feedback and support—AI can offer personalized comments and assistance primarily based totally on the learner's development and desires. For instance, in a language getting-to-know application, AI can provide positive comments on pronunciation and grammar, assisting the learner to improve. This customized assistance complements the mastering revel and facilitates beginners to attain their goals. Historical context and evolution—traditional training frequently fails to evolve to a man's or woman's desires and the possibilities of beginners. The integration of AI in adaptive mastering represents a vast advancement, presenting customized and dynamic reports that evolve with the learner. This evolution facilitates to make trainings more powerful and enjoyable, imparting beginners with the assistance and motivation they need to succeed. The integration of AI in adaptive gaining knowledge represents a large advancement, presenting customized and dynamic reviews that evolve with the learner. This evolution allows training to be more effective and enjoyable, supplying neophytes with the manual and motivation they need to succeed.

6.5 Conclusion

Generative AI is revolutionizing the pastime format with the resource of the usage of automating the advent of practical textures, dynamic environments, and procedurally generated worlds. Techniques that consist of GANs and VAEs beautify seen authenticity as AI-driven environment evolution and personalization create engaging and immersive reviews. Procedural content material cloth generation allows developers to create vast, several pastime worlds with minimal manual input, enhancing replay ability and reducing development costs. As the AI era keeps advancing, its impact on pastime format will only grow, imparting new possibilities for innovation and creativity inside the gaming industry. Generative AI is revolutionizing pastime format with the resource of the usage of automating the advent of practical textures, dynamic environments, and procedurally generated worlds. Techniques that consist of GANs and VAEs beautify seen authenticity as the AI-driven environment evolves. Generative AI is revolutionizing pastime format with the resource of the usage of automating the advent of practical textures, dynamic environments, and procedurally generated worlds. Techniques that consist of GANs and VAEs beautify seen authenticity, making virtual worlds more immersive and believable. AI-driven environment evolution and personalization create engaging and specific reviews for each player, even as procedural content material cloth generation allows the advent of vast, several pastime worlds that offer infinite exploration and replay ability. These enhancements now not only reduce the workload on developers but also open up new possibilities for creativity and innovation in a distraction format.

AI disclosure statement: The author acknowledges the use of AI-based tools for minor language editing or grammatical correction. However, all intellectual contributions, analyses, and conclusions presented in this chapter are entirely the author's own.

References

1. Rollings, A. and Adams, E., *Andrew Rollings and Ernest Adams on Game Design*, Pearson Education, New Riders Publication, 2018.
2. García-Sánchez, P., Georgios N. Yannakakis and Julian Togelius: Artificial Intelligence and Games. *Genet. Program Evolvable Mach.*, 20, 143–145, 2019, https://doi.org/10.1007/s10710-018-9337-0.

3. Liapis, A., Yannakakis, G.N., Togelius, J., *Computational Game Creativity*, Springer, 2015.
4. Silver, D., Schrittwieser, J., Simonyan, K., *et al.*, Mastering the game of Go without human knowledge. *Nature*, 550, 7676, 354–359, 2017.
5. Justesen, N., Bontrager, P., Togelius, J., *et al.*, Deep generative design: A survey of generative methods for automotive design. *IEEE Trans. Games*, 12, 3, 252–268, 2020.
6. Zook, A. and Deterding, S., Read, play, build: The nature and role of cultural intermediaries in videogame production. *Games Cult.*, 13, 5, 467–488, 2018.
7. Geroimenko, V. and Chen, H., *Virtual Reality and Augmented Reality: Myths and Realities*, Springer, 2018.
8. Billinghurst, M. and Duenser, A., Augmented reality in the classroom. *Computer*, 45, 7, 56–63, 2012.
9. Steuer, J., Defining virtual reality: Dimensions determining telepresence. *J. Commun.*, 42, 4, 73–93, 1992.
10. Anderson, L.W., Krathwohl, D.R., *et al.*, *A Taxonomy for Learning, Teaching, and Assessing: A Revision of Bloom's Taxonomy of Educational Objectives*, Allyn & Bacon, Pearson, 2001.
11. Kizony, R. and Zeilig, G., *Virtual Reality Capture Labs: Clinical, Psychometric, and Immersive Assessment of Spatial Navigation*, Springer, 2017.
12. Chang, C.H., A systematic review of research on virtual reality in education. *Themes Sci. Technol. Educ.*, 12, 2, 129–145, 2019.
13. Barab, S.A. and Duffy, T., From practice fields to communities of practice. *Theor. Found Learn. Environ.*, 2, 25–55, 2000.
14. Dawley, L., *Social Network Knowledge Construction: Emerging Virtual World Pedagogy*, IGI Global, Emerald Discover Journals, 2009.
15. McKinney, D. and Dyck, J.L., Leveraging the potential of augmented reality in education. *TechTrends*, 55, 6, 12–15, 2011.
16. Yin, C., NPCs in video games: a reflective resource for sports coaches and participant engagement. *Front. Sports Active Living, 6*, 1403829, 2024.
17. Vayadande, K., Pednekar, C.B., Khune, P.A., Prabhavalkar, V.S., Dange, V.R., GPT-3-and DALL-E-Powered Applications: A Complete Survey, in: *How Machine Learning is Innovating Today's World: A Concise Technical Guide*, pp. 329–341, 2024.
18. Yang, Z., Luo, D., You, J., Guo, Z., Yang, Z., Multimodal Conditional VAE for Zero-Shot Real-World Event Discovery, in: *International Conference on Advanced Data Mining and Applications*, Springer Nature Switzerland, Cham, pp. 644–659, 2023, August.
19. Jamal, J., II, Yusof, M.H.M., Lim, K.Y., Jamal, J.A., Improving Visual Style Classification in Digital Games Using Intercoder Reliability Assessment. *J. Inf. Commun. Technol., 22*, 2, 283–308, 2023.
20. Przegalinska, A. and Triantoro, T., *Converging Minds: The Creative Potential of Collaborative AI*. CRC Press, Taylor & Francis Group, Boca Raton, 2024.

21. Manu, A., *Transcending Imagination: Artificial Intelligence and the Future of Creativity*. CRC Press, Taylor & Francis Group, Routledge, 2024.
22. Partarakis, N. and Zabulis, X., A Review of Immersive Technologies, Knowledge Representation, and AI for Human-Centered Digital Experiences. *Electronics*, *13*, 2, 269, 2024.
23. Liu, C., Xiang, L., Yi, L., Impact of immersion experience on encountering information adoption: experimental evidence from AI virtual live streaming under the algorithmic recommendation. *Lib. Hi Tech.*, 0737–8831, 2024.
24. Liu, L., Zhang, Z., Yin, Y., Li, Y., Xie, H., Zhang, M., Zhao, Y., Kennel, R., A robust high-quality current control with fast convergence for three-level NPC converters in micro-energy systems. *IEEE Trans. Ind. Inf.*, 1–10, 2023. 10.1109/TII.2023.3241594.
25. Bharathi, G.P., Chandra, I., Sanagana, D.P.R., Tummalachervu, C.K., Rao, V.S., Neelima, S., AI-driven adaptive learning for enhancing business intelligence simulation games. *Entertain. Comput.*, *50*, 100699, 2024.
26. da Rocha Franco, A.D.O., de Carvalho, W.V., da Silva, J.W.F., Maia, J.G.R., de Castro, M.F., Managing and controlling digital role-playing game elements: A current state of affairs. *Entertain. Comput.*, *51*, 100708, 2024.
27. Kuriachan, A., Thomas, R.R., Sukanya, R., Place-Based Strategies, Multichannel Merger, and Context-Driven Alerts for Engagement With Mobile Marketing, in: *Smart and Sustainable Interactive Marketing*, pp. 198–229, IGI Global, 2024.
28. Wallner, G., Wang, L., Dormann, C., Visualizing the Spatio-Temporal Evolution of Gameplay using Storyline Visualization: A Study with League of Legends. *Proceedings of the ACM on Human-Computer Interaction*, vol. *7*, pp. 1002–1024, 2023.
29. Soliman, M.M., Ahmed, E., Darwish, A., *et al.*, Artificial intelligence powered Metaverse: analysis, challenges and future perspectives. *Artif. Intell. Rev.*, 57, 36, 2024, https://doi.org/10.1007/s10462-023-10641-x
30. Melhart, D., Togelius, J., Mikkelsen, B., Holmgård, C., Yannakakis, G.N., The ethics of AI in games. *IEEE Trans. Affective Comput.*, 50–67, 2023.
31. Hu, Z., Ding, Y., Wu, R., Li, L., Zhang, R., Hu, Y., Fan, C., Deep learning applications in games: a survey from a data perspective. *Appl. Intell.*, *53*, 24, 31129–31164, 2023.
32. Uludağlı, M.C. and Oğuz, K., Non-player character decision-making in computer games. *Artif. Intell. Rev.*, *56*, 12, 14159–14191, 2023.
33. Pretty, E.J., Fayek, H.M., Zambetta, F., A case for personalized non-player character companion design. *Int. J. Hum.–Comput. Interact.*, 1–20, 2023.
34. Toh, W., The player experience and design implications of narrative games. *Int. J. Hum.–Comput. Interact.*, *39*, 13, 2742–2769, 2023.

7

Ethical Dimensions and Societal Effects of Generative AI: The Portrayal of Ethical Issues of ChatGPT, DALL-E, and Other Systems

Bhuvaneswari Sivagnanam[1], Saranya Rajiakodi[1]*, Kathiravan Pannerselvam[1] and Bharathi Raja Chakravarthi[2]

[1]*Department of Computer Science, Central University of Tamil Nadu, Tamil Nadu, India*

[2]*School of Computer Science, University of Galway, Galway, Ireland*

Abstract

This chapter describes the ethical considerations and societal implications of developing and using Generative AI technologies such as ChatGPT, DALL-E, and similar platforms in today's society. These advanced AI systems enable users to create various kinds of content such as images, text, sounds, and more with the advantage of innovative capabilities of Generative AI. The advantages of these technologies are assistance in coding, generating blog and website content, and creating novel graphics in response to user prompts. Although there are significant benefits in using Generative AI, there are also substantial challenges and concerns for society in using Generative AI technologies. In this book chapter, we discuss about the disadvantages and challenges of using and developing Generative AI. The first section of the chapter gives a summary of Generative AI and the Deep Learning techniques that help in creating Generative AI technologies. Then, it progresses to a detailed discussion of these Generative AI technologies and their ethical and moral dimensions. Ethical issues such as fairness and bias, data privacy, justice, sustainability, dignity, and the dissemination of potentially harmful content are explored in this chapter. In addition, the legal considerations involving generative AI systems and their societal integration are also addressed in this chapter. It also highlights the importance of ethical compliance. Further, the chapter examines the positive and negative impacts

**Corresponding author:* saranya@acad.cutn.ac.in

N. Gayathri, S. Rakesh Kumar, Ramesh Chandran, Pethuru Raj Chelliah and Danilo Pelusi (eds.) Generative AI: Disruptive Technologies for Innovative Applications, (131–152) © 2025 Scrivener Publishing LLC

of Generative AI on society. A notable focus is given to the transparency of AI generated content, highlighting the necessity for these systems to be dependable, trustworthy, and operate with integrity. This discussion examines the moral difficulties and risks of using generative AI technologies. Finally, the chapter also discusses the role of various institutions and non-governmental organizations in addressing the ethical challenges of Generative AI and their guidelines and standards essential for adopting ethical AI in the field of generative AI. These recommendations aim to guarantee that these technologies are implemented and used in a way that is both responsible and advantageous to society.

Keywords: Generative AI, ethical and moral dimensions, fairness, transparency, NGOs, ChatGPT, DALL-E, data privacy

Introduction

In recent years, Artificial Intelligence (AI) has played an important role in daily life, making significant advancements in various fields and sectors such as entertainment, education, medicine, law, business, and more. Artificial intelligence is a big umbrella that has many technologies under it. It helps create more intelligent systems and novel technologies using Machine Learning, Deep Learning, Generative AI, and Natural Language Processing to perform the complex tasks associated with human beings, like reasoning, decision making, learning from experiences, and solving problems. Generative AI is one of the subfields of artificial intelligence that emerged as the most promising area in various technological advancements. It demonstrates the ability to create new human like content such as text, images, audio, and videos that cannot be easily distinguished from human creation. This uses the foundational ideas of Artificial Intelligence with the help of computational resources and algorithms to replicate human intellectual capacities. Thus, generative AI can potentially transform a wide range of fields and sectors that depend on creativity and innovation. In particular, it also made it possible to create many previously unimaginable things like digital art, adapted education services, and virtual personal assistants that function like human beings. Various models and techniques have been introduced to be incorporated into Generative AI technologies. Autoregressive models, variational autoencoders, and generative adversarial networks (GAN) are a few examples of the technologies used in generative AI [1].

Within the large AI spectrum, the foundational technology of Generative AI comprises two essential techniques. These include Machine Learning and Deep Learning. Machine Learning, a branch of Artificial Intelligence, enables the system to learn from experiences or data patterns without the need for explicit programming.

The large amount of data has been fed to machine learning algorithms, which then try to detect patterns, make decisions, and predict future outcomes. Deep Learning is the subfield of Machine Learning that utilizes neural networks with many layers to detect and predict the future automatically. Generative AI uses the highly complex models of Deep Learning to generate data. One of the technologies used by Generative AI is the Generative Adversarial Network. It has two networks: Generator and Discriminator. The generator creates fake data from a noise vector to imitate real data without direct access. The discriminator evaluates both real and generated data to distinguish between the two. Both networks improve simultaneously during the adversarial training phase until equilibrium is established. The difference between actual and false data is measured using the Earth Mover's or Wasserstein distance, which improves the GAN's capacity to generate highly realistic fake data [2].

The survey done by the researchers showed that 38% of the companies started using AI in their workplace, which is anticipated to increase to 62%. Due to advancements in automation and robotics, researchers have demonstrated that labor displacement is inevitable, and AI will replace humans in the workplace by undertaking various tasks [3]. Generative AI, especially large language models like ChatGPT, DALLE-2, Stable Diffusion, and Midjourney, created valuable content that may transform modern-day life, including entertainment, music, arts, and many professions [4]. In education, the generative AI serves as a conversational agent that gives personalized tutoring to the students and automated assessment to the teachers. Using the GPT model, AI systems can analyze complex patterns and how human language works [5]. AI systems are exceptionally trained to develop and understand human language.

In some cases, the generative AI produces content that may be inaccurate or contain false information due to insufficient training data. For instance, the GPT 3.5 model trained the content up to September 2021, so its accuracy will be reduced when the queries are based on recent events. Even humans make errors, so it is unacceptable to expect the AI to be flawless [4].

The development of Generative AI has brought back various use cases like poetry, music, writing contracts, writing scientific papers, writing emails, coding, and developing and testing software. It has also various ethical concerns and social implications [6]. In this chapter, we will discuss ethical concerns like bias, privacy, transparency, societal implications of generative AI, policies, law, legal considerations of Generative AI, and the terms and conditions to be used while developing and using Generative AI.

Generative and Discriminative Models

The Table 7.1 discusses about the difference between generative and discriminative model.

Table 7.1 Generative and discriminative model difference.

Generative model	Discriminative model
It learns to generate new data samples similar to train data.	It knows how to predict the data.
It is used in Unsupervised Machine Learning, like for image generation.	It is used in Supervised Machine Learning, like for Classification.
It uses joint probability for the actual distribution of data.	It uses conditional likelihood to learn the decision boundary for Classification and Regression.
Generative Adversarial Networks (GAN), Variational Auto Encoders (VAE), and AutoRegressive models come under this.	Support Vector Machine and Logistic Regression and Decision trees come under this.

Ethical Concerns

Ethical concerns arise when decision-making or activities in certain situations affect social principles or moral standards, necessitating careful attention. In Generative AI, the ethical concerns include the consumers' data privacy, leakage, or inappropriate data usage. Hallucination is one of the problems where AI tools produce results without any solid basis or information regarding the queries, or generating offensive images and content without being asked explicitly, even giving racial and gender-offensive remarks concerning human rights issues of ethical concerns and limited transparency.

Bias and fairness

Bias arises when a Generative AI system gives the output (response), and that output contains a systematic error due to the biased decision-making processes, thus resulting in unfair outcomes. Serious consequences may occur due to biased outputs, such as during the recruitment of professionals. Decision-making may be unfair due to bias and discrimination against certain individuals [7]. There are various sources of bias, as shown in Figure 7.1 [8].

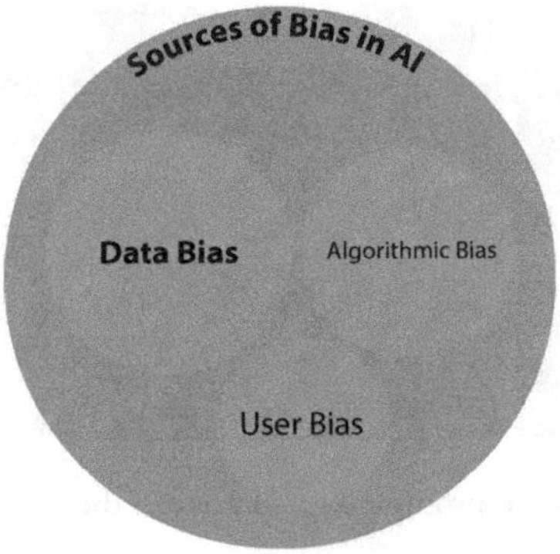

Figure 7.1 Sources of bias in AI.

Data Bias: When the dataset used to train the Generative model is incomplete and non-representative, this results in biased outputs. This occurs when data collection is biased toward a particular group of people or objects or when it contains inaccurate information [8].

Algorithmic Bias: This bias occurs when the model's algorithm has built biases shown in their results. This situation occurs when an algorithm operates on prejudiced assumptions and uses biased standards for decision-making [8].

User Bias: It occurs when the user intentionally or unintentionally introduces their own bias or prejudice into the system due to their experiences that are biased towards particular things [8].

Fairness in a system is characterized by the absence of biases, ensuring that no preferential treatment is given based on race, such as favoring white individuals over black individuals, or gender, such as discriminating against women in the hiring processes. It also eliminates decision-making biases resulting from models disproportionately leaning toward certain groups [9]. Fairness attempts to correct the systematic bias in algorithms that will affect people's lives. Hence, the service providers use unbiased data and put effort into these biased problems to rectify them [10].

Figure 7.2 and Figure 7.3 show when the prompt is given to the Generative AI tool for generating images and how biased the response is produced. The prompt is something like the input or instruction we give to the AI tools, and the Response is the output produced by the AI. Here, the example is based on gender bias. When asked for the "Image of the Doctor," the system produced only the image of the male doctor.

Figure 7.2 Biased image when prompted for "Image of the Doctor".

Figure 7.3 Biased image when prompted for "Image of the Teacher".

When prompted "Image of the Teacher", it created the results with the female gender. Thus, Bias occurs in Generative AI.

The detection of bias in ethical AI plays a significant role in developing and deploying generative AI systems. Bias detection involves analyzing the output of the system to identify any biased behaviors, such as gender bias, community bias, race bias, or religious bias [11]. In particular, gender bias has long been noticed in transformer-based models, where certain occupations are considered suitable only for a specific gender. Here, bias starts from the imbalance of male-to-female data in the dataset, thus resulting in generative AI systems producing offensive or biased results. For example, occupations such as "doctor" may mainly be associated with the male gender, while the occupation "teacher" may be related to the female gender because of the training data or the lack of data; and thus, causes stereotypes to occur in the produced results [12]. Sources of bias in generative AI systems are data bias, annotation bias, model bias, and bias from input representations [12]. To overcome these biases, we can employ statistical analysis, correlation studies, and fairness metrics in generative AI systems. These fairness metrics include disparate impact analysis, demographic parity, and equalized odds which help to evaluate the fairness of system responses across different demographic groups [11, 13]. Thus, detecting and mitigating bias in generative AI systems is crucial for ensuring fairness and equity in their outcomes. By employing rigorous statistical analysis and fairness metrics, developers can work towards creating generative AI systems that produce unbiased and equitable results across diverse demographic groups. However, continuous research and development are essential to address the complex challenges associated with bias and fairness in generative AI systems [13].

Transparency and Explainability

In the field of artificial intelligence (AI), explainability refers to the ability of an AI system to clarify its outcomes and decision-making processes [14]. There are mainly four components involved in this aspect of AI comprehension and explainability of AI. They are addresses, aspects, contexts, and explainers. Here, addresses refer to the intended recipients of explanations including various stakeholders such as customers, users, employees, and developers including behavioral patterns within the system's operation. Aspects describe the meaningful content of explanations by covering the considerate details about the AI system's purpose, the functionality of its capabilities, the nature of inputs and outputs, behavioral tendencies, its underlying algorithms, utilized data, and constraints inherent in the AI system's operations. Contexts explain the circumstances under which explanations are necessary, spanning the phases of utilizing, constructing, testing, and auditing the AI system.

More realistically, explainability within AI is a link for fostering transparency, accountability, and trustworthiness. It enhances user comprehension and confidence by providing insights into the decision-making rationale of AI systems. In addition to that, it also aids in regulatory compliance and ethical oversight. Moreover, understanding the inner workings of AI algorithms and processes can lessen the risks of unintended biases, errors, or any adverse consequences. Thus, promoting a more equitable and responsible implementation of AI technologies across various domains and applications. As a result, the demand for AI systems continues to increase across various sectors and the need for robust explainability mechanisms becomes increasingly salient. This ensures that AI-driven projects are ethical and have operational integrity [14].

Privacy

In Ethical AI [15], privacy pertains to examining a system's capacity to refrain from utilizing, retaining, analyzing or delving into users' private data and steering clear of sensitive subjects. Privacy assessment involves scrutinizing how a generative AI system manages user data, encompassing practices related to data collection, storage and sharing. The established privacy guidelines like the General Data Protection Regulation (GDPR) and the Health Insurance Portability and Accountability Act (HIPAA) can act as regulatory frameworks to safeguard user privacy within the system [15].

Privacy is important in the ethical discourse as it intersects with fundamental rights, ethical principles, and legal requirements involving AI. Respecting user privacy [16] shows that AI systems value individual autonomy, dignity, and confidentiality. By prioritizing privacy principles, we can develop trust and foster positive user experiences which helps society to accept and adopt AI technologies. From an ethical standpoint, prioritizing privacy within AI systems displays a commitment to responsible and accountable AI deployment and mitigating the risks of unauthorized access, data breaches, or misuse of personal information.

In scholarly discourse, discussions on privacy within AI frameworks often focus on managing data, obtaining user consent, information anonymity, and ensuring accountability. The researchers are engaged in developing privacy preserving methodologies, standards, and methods for the challenge posed by AI systems. By integrating privacy considerations into the design, development, and deployment phases of AI projects, stakeholders endeavor to strike a balance between innovation and ethical stewardship, thereby advancing the ethical frontier of AI technology while safeguarding user privacy rights.

Intellectual Property

The variety of data generated by AI systems often leads to copyright concerns, raising the question of ownership: Who will be the copyright owner? AI systems or the human who prompted that? [17] The researcher discusses the copyright issues under various countries' legislation, leading many nations to determine that ownership belongs to humans, as they are the ones prompting

In contrast, some argue that authorship copyright should extend to non-human entities. This AI-generated content raises concerns about the role and rights of those who do not use creation systems, particularly in the context of AI systems [18]. Countries like India, Ireland, the UK, South Africa, Hong Kong, and New Zealand have created copyright laws in which the copyright belongs to the person who created the work with the help of AI. In the United Kingdom, an individual's work is only eligible for copyright protection if it was not previously made by anybody else.

Identity Theft

Identity theft is stealing someone's identity using generative AI. In 2018, Buzzfeed released a deep fake video of former President Obama giving a speech on a particular subject. Reddit users also raised concerns regarding the impersonation and the spread of misinformation on social media. These are morphing the faces of the actress using the Generative AI and releasing the videos in the porn. Many such videos started spreading in the industry after that [19]. This new article releases the news of the women blackmailed by saying they kidnapped the child by using the child voice sample data and created the same voice using Generative AI. There is also the chance of generative AI breaking the authentication. With the help of learning the process of finding the patterns of the user's password, they will be able to find the other credentials [20].

Societal implications

Societal implications refer to how the actions and usage of Generative AI affect social norms and cultural practices. Generative models have the risk of giving fictional references that reduce their reliability. Due to its generative capabilities, there is an issue of copyright and getting profit from this content without even considering whether it is under copyright protection. When using generative tools in academics, academic guidelines should be followed so that students and teachers may not be implicated [21].

Job Displacement

AI has surpassed humans at various tasks, such as games like Go and video games. However, there are certain things only humans can do, with the assistance of AI, like the job of a lawyer. One of the reasons for job displacement is dependence on technology [22, 23]. Creating arts and novelty ideas may be automated in a few decades in AI systems. Jobs that require social skills, like cashiers and telemarketers, can be replaced by AI systems, as they do not demand a high level of social intelligence [24]. Employing AI systems in the workplace is cost-effective because it does more work than humans due to the 90-10 wage distribution. Task or job automation driven by AI systems leads to a decline in human jobs. To avoid these issues, new kinds of tasks should be included. New technologies and policies that depend on our innovation ability, demographics, government policies, and taxes are needed [25–27]. Nowadays, organizations prefer AI-generated images over artists because they are cost-effective and less time-consuming, resulting in the decline of many artists' jobs [28].

Art and Creativity

Recent AI advancements, such as Midjouney and DALLE-2, in the fields of fine arts like painting, music, architecture, and dance have given rise to the issues of transparency, copyrights, and authorship. With technology like chatbots and Stable Diffusion, AI systems have taken over the tasks of humans, which require high precision and creativity. Researchers stated that students and facilities from various art institutes could not differentiate the work generated by AI and humans regarding music and arts because they are based on abstract human work. AI systems can identify and authenticate the paintings and artworks and give detailed explanations of them. Even though AI can perform better in creating art, the copyrights and authorship are still questioned [29]. Many professional artists have raised the concern about the harm caused by AI-generated art includes plagiarism, copyrights, economic loss, and reputational damage. Since numerous images can be generated easily by AI systems, like Japanese anime created by the AI by Netflix Japan, the artists need help to get jobs, causing economic loss. Artists also said Stable Diffusion was trained on the dataset containing their works without consent. Some works of art were created using specific artists' names, resulting in their displeasure of having their name associated with the created image but not having their style, thus causing reputational damage [28].

Cultural Impact

The impact of artificial intelligence (AI) on culture and society has been widely discussed because of its potential to perform jobs that are usually connected with human empathy and the development of great arts [29]. These philosophers strongly emphasize human experience and culture's role in creating and understanding art. They contend that human-made art is more meaningful and gratifying because it has a solid basis in the diversity of human perception, emotion, and cultural context. On the other hand, because AI-generated art is produced using algorithms rather than human intuition and feeling, it might be viewed as lacking authenticity and soul [28].

Education and Literacy

Applications of AI in education have a variety of benefits, like adaptive learning systems in which students can interact with the systems and focus on the topic that they can work on due to the system's adaptiveness, which resulted in massive progress in students' education—automated grading system to help the graders to correct the answers automatically. Although the advantage is there, it raises ethical concerns, such as students or teachers consenting to using their personal information when working on AI tools. Their privacy may be violated, and monitoring and tracking students may result in access to all information, like personal and friendship details [30]. AI tools also lead to the concepts of cheating in writing essays; the students can ask the ChatGPT, and they will get the answers, solving the homework problems with the help of AI, and it is difficult to detect since the homework content is too perfect. This dependency on AI tools may reduce the students' creativity in organizing concepts. There is also the risk of getting error-prone answers due to hallucination [4, 5].

Ethical Considerations in AI-Driven Recruitment: Video and Image Interviews

Traditional AI systems scan resume keywords and extract the interviewee's skills. Nowadays, the trend has changed towards video-interview analysis. In spite of that, this trend has many biases and issues that lead to Ethical concerns [3]. The ethical considerations of the AI driven recruitment process have been depicted in Figure 7.4.

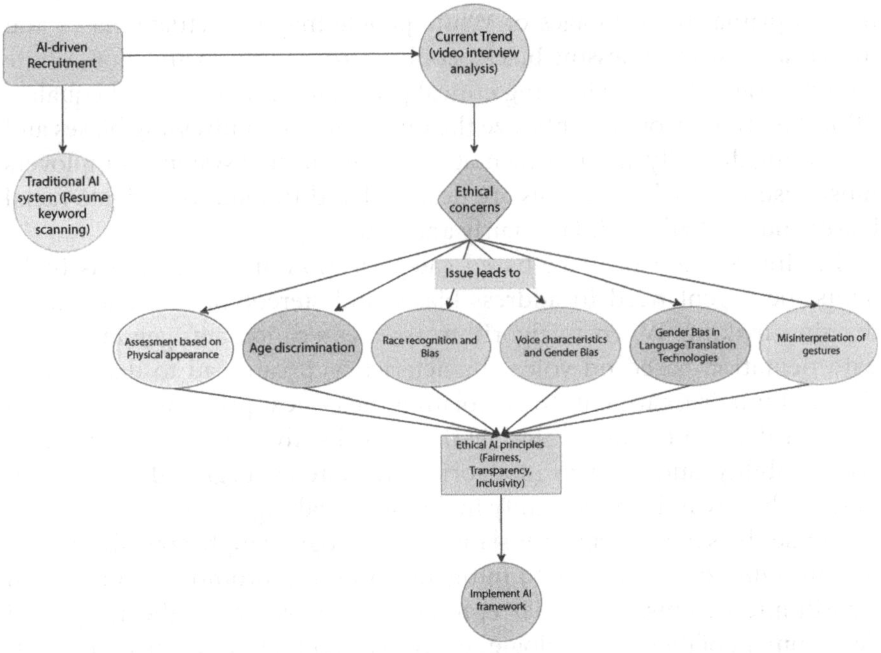

Figure 7.4 Framework on ethical considerations of AI-driven recruitment process.

Ethically, job applicants being assessed based on physical attractiveness raised concerns regarding fairness and objectivity. It goes against the concept of the principle of fairness and equality in hiring processes. Criteria such as facial symmetry have been employed in many companies to evaluate candidates and this leads to societal biases and beauty standards. It also causes disadvantage to certain individuals who do not conform to these standards. Thus, the integration of ethical AI principles in the recruitment process dictates the need for fairness, transparency, and inclusivity in algorithmic decision-making, urging caution against using personal opinions of attractiveness in recruitment [3].

The issue of age discrimination underscores the importance of adhering to ethical principles of non-discrimination and equal opportunity. Using physical appearance as a proxy for age may lead to biases against older candidates, contradicting the principle of fairness. Ethical AI frameworks advocate for mitigating bias and ensuring diversity and inclusion in algorithmic systems. Employers should strive to evaluate candidates based on their skills, qualifications, and experience rather than on age related physical characteristics, aligning with ethical principles of meritocracy and fairness [3].

Racial bias in video image hiring tools raises significant ethical concerns regarding fairness, equity, and non-discrimination. Algorithms trained primarily on images of White people may perpetuate biases and inaccuracies when assessing black people (Afro-American and Non-White communities) thereby violating ethical principles of fairness and equality. Ethical AI frameworks emphasize the importance of addressing biases and promoting diversity and representation in algorithmic systems. Employers must ensure their hiring tools are designed and trained to mitigate racial biases and treat all candidates fairly and equitably.

The intersection of voice-based categorization and gender bias highlights the urgent need to address biases and stereotypes in algorithmic decision-making. When an algorithm assesses a candidate's gender or sexual orientation based on voice characteristics, it can lead to discrimination and unfair treatment, thus violating the ethical principles of fairness and non-discrimination. Ethical AI frameworks advocate for transparency, accountability, and fairness in algorithmic systems, urging developers to mitigate biases and ensure equity in decision-making processes.

Gender bias in language translation technologies emphasizes the ethical responsibility of developers to mitigate biases and promote inclusivity in algorithmic systems. The underrepresentation of women in the design and development of these technologies exacerbates gender imbalances in translation outputs, violating ethical principles of diversity and representation.

Ethical AI frameworks emphasize the need for diverse and inclusive development teams, transparent algorithms, and ongoing bias mitigation efforts to ensure fairness and equity in algorithmic systems.

The potential misinterpretation of gestures in video interviews highlights the importance of ethical principles to ensure accuracy, transparency, and fairness in algorithmic decision-making. Biases or inaccuracies in assessing candidates' non-verbal cues may lead to unfair treatment and discrimination violating ethical principles of fairness and equity. Ethical AI frameworks stress the importance of algorithmic transparency, accountability, and bias mitigation strategies to address potential biases and ensure fairness in decision-making processes.

Law and legal considerations of Generative AI

According to the firm FASKEN [31, 32], it is advisable for organizations not to put confidential information or personal data into generative AI systems because it is a breach of confidentiality under the data protection law. Since the organization cannot ensure how the data will be used, it must abide by the law for the security of the data.

Responses received from the generative AI system should be verified using reliable sources and treated with caution because there may be cases where a particular organization or person claims the responses from the AI for defamation, misinterpretation, liability for negligence, and breach of contract. To have responsible AI, organizations should create policies and specific training systems to train the tool, and a security risk assessment will be needed. Many countries have started to enact AI-specific laws for product safety, employment, cyber security, and consumer production. There should be intellectual and copyright considerations to the data generated by the AI, such as what type of data to train the AI. Even though the public domain data are not confidential, they may be under copyright law. So, AI should not violate that. Generative AI will be used in assistance and decision-making processes, so in the process of doing the tasks, there may be potential harm to specific individuals, which may cause the service provider to be responsible for the negligence of the claim.

Terms and conditions

According to Deloitte [33], specific points need to be considered when creating generative systems.

1. Generative AI may be used in many businesses in a day-to-day process, so the unavailability of GenAI tools should be mentioned in the contracts in a timely manner.

Figure 7.5 Policy breach in respond to a ChatGPT inquiry.

2. Many organizations have created specific AI regulations. It is necessary to resolve any regulations that might run in conflict with the agreement based on those regulations.
3. Confidentiality and Data Privacy should be in any contractual framework for GenAI services.
4. The Generative AI service providers will be held responsible in case of IP infringements, data privacy leakage, and confidentiality. These issues should be mentioned in the contracts.
5. If problems arise, they should address whether there is a way to claim any insurance.

Policies of various organizations

The following Figure 7.5 shows a violation of the policy framework in answer to questions that are judged as violating the rules that govern ChatGPT's protocols for interaction.

UNESCO

UNESCO is an organization that establishes standards for various scientific research fields, such as climate engineering, neurotechnology, and artificial intelligence. These standards are designed to optimize the advantages while minimizing potential risks. Furthermore, this organization is responsible for establishing the initial global ethics standards in artificial intelligence.

In November 2021, UNESCO unveiled the first-ever universal AI ethics standard, the 'Recommendation on the Ethics of Artificial Intelligence.' This framework garnered unanimous adoption from all 193 Member States. The cornerstone of the Recommendation lies in safeguarding human rights and dignity, which is rooted in promoting fundamental principles like transparency and fairness. It consistently emphasizes the significance of human oversight in AI systems.

Nonetheless, the Recommendation's remarkable applicability stems from its comprehensive Policy Action Areas. These areas empower policymakers to translate the core values and principles into tangible actions concerning data governance, environment and ecosystems, gender, education and research, and health and social wellbeing. These guidelines are based on the four core values [34]. They are:

1. Human rights and human dignity
2. Living in a peace
3. Ensuring diversity
4. Promoting environmental and ecosystem flourishing [34, 35]

AI should be utilized lawfully, and identifying potential risks should be employed to prevent any harm caused by AI. The responsibility for assessing the safety and security risks should rest with those involved in AI. It is essential to establish an effective system for safeguarding data to protect privacy. When using data, respecting international law and national sovereignty is crucial. Furthermore, inclusive approaches to AI governance require the involvement of diverse stakeholders. AI systems should be auditable and traceable to avoid conflicts with human rights norms and environmental threats. Oversight, impact assessment, audit, and due diligence mechanisms should be implemented. Maintaining transparency and explainability are essential. They ensure that AI does not replace human responsibility and that accountability is vital. Promoting awareness and literacy of AI should be encouraged publicly. While fostering an inclusive approach, AI actors should advocate for social justice, fairness, and non-discrimination to make AI's benefits accessible to all. The impact of AI technologies on "sustainability" should be assessed, considering the UN's Sustainable Development Goals as a guide [35].

Eleven critical areas for policy actions [35]:

1. Ethical impact assessment
2. Ethical governance and stewardship
3. Data policy
4. Development and international cooperation
5. Environment and ecosystem
6. Gender
7. Culture
8. Education and research
9. Communication and information
10. Economy and Labor
11. Health and Social Wellbeing

UNESCO has developed two following practical methodologies to implement the recommendations:

1. The Readiness Assessment Methodology (RAM) employs a variety of quantitative and qualitative questions designed to collect data on different dimensions of a country's AI ecosystem. These facets include legal and regulatory frameworks, social and cultural aspects, economic conditions, scientific and educational factors, and technological and infrastructural dimensions. Each dimension feature in RAM comprises a series of quantitative and qualitative assessment questions, unlike the other readiness assessment tools [34, 36]. The implementation of the RAM is adapted to the unique circumstances and characteristics of the country, as well as the budget available for the project. The RAM is expected to be carried out by an independent consultant or research organization, supported by a national team comprising a variety of stakeholders, such as personnel from the UNESCO Secretariat and UNESCO National Commission, as well as representatives from the country's government, the academic community, civil society, and the private sector, among others [36, 37]. In addition to the completion of the RAM questionnaire itself, the final output of the RAM exercise includes the creation of a country report that provides
    - A comprehensive analysis of the status of AI readiness in the country,
    - Summarizing the country's standing on each dimension,
    - Detailed current activities,
    - Overview of the state-of-the-art and
    - Providing concrete policy recommendations on how to address governance gaps.

   This report is instrumental in identifying the necessary institutional changes required to enhance or develop a national AI strategy and enable UNESCO to customize capacity-building efforts to the country's needs [36].

2. Ethical Impact Assessment (EIA) is a tool that prioritizes ethical guidelines and transparent risk assessment to help developers make the tools without harming the public, because some AI tools are available to the public without considering the transparency and potential risks they cause.

WHO (World Health Organization)

The World Health Organization (WHO) is dedicated to ensuring universal healthcare access. It plays a pivotal role in coordinating and leading initiatives during health crises. By partnering with a diverse group of experts, such as academics, scientists, researchers, and medical practitioners, the WHO is committed to advancing public health and safety. Furthermore, it has released AI ethics and governance guidelines specifically for Large Language Models (LLMs) [38]. They are:

1. Developers should consider using the Ethics certification and train the programmers so the consumers will trust the product and services regarding health care, medicine, and scientific research.
2. "Data Protection impact assessments" should be taken before processing the data to prevent data leakage and privacy breaches of the individual and the associated risk.
3. The developers should train the LLm data under the data protection rules.
4. Data directly collected or used by third parties should be kept up to date to train the model.
5. Developers should be transparent about the data, so that when others are training or fine-tuning it, they will be aware of data insufficiency and incompleteness.
6. Data workers should be well paid and provided with counseling when experiencing stress.
7. The LLM should be developed by the developers, scientists, professors, and stakeholders relevant to the field to raise ethical issues and concerns.
8. Developers should ensure the LLM works accurately and reliably regarding healthcare and patient well-being. Premortems and red teaming techniques can be used for this.
9. The government should have laws and regulations to protect the data, give people their rights, and get their consent.

Conclusion

In conclusion, it is said that the integration of Generative AI within our human community and societal structure needs careful consideration to lessen the ethical and social impact including bias across various aspects– job displacement, copyright issues, and privacy breaches. For the benefit of society, our efforts must prioritize the values of fairness, transparency, and enhancement of human well-being to harness the transformative potential of Generative AI. However, this also needs to comply with strict laws and regulations to curb the spread of bias, misinformation, and misuse. It is equally important to promote awareness and widespread education about Generative AI by encouraging users to engage with these technologies responsibly. Through this multifaceted approach, we pave the way toward a future where Generative AI contributes to sustainable progress and equity.

Acknowledgments

The author Bharathi Raja Chakravarthi received support in part through a research grant from Science Foundation Ireland (SFI) under Grant No. SFI/12/RC/2289_P2(Insight_2).

AI disclosure statement: The author acknowledges the use of AI-based tools for minor language editing or grammatical correction. However, all intellectual contributions, analyses, and conclusions presented in this chapter are entirely the author's own.

References

1. Feuerriegel, S., Hartmann, J., Janiesch, C., Zschech, P., Generative AI. *Bus. Inf. Syst. Eng.*, 66, 1, 111–126, Feb. 2024, doi: 10.1007/s12599-023-00834-7.
2. Konidaris, F., Tagaris, T., Sdraka, M., Stafylopatis, A., Generative Adversarial Networks as an Advanced Data Augmentation Technique for MRI Data, in: *Proceedings of the 14th International Joint Conference on Computer Vision, Imaging and Computer Graphics Theory and Applications*, pp. 48–59, SCITEPRESS - Science and Technology Publications, Prague, Czech Republic, 2019, doi: 10.5220/0007363900480059.
3. Fernández-Martínez, C. and Fernández, A., AI and recruiting software: Ethical and legal implications. *Paladyn J. Behav. Robot.*, 11, 1, 199–216, May 2020, doi: 10.1515/pjbr-2020-0030.
4. Morris, M.R., Scientists' Perspectives on the Potential for Generative AI in their Fields, 2023, ArXiv Prepr. ArXiv230401420.
5. Bozkurt, A., Generative artificial intelligence (AI) powered conversational educational agents: The inevitable paradigm shift. *Asian J. Distance Educ.*, 18, 1, 2023, http://www.asianjde.com/ojs/index.php/AsianJDE/article/view/718.
6. Dwivedi, Y.K., *et al.*, Opinion Paper: 'So what if ChatGPT wrote it?' Multidisciplinary perspectives on opportunities, challenges and implications

of generative conversational AI for research, practice and policy. *Int. J. Inf. Manag.*, 71, 102642, Aug. 2023, doi: 10.1016/j.ijinfomgt.2023.102642.

7. Srivastava, S. and Sinha, K., From Bias to Fairness: A Review of Ethical Considerations and Mitigation Strategies in Artificial Intelligence. *Int. J. Res. Appl. Sci. Eng. Technol.*, 11, 3, 2247–2251, Mar. 2023, doi: 10.22214/ijraset.2023.49990.
8. Ferrara, E., Fairness and bias in artificial intelligence: A brief survey of sources, impacts, and mitigation strategies. *Sci*, 6, 1, 3, 2023.
9. Petrozzino, C. and Shapiro, S., Actionable Ethics for Fairness in AI.
10. Caccavale, F., Gargalo, C.L., Gernaey, K., Krühne, U., To be fAIr: ethical and fair application of artificial intelligence in virtual laboratories, in: *Towards a new future in engineering education, new scenarios that european alliances of tech universities open up*, pp. 1022–1030, Universitat Politècnica de Catalunya, Barcelona, Spain, 2022.
11. Ray, P.P., Benchmarking, ethical alignment, and evaluation framework for conversational AI: Advancing responsible development of ChatGPT. *BenchCouncil Trans. Benchmarks Stand. Eval.*, 3, 3, 100136, Sep. 2023, doi: 10.1016/j.tbench.2023.100136.
12. Nemani, P., Joel, Y.D., Vijay, P., Liza, F.F., Gender bias in transformers: A comprehensive review of detection and mitigation strategies. *Nat. Lang. Process. J.*, 6, 100047, Mar. 2024, doi: 10.1016/j.nlp.2023.100047.
13. Bellamy, R.K., *et al.*, AI Fairness 360: An extensible toolkit for detecting and mitigating algorithmic bias. *IBM J. Res. Dev.*, 63.4/5, 4–1, 2019.
14. Balasubramaniam, N., Kauppinen, M., Rannisto, A., Hiekkanen, K., Kujala, S., Transparency and explainability of AI systems: From ethical guidelines to requirements. *Inf. Softw. Technol.*, 159, 107197, 2023.
15. Wu, X., Duan, R., Ni, J., Unveiling security, privacy, and ethical concerns of ChatGPT. *J. Inf. Intell.*, S2949715923000707, 2, 2, 102–115, Oct. 2023, doi: 10.1016/j.jiixd.2023.10.007.
16. Mennella, C., Maniscalco, U., De Pietro, G., Esposito, M., Ethical and regulatory challenges of AI technologies in healthcare: A narrative review. *Heliyon*, Elsevier, 10, 4, Feb. 2024, https://doi.org/10.1016/j.heliyon.2024.e26297
17. Ihalainen, J., Computer creativity: artificial intelligence and copyright. *J. Intellect. Prop. Law Pract.*, 13, 9, 724–728, Sep. 2018, doi: 10.1093/jiplp/jpy031.
18. Sturm, B.L., Iglesias, M., Ben-Tal, O., Miron, M., Gómez, E., Artificial intelligence and music: open questions of copyright law and engineering praxis, in: *Arts*, vol. 8, no. 3, p. 115, MDPI, 2019.
19. Mirsky, Y. and Lee, W., The Creation and Detection of Deepfakes: A Survey. *ACM Comput. Surv.*, 54, 1, 1–41, Jan. 2022, doi: 10.1145/3425780.
20. The growing impact of generative AI on cybersecurity and identity theft | VentureBeat, Accessed: Jun. 21, 2024. [Online]. Available: https://venturebeat.com/security/the-growing-impact-of-generative-ai-on-cybersecurity-and-identity-theft/.

21. Baldassarre, M.T., Caivano, D., Fernandez Nieto, B., Gigante, D., Ragone, A., The social impact of generative AI: An analysis on chatgpt. *Proceedings of the 2023 ACM Conference on Information Technology for Social Good*, pp. 363–373, 2023.
22. Gruetzemacher, R., Paradice, D., Lee, K.B., Forecasting extreme labor displacement: A survey of AI practitioners. *Technol. Forecast. Soc. Change*, 161, 120323, Dec. 2020, doi: 10.1016/j.techfore.2020.120323.
23. Khogali, H.O. and Mekid, S., The blended future of automation and AI: Examining some long-term societal and ethical impact features. *Technol. Soc.*, 73, 102232, May 2023, doi: 10.1016/j.techsoc.2023.102232.
24. Frey, C.B. and Osborne, M.A., The future of employment: How susceptible are jobs to computerisation? *Technol. Forecast. Soc. Change*, 114, 254–280, Jan. 2017, doi: 10.1016/j.techfore.2016.08.019.
25. Acemoglu, D. and Restrepo, P., Robots and jobs: Evidence from US labor markets. *J. Polit. Econ.*, 128, 6, 2188–2244, 2020.
26. Acemoglu, D. and Restrepo, P., Robots and jobs: evidence from US labor markets. *NBER Work. Pap.*, no. 23285, 2016.
27. Acemoglu, D. and Restrepo, P., Automation and new tasks: How technology displaces and reinstates labor. *J. Econ. Perspect.*, 33, 2, 3–30, 2019.
28. Jiang, H.H., *et al.*, AI Art and its Impact on Artists, in: *Proceedings of the 2023 AAAI/ACM Conference on AI, Ethics, and Society*, pp. 363–374, ACM, Montreal QC Canada, Aug. 2023, doi: 10.1145/3600211.3604681.
29. Oksanen, A., *et al.*, Artificial intelligence in fine arts: A systematic review of empirical research. *Comput. Hum. Behav. Artif. Hum.*, 1, 2, 100004, 2023, doi: 10.1016/j.chbah.2023.100004.
30. Akgun, S. and Greenhow, C., Artificial intelligence in education: Addressing ethical challenges in K-12 settings. *AI Ethics*, 2, 3, 431–440, Aug. 2022, doi: 10.1007/s43681-021-00096-7.
31. Regulation, Generative AI, and legal considerations | Knowledge | Fasken, Accessed: Jun. 21, 2024. [Online]. Available: https://www.fasken.com/en/knowledge/2023/10/regulation-generative-ai-and-legal-considerations.
32. 7 AI legal issues and how to deal with them, Accessed: Jun. 21, 2024. [Online]. Available: https://www.walkme.com/blog/ai-legal-issues/.
33. The legal implications of Generative AI | Legal | Deloitte Global, Accessed: Jun. 21, 2024. [Online]. Available: https://www.deloitte.com/global/en/services/legal/services/legal-implications-of-generative-ai.html.
34. Ethics of Artificial Intelligence | UNESCO, Accessed: Jun. 21, 2024. [Online]. Available: https://www.unesco.org/en/artificial-intelligence/recommendation-ethics.
35. UNESCO's Recommendation on the Ethics of Artificial Intelligence: key facts - UNESCO Digital Library, Accessed: Jun. 21, 2024. [Online]. Available: https://unesdoc.unesco.org/ark:/48223/pf0000385082.
36. Readiness assessment methodology: a tool of the Recommendation on the Ethics of Artificial Intelligence - UNESCO Digital Library, Accessed:

Jun. 21, 2024. [Online]. Available: https://unesdoc.unesco.org/ark:/48223/pf0000385198.

37. Paraman, P. and Anamalah, S., Ethical artificial intelligence framework for a good AI society: principles, opportunities and perils. *AI Soc.*, 38, 2, 595–611, 2023.
38. WHO releases AI ethics and governance guidance for large multi-modal models, Accessed: Jun. 21, 2024. [Online]. Available: https://www.who.int/news/item/18-01-2024-who-releases-ai-ethics-and-governance-guidance-for-large-multi-modal-models.

8

Generative Artificial Intelligence for Social Good and Sustainable Development

Wasswa Shafik[1,2]

[1]*School of Digital Science, Universiti Brunei Darussalam, Jalan Tungku Link, Gadong, Bandar Seri Begawan, Brunei Darussalam*
[2]*Dig Connectivity Research Laboratory (DCRLab), Kampala, Uganda*

Abstract

Generative artificial intelligence (GAI) occupies a prominent position within the field of AI, offering a powerful instrument for tackling the urgent global issues related to enhancing societal well-being and promoting sustainable development. This study examines the diverse and intricate impact of GAI on the progress of societal well-being and the principles of sustainability. GAI possesses an inherent capability to generate a wide range of data-driven content, including varied modalities like text, graphics, music, and other forms. The study presents a range of applications that make use of generative AI. These applications span various domains, including personalized healthcare, equitable education, disaster response, and humanitarian aid. The study also highlights the significant influence of generative AI in fostering social equity and enhancing the well-being of marginalized communities. The study's investigation encompasses the complex interrelation between GAI for Sustainable Development and the Sustainable Development Goals (SDGs) established by the United Nations. This analysis unveils generative AI as a valuable partner in tackling environmental issues such as mitigating climate change, managing resources, and developing clean energy solutions. The focal point of attention is placed on ethical considerations, which encompass the examination of potential biases, concerns regarding data privacy, and the fundamental requirement for transparency and fairness. It demonstrates the opportunities and innovations that focus on emerging technologies and potential policy frameworks that show promise for the future. To solidify these principles, we present empirical case studies that demonstrate the significant effects of generative artificial intelligence in practical settings. In anticipation of future developments,

Email: wasswashafik@ieee.org; ORCID: 0000-0002-9320-3186

N. Gayathri, S. Rakesh Kumar, Ramesh Chandran, Pethuru Raj Chelliah and Danilo Pelusi (eds.) Generative AI: Disruptive Technologies for Innovative Applications, (153–186) © 2025 Scrivener Publishing LLC

the future directions delineate the trajectory for more scholarly investigations, placing significant emphasis on the importance of multidisciplinary cooperation and continuous advancement. In summary, this paper highlights the significant contribution of generative AI in promoting social welfare and sustainable progress. Finally, it presents GAI as a catalyst for positive global transformation, aiming to inspire additional research and innovation that can contribute to a fairer and more sustainable future for all individuals.

Keywords: Generative artificial intelligence, sustainable development, social good, natural language processing, ethical and security, openAI

8.1 Introduction

This disruptive technology is known as generative artificial intelligence[1] (GAI) possessing the ability to independently generate information, rendering it a potent catalyst in tackling a diverse array of societal and environmental issues. Consequently, it assumes a crucial role in promoting social welfare and facilitating sustainable development [1]. The revolutionary capacity of this technology extends well beyond mere automation, offering a unique opportunity to leverage innovation for the advancement of society and the preservation of the planet. In the subsequent paragraphs, we examine eight discrete aspects of GAI's inclination toward advancing societal welfare and sustainability, thoroughly investigating each dimension [2].

The utilization of GAI has the promise of transforming the healthcare sector through its ability to facilitate the development of individualized treatment regimens, predict the occurrence of disease outbreaks, and accelerate the process of discovering new drugs. By conducting a comprehensive examination of vast medical data, this process provides healthcare practitioners with the necessary resources to make informed judgments based on data, which could enhance patient outcomes, mitigate mortality rates, and alleviate the economic strain on healthcare systems [3]. In the field of education, GAI possesses the potential to revolutionize the learning process by producing customized instructional resources that surpass language boundaries. This enables educators to provide tailored information that caters to everyone's unique learning preferences, thereby promoting equal access to excellent education and nurturing a culture of continuous learning for people across the globe [4].

The utilization of GAI holds significant importance in the progression of environmental conservation and the promotion of sustainability.

[1]https://generativeai.net/

Through the examination of comprehensive datasets, the capability to forecast climatic patterns, discern endangered species, and enhance resource management can be achieved. This technology plays a crucial role in tackling pressing concerns such as climate change, the preservation of biodiversity, and the sustainable exploitation of resources; hence, making a significant contribution towards achieving a more ecologically balanced global environment [5]. Also, the use of GAI holds significant potential in facilitating the advancement towards the attainment of the Sustainable Development Goals[2] (SDGs) set out by the United Nations. The clear potential for innovation is observed in the domains of renewable energy, waste mitigation, and sustainable agriculture. GAI plays a pivotal role in facilitating advancements in various domains, thereby contributing to the establishment of a global society that is characterized by fairness and long-term viability [6].

The multilingual capabilities of generative AI have the potential to revolutionize global communication by facilitating effortless translation of content across different languages. This phenomenon surpasses linguistic barriers, hence facilitating the accessibility of information to a wide range of individuals, increasing intercultural interaction, and cultivating a more profound comprehension among various societies [7]. The potential of GAI in producing inclusive material, such as braille papers and audio descriptions, has a notable impact on enhancing the quality of life for those with disabilities. It promotes the value of inclusivity, dismantling obstacles and enabling universal access to knowledge, thus cultivating a society that is fairer and more empathetic [8].

GAI facilitates the establishment of ethical parameters for content creation, thereby promoting the conscientious acknowledgment of personal preferences and permission by users. This ethical framework aims to foster responsible content creation in several fields, such as marketing, media, and entertainment, as illustrated in Figure 8.1, by endorsing content that is in accordance with social values and ethical norms [9]. GAI has the potential to offer invaluable decision-making assistance in various fields, encompassing areas such as financial analysis and legal procedures. The optimization of productivity and efficiency, as well as the ethical and responsible utilization of AI, particularly in high-stakes situations where human judgment is crucial, can be achieved through the establishment of well-defined limits for human-AI collaboration [10].

---

[2]https://sdgs.un.org/goals

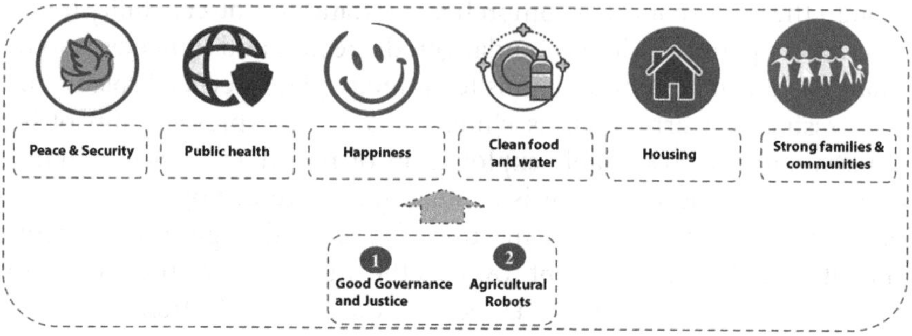

Figure 8.1 Benefits of good governance and justice and agricultural robots.

8.1.1 Motivation of Generative Artificial Intelligence

The potential of generative AI to drive positive social impact and promote sustainable development is significant, motivating us to leverage its capacities for the advancement of society and the environment. By enabling GAI to produce important content, we may augment the field of healthcare by providing individualized treatment recommendations, facilitate the domain of education by generating customized learning materials, and strengthen initiatives in environmental conservation through the analysis and prediction of data. Moreover, the utilization of GAI has the potential to foster innovation in tackling climate change, resource management, and the global concerns that have been delineated in the SDGs established by the United Nations. The utilization of technology has the potential to enhance the accessibility of information, overcome linguistic obstacles, and cultivate inclusivity, thus contributing to the establishment of a more equitable global society. Nevertheless, it is imperative to approach this potential with a sense of ethical responsibility, transparency, and the mitigation of bias. This approach is crucial not only to promote the progress of Generative AI in terms of social welfare and sustainability but also to uphold fundamental principles such as fairness, accountability, and respect for individual privacy. By doing so, we can maximize the positive impact of GAI on our collective future.

8.1.2 The Contribution of the Chapter

The contributions of the chapter are summarized below.

- The chapter describes generative AI and its applications and establishes the significance of social good and sustainable

development as crucial goals, presenting diverse case studies showcasing the use of generative AI in fields like healthcare, education, and disaster response and highlighting the transformative impact of generative AI on marginalized communities.
- The chapter explores the role of generative AI in addressing sustainable development goals related to environmental challenges and clean energy and provides examples of AI-driven solutions for environmental issues. It examines the ethical and regulatory concerns associated with generative AI, including biases, data privacy, fairness, and transparency.
- The chapter dissects the challenges and limitations in the widespread implementation of generative AI for social good and sustainability, exploring emerging technologies and potential policy frameworks in the field of generative AI and highlighting innovative approaches to overcome challenges.
- Finally, the chapter proposes potential research directions and emphasizes the importance of interdisciplinary collaboration and innovation, demonstrating some lessons learned from the chapter and the conclusion.

8.1.3 The Organization of the Chapter

Section 8.2 provides an overview of generative artificial intelligence and its applications. Section 8.3 illustrates generative artificial intelligence for social good. Section 8.4 broadly presents generative artificial intelligence for sustainable development. Section 8.5 presents ethical and regulatory considerations. Section 8.6 illustrates the limitations of generative artificial intelligence. Section 8.7 presents future research directions. Section 8.8 presents lessons learned from the chapter and the conclusion.

8.2 An Overview of Generative Artificial Intelligence and Its Applications

Generative AI is a specific domain within the field of AI that centers on the creation and generation of various types of material, such as text, images, music, and other forms of data. This is accomplished through the utilization of algorithms and neural networks. In contrast to conventional AI systems that are primarily developed for categorization and forecasting, GAI endeavors to generate novel and innovative data without relying on explicit programming or pre-existing information. The system functions by acquiring knowledge of patterns and structures from preexisting data and, after that, creating novel material that adheres to such patterns.

8.2.1 Text Generation

GAI models, like GPT-4[3], serve as a testament to the significant advancements made in comprehending and producing text that closely resembles human language. The ability to comprehend and interpret contextual information, subtle distinctions, and intricate aspects of language enables the production of content that is cohesive and contextually appropriate [11]. This technology confers significant advantages to both businesses and content creators. The technology is currently employed to generate content, automate writing processes, and enhance consumer engagements via chatbots. The ramifications of this transformation are significant, as they fundamentally alter the modes of communication and content production within businesses. The utilization of generative text AI facilitates enhanced efficiency and scalability for enterprises, enabling them to effectively communicate with their target audiences through personalized and responsive means [12]. This encompasses a wide range of tasks, including creating marketing materials and providing customer support by addressing inquiries.

8.2.2 Image Generation

The advent of GANs[4] has brought about a paradigm shift in the field of picture production. The system comprises two neural networks, namely a generator and a discriminator, which collaborate to generate and assess images. GANs exhibit a diverse array of applications encompassing the creation of deepfakes, wherein the realistic overlay of one individual's appearance onto another is achieved, as well as the generation of digital art, simulation of virtual environments in video games, and production of photorealistic computer-generated imagery[5] (CGI) for films and animations [13]. This technology enables individuals in the fields of art, design, and film to delve into uncharted territories of innovation while

---

[3]https://openai.com/gpt-4

[4]https://developer.ibm.com/articles/generative-adversarial-networks-explained/

[5]https://www.3ds.com/products/3dexcite/commercial-content-creation/cgi

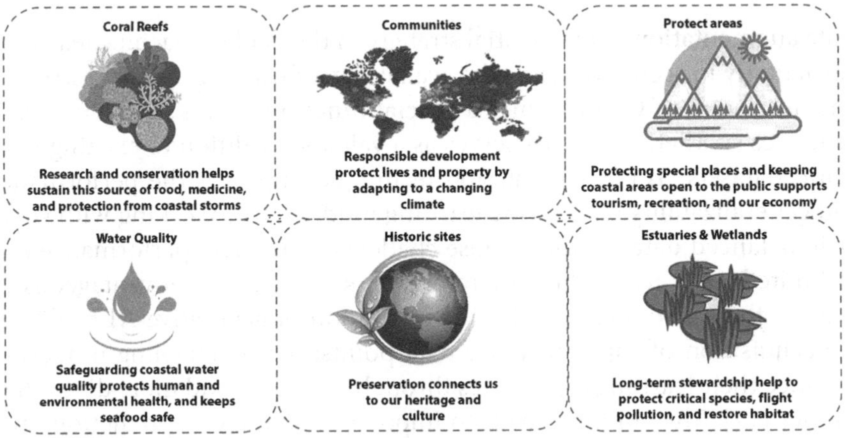

Figure 8.2 Top six contributing aspects of sustainable environment.

also offering robust resources for the entertainment sector. Nevertheless, this phenomenon also gives rise to ethical concerns regarding the integrity of visual content in the era of digital technology; key critical aspects are presented in Figure 8.2.

8.2.3 Audio and Music Generation

AI models have demonstrated exceptional capabilities in the generation of novel musical compositions. The models have undergone training using extensive datasets comprising diverse musical patterns and styles, thereby enabling them to generate music across a range of genres, moods, and styles. The utilization of generative AI has been widely adopted by musicians, content creators, and the entertainment sector due to its capacity to enhance the efficiency of music composition procedures [14]. The software is utilized in the production of soundtracks for various forms of media, including movies, video games, and multimedia projects, thereby presenting a multitude of opportunities for artistic innovation and imaginative exploration. The utilization of GAI in the realm of music has the potential to serve as a source of inspiration for musicians, facilitate the production of background scores for cinematic works, and offer a vast array of opportunities for the advancement of audio content creation in the foreseeable future [15].

8.2.4 Data Augmentation

Data augmentation is an essential strategy in the field of machine learning, particularly in scenarios when the availability of training data is restricted. The utilization of GAI assumes a crucial function in this procedure, as it generates synthetic data that serves as a valuable addition to existing real-world datasets. This augmentation technique improves the performance and generalizability of machine learning models [16]. Working with small or imbalanced datasets might pose challenges to model performance due to limited data availability. Therefore, it is particularly advantageous to address these issues effectively. The utilization of generative AI facilitates the acquisition of supplementary data points; hence, enabling models to enhance their learning capabilities through a broader and more diversified dataset [17]. This, in turn, leads to improved accuracy in predictions and classifications.

8.2.5 Video and Animation Generation

GANs have garnered significant attention for their ability to produce highly realistic animations and special effects. These models generate character animations for video games that exhibit a remarkably high degree of realism while also being able to create visually impressive effects in movies and animations. Consequently, they have emerged as vital instruments within the entertainment sector, providing enhanced efficacy and economical means to produce dynamic content [18]. The application of generative AI in the domains of video and animation production offers a wide range of possibilities, allowing animators, filmmakers, and game developers to enhance their creative pursuits to unprecedented levels. This technological advancement expedites the duration of production schedules.

8.2.6 Drug Discovery

The application of GAI expedites the discovery and advancement of innovative drugs by forecasting the characteristics and therapeutic advantages of newly synthesized chemical compounds. This technology enables researchers to investigate a wide range of chemical compositions efficiently and expeditiously, thereby diminishing the temporal and financial resources necessary for the development and commercialization of novel pharmaceuticals [19]. Moreover, the utilization of GAI plays a significant role in enhancing the development of pharmaceuticals that are both safer and more productive. This is achieved through the prediction of potential adverse effects and interactions. The significance of generative AI in the field of drug discovery is particularly pronounced due to the persistent global need for novel and efficacious medicines.

8.2.7 Content Recommendation

Generative AI-based content recommendation systems play a crucial role in the functioning of digital platforms, encompassing a wide range of applications such as streaming services and e-commerce websites. These systems employ algorithms to assess user behavior, preferences, and historical data to produce personalized content recommendations. The implementation of personalization strategies contributes to increased user engagement, facilitates content discovery, and ultimately fosters customer happiness and corporate prosperity [20]. By utilizing GAI in the context of content suggestion, platforms have the potential to provide users with a more carefully selected and pertinent experience. Streaming services utilize this technology to provide personalized recommendations for movies, music, and shows, contemplating the user's viewing history and tastes. E-commerce platforms provide product recommendations based on the alignment of a shopper's interests and purchasing patterns [21].

8.2.8 Language Translation

The utilization of transformer topologies in GAI models has brought about a significant transformation in the field of machine translation. These models can produce translations that are not only precise but also contextually appropriate across different languages. The implementation of this technology has effectively overcome the obstacles posed by language differences, enabling seamless cross-linguistic communication and facilitating access to information [2]. The enhancement in the quality of translation, primarily ascribed to GAI, holds significant ramifications for worldwide communication, international commerce, and the accessibility of content. For instance, it facilitates individuals in comprehending and interpreting diverse cultural and linguistic materials without relying on manual translation. In the context of international business, it facilitates effective communication with global partners and customers.

8.2.9 Humanoid Robots and Avatars

GAI improves the caliber of interactions between humans and computers, rendering them more captivating, organic, and user-centric. Generative AI is facilitating the development of applications in diverse domains by empowering robots and avatars to produce realistic and contextually appropriate answers. In the context of customer service, the utilization of GAI-powered avatars enables the provision of immediate support and prompt responses to consumer requests [3]. Within virtual reality environments, avatars can fulfill roles as tour guides or educators, so augmenting the immersive nature of the user experience. The utilization of GAI in humanoid robots and avatars is currently at the forefront of developing interactive and personalized experiences for consumers.

8.2.10 Design and Creativity

The utilization of GAI has become increasingly prominent among creative practitioners, encompassing individuals such as graphic designers, architects, and artists. AI solutions can facilitate the process of creativity and concept production by offering novel ideas and stimulating creative inspiration. GAI has the potential to assist graphic designers in generating design concepts, thereby aiding in the resolution of creative obstacles, and enhancing the efficiency of the design workflow [4]. Within the field of architecture, AI models can propose novel ideas and configurations by reflecting specified criteria and limitations. Moreover, the utilization of generative AI promotes the cultivation of creativity and originality by presenting alternate viewpoints and concepts that may not have been clearly discernible to human originators [5]. This technological advancement fosters a collaborative environment between AI-enabled systems and human designers, resulting in the generation of increasingly original and imaginative outcomes.

8.3 Generative AI for Social Good

The use of GAI for social good involves utilizing advanced computational techniques to tackle urgent societal issues, foster constructive transformations, and enhance the overall welfare of both individuals and communities. The utilization of generative AI in this context is distinguished by its ability to generate content based on data, with a primary objective of promoting societal welfare, particularly by addressing issues of fairness, inclusivity, and societal influence [1, 3]. The factors depicted promote the development of new ideas, the incorporation of diverse perspectives, and the preservation of resources, ultimately resulting in a fair and empathetic society. Nevertheless, it is imperative to meticulously address ethical considerations, including but not limited to privacy, transparency, and biases, to guarantee the responsible and equitable utilization of these technologies.

8.3.1 Personalized Healthcare Interventions

The utilization of AI in the healthcare sector is causing a significant transformation by means of examining specific patient data and producing treatment plans that are tailored to the individual's unique needs. AI models can propose personalized pharmaceutical plans, forecast the advancement of diseases, and enhance treatment approaches by reflecting a patient's medical history, genetic factors, and present state of health. The use of a tailored strategy not only enhances the effectiveness of medical interventions but also contributes to the mitigation of healthcare expenditures [4]. Moreover, it confers authority to both healthcare providers and patients through evidence-based insights, thereby augmenting the overall standard of patient care while furthering the objective of societal benefit.

8.3.2 Equitable Education Access

Within the domain of education, the utilization of generative artificial intelligence (AI) has promised to address the disparities that exist in both the accessibility and quality of education. AI-driven adaptive learning solutions utilize data analytics to get insights into individuals' individual learning preferences, areas of proficiency, and areas for improvement. As a result, the system produces tailored educational materials, guaranteeing that each student receives training that is tailored to their individual requirements and learning speed [5]. This technology facilitates educational equity by accommodating a range of learning styles and skills, therefore fostering an inclusive educational setting that equalizes opportunities for students from diverse backgrounds.

8.3.3 Disaster Response and Humanitarian Aid

GAI plays a pivotal and indispensable function in the realm of disaster response and humanitarian relief endeavors. Through the examination of historical data, meteorological patterns, and pertinent data, AI can forecast the trajectory and ramifications of natural calamities. The system produces crisis response plans in real-time, maximizing the allocation of resources and facilitating prompt evacuations and coordination of emergency responses [6]. Utilizing this technology enhances the efficacy and proficiency of disaster response efforts and contributes to the preservation of human life and the alleviation of distress during emergencies.

8.3.4 Accessible Information for Diverse Audiences

The system can produce material in a range of formats that are easily accessible, including Braille papers, sign language films, and audio descriptions specifically designed for individuals with visual and hearing impairments. Implementing this approach guarantees that individuals with disabilities can effectively access and comprehend information, actively engage in educational activities, and interact with digital content on an equitable basis with their non-disabled counterparts [8]. The statement above underscores the significance of technology in fostering social equality by fostering inclusion and ensuring equitable access to information and services.

8.3.5 Mental Health Support and Therapy

The utilization of AI in the mental health sector facilitates the provision of prompt assistance and access to resources for persons grappling with mental health difficulties. AI-driven chatbots and virtual mental health aides have the potential to provide treatments, emotional support, and crisis intervention services. These platforms not only facilitate early intervention but also enable individuals to access expert assistance when necessary [10]. Technological advancements have a pivotal role in promoting positive mental health outcomes and facilitating greater accessibility to mental health services. This significant contribution addresses a crucial dimension of social well-being, simultaneously mitigating the societal stigma surrounding the act of seeking mental health help.

8.3.6 Language Translation for Communication and Diplomacy

Within the field of international diplomacy, the utilization of GAI effectively addresses and surmounts the challenges posed by language limitations. By providing instantaneous and precise language translation, it enhances the efficacy of communication between diplomats and leaders who possess diverse linguistic and cultural backgrounds. This technological advancement facilitates the cultivation of worldwide comprehension and cooperation, thereby nurturing diplomacy, commerce, and international connections [7]. The function of this entity is to act as a conduit for communication and interaction between different countries, facilitating significant exchanges and agreements. Within the realm of social welfare, this innovation plays a significant role in fostering harmonious international relations, facilitating economic alliances, and supporting humanitarian endeavors on a worldwide level.

8.3.7 Environmental Conservation and Sustainability

The utilization of GAI models is significantly impacting environmental conservation and sustainability initiatives through the examination of extensive datasets pertaining to climate, ecosystems, and biodiversity. By use of data analysis, AI produces valuable insights that contribute to the development of sustainable resource management practices, conservation measures, and efforts to mitigate climate change. The utilization of a data-driven methodology facilitates the implementation of evidence-based decision-making processes and the development of optimum environmental policies [22]. GAI improves social good and promotes the sustainability of the globe for future generations by endorsing programs that seek to save the ecosystems of the Earth and mitigate the effects of climate change.

8.3.8 Crisis Counseling and Suicide Prevention

GAI-powered chatbots and virtual assistants offer prompt emotional assistance and access to resources for persons experiencing distress, including those who are contemplating suicide. Through the provision of crisis intervention tactics, sympathetic answers, and recommendations to mental health specialists, these AI systems can effectively preserve lives and facilitate timely access to necessary assistance for those in distress [23]. Technology serves a vital function in promoting social well-being by providing prompt and easily available aid during critical situations, hence highlighting its significance in bolstering mental health and facilitating crisis management to achieve the SDG requirements, as demonstrated in Figure 8.3.

8.3.9 Promoting Social Equity Through Policy Insights

The utilization of GAI advances social justice through the provision of policy insights that are rooted in data. The process involves the examination of intricate socioeconomic data to produce policy proposals and insights that have the potential to tackle social inequality effectively. These insights

Figure 8.3 Signs of realizing the SDGs.

provide valuable information for making evidence-based policy decisions and enable the successful implementation of effective interventions that can have positive impacts on underrepresented populations [24]. Using AI's analytical powers, policymakers may make well-informed decisions to enhance the accessibility of resources, economic prospects, and social services for marginalized people.

8.3.10 Content Creation for Nonprofits and Humanitarian Organizations

The system can produce a diverse array of content, encompassing reports, social media campaigns, and materials for fundraising purposes. Through the implementation of GAI, companies streamline content development processes, allowing them to allocate more resources toward their fundamental objectives and outreach endeavors. This enhances the operational effectiveness of nonprofit organizations and humanitarian endeavors, enabling them to extend their outreach to a wider demographic and generate a more substantial influence [25]. The utilization of technology ensures the efficient allocation of scarce resources to promote social welfare, facilitate the gathering of financial support, and enhance public understanding of pressing matters.

8.4 Generative Artificial Intelligence for Sustainable Development

The field of GAI for sustainable development is currently gaining prominence as it utilizes AI technology to tackle worldwide issues pertaining to sustainability, environmental preservation, and fair socioeconomic advancement. The primary objective of employing generative AI in this context is to advance sustainable practices, mitigate environmental consequences, and contribute to the achievement of the SDGs set forth by the United Nations. Generative AI for sustainable development offers a potent tool for addressing the complex concerns of environmental protection, resource management, and fair socioeconomic progress.

8.4.1 Renewable Energy Optimization

Machine learning models can predict energy output by utilizing both historical and real-time data while considering factors such as weather patterns, energy consumption, and the capacity of renewable sources. This data contributes to improved grid management and storage options, hence assuring a reliable energy supply [2]. Furthermore, GAI has the potential to enhance the efficiency and effectiveness of renewable energy installations by optimizing their placement and design, resulting in cost reduction and minimized environmental impact. These technological developments facilitate the rapid adoption of environmentally friendly energy sources and contribute to the promotion of sustainable development through the mitigation of climate change [3]. GAI enhances the efficiency and effectiveness of renewable energy sources, thereby facilitating the global shift towards affordable, reliable, and environmentally sustainable energy systems, as articulated in SDG 7[6]. This optimization strategy aims to mitigate greenhouse gas emissions and effectively tackle climate change, SDG 13[7], while simultaneously promoting sustainable industrialization (SDG 9).

8.4.2 Smart Resource Management

The implementation of sustainable resource management practices plays a critical role in mitigating waste generation and preserving essential resources. GAI models employ data analytics techniques to forecast

[6]https://sdgs.un.org/goals/goal7
[7]https://sdgs.un.org/goals/goal13

resource demand, encompassing vital resources like water and energy. This capability facilitates the optimal allocation of resources by enterprises and governments, hence enhancing efficiency. GAI significantly impacts environmental conservation and cost reduction by effectively utilizing resources and eliminating wastage [4]. This technique additionally guarantees a fairer allocation of resources in accordance with sustainable development objectives that prioritize the reduction of resource disparities. GAI facilitates climate action by offering data-centric insights that inform the development of solutions aimed at minimizing the adverse effects of climate change [5].

8.4.3 Climate Change Mitigation

The capacity of AI to evaluate vast datasets plays a crucial role in enhancing comprehension of the intricate dynamics associated with climate change. Through the identification of patterns and the recognition of trends, AI-enabled models possess the capability to offer significant insights to policymakers and researchers [6]. These observations provide valuable information for the formulation of climate change mitigation measures and the establishment of sustainable policies. AI assesses the efficacy of these tactics, facilitating the process of adapting and refining activities to tackle the continuously increasing difficulties posed by global warming effectively [7]. The statement aligns with the objectives of SDG 15, which seeks to safeguard, restore, and promote the sustainable utilization of terrestrial ecosystems. Additionally, it is in line with the aims of SDG 14[8], which focuses on the conservation and sustainable utilization of marine resources.

8.4.4 Ecosystem Monitoring and Conservation

Ecosystems have a crucial role in maintaining biodiversity, and the utilization of GAI is of utmost importance in the monitoring and conservation efforts of these natural environments. By utilizing satellite images and sensor data, artificial intelligence models can monitor and analyze alterations occurring within ecosystems. This enables the identification of potential risks and hazards that may pose a danger to biodiversity and habitats [9]. These insights enhance conservation efforts by facilitating the implementation of more focused and efficient preservation strategies. GAI safeguards endangered species by tracking their movements and monitoring potential dangers, which, in turn, contributes to the sustainable management of natural resources.

---

[8]https://sdgs.un.org/goals/goal14

8.4.5 Circular Economy Promotion

The fundamental focus of the circular economy concept lies in the minimization of waste, the recycling of materials, and the promotion of sustainable resource utilization. The utilization of generative AI plays a crucial role in the attainment of this objective through the optimization of recycling procedures, the improvement of product design to enhance recyclability, and the mitigation of waste generation in the manufacturing sector [13]. By leveraging AI-powered analysis, enterprises have the potential to optimize their operational processes, diminish their ecological impact, and actively contribute to the establishment of a more sustainable and resource-efficient economy. SDG 12[9], also known as the SDG on Responsible Consumption and Production, focuses on promoting sustainable patterns of consumption and production. GAI demonstrates alignment with SDG 12 by advocating for waste reduction and the promotion of recycling, thus supporting the establishment of sustainable consumption and production practices [19]. This phenomenon facilitates the development of a circular economy that is characterized by enhanced resource efficiency.

8.4.6 Sustainable Agriculture and Food Security

GAI enhances precision agriculture through the analysis of data collected from various sources such as sensors, drones, and satellites. This technology has the potential to offer agricultural practitioners valuable information pertaining to soil quality, crop development, and the control of pests. The utilization of GAI in agricultural practices enables farmers to effectively enhance irrigation techniques, minimize pesticide application, and achieve sustainable growth in crop yields [26]. This technology contributes to the enhancement of food security by facilitating a more reliable and streamlined food production system, thereby harmonizing with the objectives of sustainable development. The utilization of GAI optimizes agricultural practices, thereby contributing significantly to the attainment of Sustainable Development Goal 2[10], which aims to eradicate hunger and achieve food security [27]. Implementing strategies to enhance crop productivity and advocating for the use of sustainable agricultural methods contributes to the maintenance of food security and the improvement of nutritional outcomes, as demonstrated in Figure 8.4.

---

[9]https://sdgs.un.org/goals/goal12
[10]https://sdgs.un.org/goals/goal2

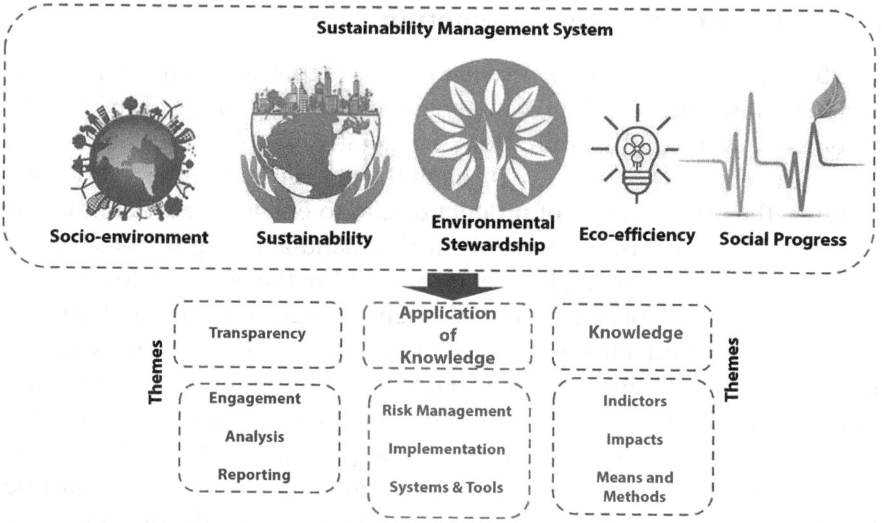

Figure 8.4 Sustainable management systems.

8.4.7 Urban Planning and Smart Cities

The management of rapid urbanization necessitates the use of sustainable urban development practices. GAI develops smart cities that emphasize energy efficiency, public transit, and the integration of renewable energy resources. The utilization of artificial intelligence in urban planning facilitates the optimization of traffic flow, the reduction of energy consumption in buildings, and the enhancement of public services [28]. These measures play a significant role in fostering the development of urban settings that are more sustainable and conducive to human habitation, hence enhancing the overall well-being and satisfaction of urban dwellers.

8.4.8 Water Resource Management

The effective and sustainable governance of water resources plays a pivotal role in guaranteeing dependable and uncontaminated water provision. GAI models are utilized for the purpose of monitoring water quality, making predictions on water scarcity, and optimizing the distribution of water resources. GAI mitigates water-related emergencies and promotes the preservation of this valuable resource by offering up-to-date information and valuable insights [27]. The effective management of water resources in a sustainable manner is a fundamental element of SDG 6[11]. GAI facilitates the provision of clean water and sanitation by actively monitoring water quality, accurately forecasting instances of scarcity, and optimizing the distribution of water resources.

8.4.9 Global Supply Chain Sustainability

The establishment of sustainable supply chains is necessary to mitigate the environmental consequences associated with worldwide commerce. GAI analyzes supply chain data with the aim of identifying potential avenues for carbon emissions reduction, logistics optimization, and the promotion of sustainable sourcing and manufacturing methods. The integration of GAI in supply chains contributes to the attainment of corporate social responsibility objectives and facilitates the worldwide transition towards more conscientious and ethical business methodologies [29]. The alignment between sustainable supply chain management and SDG 12[12] (responsible consumption and production), as well as SDG 9[13] (industry, innovation, and infrastructure), is evident. The promotion of responsible consumption and production is accompanied by the advancement of industry, innovation, and infrastructure to foster sustainable development.

8.4.10 Environmental Education and Advocacy

The utilization of GAI in content generation and recommendation systems provides valuable assistance to environmental education and advocacy endeavors. The utilization of GAI facilitates the dissemination of tailored content and suggestions, thereby enhancing the consciousness surrounding environmental concerns and motivating individuals to embrace sustainable practices. GAI systems play a crucial role in enabling individuals to make well-informed decisions that are in line with sustainable development objectives and contribute to the advancement of an environmentally conscious society. SDG 4[14], which pertains to Quality Education, and SDG 17[15], which focuses on Partnerships for the Goals, are two SDGs outlined by the United Nations. GAI contributes to the advancement of quality education, as outlined in SDG 4, by its ability to deliver tailored educational

---

[11]https://sdgs.un.org/goals/goal6
[12]https://sdgs.un.org/goals/goal12
[13]https://sdgs.un.org/goals/goal9
[14]https://sdgs.un.org/goals/goal4
[15]https://sdgs.un.org/goals/goal17

materials for environmental education [30]. Furthermore, it promotes the establishment of partnerships to achieve SDG 17[16]. This is accomplished through the encouragement of joint endeavors aimed at increasing awareness and advocating for the adoption of sustainable practices.

8.5 Ethical and Regulatory Considerations

This section presents ethical and regulatory concerns of GAI as they appear in social good and sustainable development.

8.5.1 Data Privacy and Security

The preservation of data privacy is a critical consideration while utilizing GAI. Sustainable development programs frequently encompass the collection and analysis of extensive datasets, which may encompass confidential information. To uphold ethical standards, enterprises must demonstrate respect for individuals' privacy by strict adherence to data protection legislation. This encompasses the processes of acquiring informed consent, anonymizing personal data, and installing strong encryption and access control systems [31]. The alignment between the enforcement of data privacy and security and SDG 16[17] (Peace, Justice, and Strong Institutions) may be observed. This goal emphasizes the importance of upholding the rule of law and safeguarding data to promote peace and justice.

8.5.2 Fairness and Bias

The ethical utilization of generative AI, particularly within the realm of sustainable development, necessitates a significant focus on the concepts of fairness and prejudice. In this context, the principles of justice and inclusivity hold utmost importance. GAI-enabled models have the potential to unintentionally sustain biases that exist within their training data, which may result in unjust conclusions. To address biases in AI systems, conscientious AI developers must utilize methodologies such as fairness-aware machine learning [32]. This approach aims to eliminate biases and promote equitable treatment of all individuals and groups inside AI systems. The pursuit of equity in AI is congruent with SDG 10 (Reduced Inequalities), which seeks to diminish disparities both within and between nations.

---

[16]https://sdgs.un.org/goals/goal17
[17]https://sdgs.un.org/goals/goal16

8.5.3 Explainability and Transparency

The transparency and explainability of GAI models are crucial factors in establishing confidence and ensuring accountability. In the context of sustainable development, stakeholders must possess a comprehensive understanding of the decision-making processes powered by AI, particularly in relation to the allocation of resources and the formulation of policy recommendations. Organizations should utilize methodologies that provide transparency into the decision-making mechanisms of GAI models [33]. The openness and explainability of AI systems are in accordance with the fundamental principles of accountability and ethical utilization of AI.

8.5.4 Accountability

The establishment of a clear definition of accountability within AI systems is of utmost importance. The identification of the individuals or entities accountable for errors, biases, or unexpected consequences is crucial to ensure ethical conduct and adherence to regulatory standards. The establishment of well-defined lines of responsibility serves to mitigate the risk of unattended ethical transgressions and fosters a heightened level of confidence in GAI systems [34]. The relevance of this feature is particularly notable in relation to SDG 16[18], which emphasizes the importance of establishing effective, accountable, and transparent institutions.

8.5.5 Environmental Impact

The escalating apprehension revolves around the ecological ramifications of artificial intelligence (AI), specifically pertaining to the training of extensive models. The carbon footprint of GAI is influenced by factors such as energy consumption, carbon emissions, and the utilization of finite resources during the training of AI models. The concepts of sustainable development advocate for the adoption of ecologically responsible activities [35]. Organizations could investigate energy-efficient training techniques, employ renewable energy sources, and allocate resources towards carbon offsetting to mitigate the environmental consequences associated with generative AI. These efforts align with SDG 13[19] (Climate Action).

---

[18]https://sdgs.un.org/goals/goal16
[19]https://sdgs.un.org/goals/goal13

8.5.6 Ethical Use Cases

The process of identifying ethical use cases for generative AI in the context of sustainable development is a decision that is guided by principles. By giving precedence to applications that actively contribute to the SDGs set by the United Nations, such as clean energy, environmental conservation, fair resource allocation, and enhanced healthcare, it guarantees that technology is utilized for the betterment of society at large [36]. This emphasis is in accordance with the principles of sustainability and the ethical deployment of artificial intelligence.

8.5.7 Global Collaboration

The establishment of a worldwide framework for the ethical and regulatory utilization of generative AI in sustainable development necessitates imperative collaboration among countries, organizations, and stakeholders. Sustainable development is a worldwide undertaking, necessitating collective endeavors to tackle ethical and regulatory obstacles. Collaborative frameworks play a crucial role in promoting the harmonization of standards and facilitating the consistent and ethical utilization of AI technology across international boundaries [37]. This alignment with the global nature of the SDGs underscores the significance of such frameworks in fostering responsible and sustainable AI practices.

8.5.8 Ethical Artificial Intelligent Education

It is imperative to cultivate comprehension and awareness of the ethical implications associated with generative artificial intelligence. Ethical AI education initiatives possess the potential to enhance the consciousness of developers, users, and decision-makers, thus fostering the adoption of responsible and ethical practices in the field of AI [38]. These systems facilitate the identification of ethical quandaries and guide individuals in making proper decisions, hence promoting the ethical utilization of artificial intelligence within the framework of sustainable development.

8.5.9 Public Engagement, Input and Global Governance

The inclusion of the public and pertinent stakeholders in deliberations concerning the ethical and regulatory dimensions of GAI fosters greater levels of openness and accountability. The inclusion of public involvement in the development and implementation of AI technology serves to assure its alignment with prevailing social values and goals. Stakeholder interactions play a crucial role in the identification and proactive addressing of ethical concerns, hence fostering the development of trust in GAI systems [39]. The construction of global governance frameworks for GAI, particularly in domains with transnational ramifications such as climate change or biodiversity protection, is imperative. Global governance frameworks play a crucial role in promoting international cooperation and fostering the harmonization of GAI standards [40]. They assist in resolving ethical and regulatory dilemmas on a worldwide level in accordance with the broad reach of Sustainable Development.

8.6 Generative Artificial Intelligence Limitations

The field of GAI exhibits significant promise, although it is accompanied by various constraints and obstacles that necessitate thorough examination. It is vital to comprehend these constraints in order to engage in conscientious creation and implementation.

8.6.1 Data Dependence

The training of generative AI is strongly dependent on the availability and utilization of data. In domains characterized by scarcity or partiality of data, these models encounter a significant constraint. The outcome exhibits a dual nature, characterized by a decline in their performance and the potential reinforcement and exacerbation of preexisting biases and inequities within the data [20]. The constraint above highlights the importance of gathering a wide range of impartial data and employing strategies to reduce bias in artificial intelligence algorithms. In sectors such as healthcare and finance, where choices can have substantial consequences for individuals, the reliance on data gives rise to ethical and fairness considerations [17]. As a result, it becomes imperative to subject model outputs to thorough and rigorous examination.

8.6.2 Bias and Fairness

The existence of biases inside models of GAI represents a complex and multi-dimensional constraint. These models have the potential to unintentionally adopt and disseminate biases that exist within their training data, resulting in discriminatory consequences, particularly in critical domains such as criminal justice or healthcare. The task of acknowledging and reducing bias is a multifaceted endeavor, typically encompassing the reassessment of training data, enhancements to algorithms, and the establishment of ethical principles [12]. The pursuit of fairness in AI systems continues to be a crucial objective, as the establishment of unbiased and equitable decision-making is essential for the responsible use of AI.

8.6.3 Ethical Concerns

The ability of GAI to produce deepfakes and modified information gives rise to significant ethical considerations. The persistent difficulty faced by regulators, organizations, and society at large pertains to the generation of deceptive information and the vicious exploitation of technology. The proper utilization of GAI requires the establishment of ethical frameworks and norms that serve the dual purpose of preventing misuse and safeguarding the principles of freedom of expression and creativity [9]. Achieving a harmonious equilibrium between innovation and responsibility is an ongoing pursuit, underscoring the significance of openness and accountability in the realm of AI-powered content development.

8.6.4 Lack of Creativity and Common Sense

The limits of GAI, in terms of its ability to exhibit genuine creativity and common-sense reasoning, can be attributed to the inherent characteristics of AI models. Although they demonstrate proficiency in pattern recognition and data synthesis, their outputs frequently exhibit a deficiency in actual creativity, novelty, and contextual comprehension, qualities that are inherent to human capabilities [13]. As a result, these models function as valuable instruments for generating content. However, they do not supplant the role of human creativity. Consequently, it is imperative to perceive them as tools that foster collaboration among artists, authors, and designers rather than serving as substitutes for creative endeavors [16]. Investigating the mutually beneficial interaction between AI and human creativity presents a highly promising domain for fostering innovation.

8.6.5 Resource Intensive

The considerable demand for resources that is inherent in GAI poses a notable constraint in relation to both the capacity to access it and its long-term viability. The utilization of large GAI-enabled models necessitates significant computational resources, so creating an accessibility disparity that limits their adoption to enterprises with abundant financial and technological means. Furthermore, the energy consumption linked to the training and execution of these models gives rise to environmental apprehensions [20]. Addressing this challenge entails developing energy-efficient training techniques, employing renewable energy sources, and investing in carbon offsetting to minimize the environmental impact and democratize access to GAI technology.

8.6.6 Interpretability and Transparency

The absence of interpretability and openness in GAI presents a notable obstacle in terms of ensuring accountability and fostering confidence. Numerous models of GAI exhibit intricate opaque structures, hence posing challenges in comprehending the underlying logic behind their generated outputs. The enhancement of methods aimed at improving the interpretability and transparency of models is crucial to overcome this constraint. Interpretable AI models provide users with the ability to acquire a deeper understanding of the decision-making process, facilitating the identification and resolution of potential biases, errors, or ethical considerations [40]. This is consistent with the overarching objective of developing AI systems that are responsible and accountable.

8.6.7 Overfitting

Overfitting poses a constraint that hinders the ability of GAI to generalize its learned knowledge to novel data instances effectively. Although these models demonstrate exceptional performance when trained on specific data, they may encounter difficulties when confronted with unfamiliar data or unique scenarios. From a practical standpoint, this constraint implies that GAI models may exhibit reduced efficacy when applied to real-world situations. Ongoing research is necessary to address the challenges of overfitting prevention and model adaptability enhancement [39]. Techniques such as regularization, transfer learning, and domain adaptation are being explored to increase the practicality of these approaches in real-world scenarios. Mitigating overfitting is of utmost importance to ensure the reliable and ethical performance of GAI systems across a wide range of situations.

8.7 Future Research Directions

Within this section, we present the identified future research directions.

Subsequent investigations ought to prioritize the augmentation of interpretability and explainability in GAI models. The elucidation of decision-making mechanisms employed by intricate AI models is of paramount importance. The process entails the development of visual representations and storytelling techniques that enhance the comprehensibility of AI-generated outcomes [2]. This empowers users to get insights into the underlying factors that lead to a certain outcome produced by the model. Conducting such research is crucial to establishing accountability, mitigating prejudice, and fostering confidence in AI systems, particularly in domains where interpretability has significant importance, such as healthcare and finance [4]. This path is in accordance with the overarching objective of responsible AI implementation and satisfies the growing need for ethical AI systems.

The investigation of bias mitigation and the promotion of fairness in GAI models is a critical and urgent field of study. The development of methodologies aimed at detecting and addressing biases, both within the training data and the model itself, is of utmost importance. Researchers should explore novel methodologies, such as adversarial debiasing and bias-aware training, to minimize discrimination in AI-generated material [9]. Future research should focus on the establishment of universally accepted fairness criteria for General Artificial Intelligence (GAI) and the integration of fairness considerations into the development process. This will ensure that equal outcomes are achieved across different domains. Emphasizing the ethical considerations in the field of artificial intelligence (AI) research, as well as ensuring diversity in the collection of datasets, can play a crucial role in addressing bias and promoting responsible utilization of General Artificial Intelligence (GAI) [11].

The energy consumption and environmental effects of GAI models, particularly during the training process, give rise to issues due to their resource-intensive nature. Subsequent investigations should prioritize the advancement of energy-efficient training methodologies, the exploration of model quantization, knowledge distillation, and architectural enhancements. Furthermore, it is imperative to optimize inference techniques to minimize energy consumption during real-time utilization. These improvements are in line with sustainability objectives since they aim to make GAI technology more accessible to a wider array of businesses while also reducing its environmental impact [14]. The focal point of this research direction revolves around the establishment of optimal strategies for responsible management of AI resources.

The exploration of enhancing the capacities of General Artificial Intelligence (GAI) to comprehend and produce material across several languages and modalities, including text, graphics, and speech, is a stimulating path for academic investigation. This encompasses the enhancement of translation quality, the facilitation of seamless cross-modal content development, and the augmentation of multilingual proficiency in GAI models [17]. Furthermore, it is crucial to acknowledge and tackle the obstacles associated with low-resource languages and dialects to advance the principles of inclusion and enhance the worldwide availability of GAI-powered apps. This study direction facilitates intercultural communication, education, and accessibility to AI technology, hence supporting the United Nations' Sustainable Development Goal of promoting inclusive and high-quality education for all individuals [21].

8.8 Lessons Learned and the Conclusion

Within this section, we present the lessons learned from the chapter and the conclusion.

8.8.1 Lessons

The study's findings offer significant insights for researchers, developers, politicians, and organizations involved in the advancement and implementation of GAI for social welfare and sustainable development. The need for responsible and ethical behaviors in the field of artificial intelligence is emphasized, particularly in relation to harnessing the potential of GAI for beneficial effects on society.

- This study highlights the significant significance of diverse and good-quality training data. The efficacy and fairness of GAI models are heavily reliant on data, with the quality of the data directly impacting these models. Researchers and practitioners must give utmost importance to the collection and curation of data to mitigate bias and guarantee that GAI systems encompass a diverse array of perspectives and circumstances.
- The ethical ramifications of applications involving GAI are of utmost significance and should not be underestimated. It is imperative to establish ethical rules and protections across various domains, ranging from content development to healthcare. The study highlights the importance of

prioritizing ethical considerations, privacy, and transparency in the responsible development and utilization of GAI.

- The development and implementation of GAI frequently requires the collaborative efforts of experts in the field of AI, specialists in specific domains, ethicists, and professionals in regulatory matters. The necessity of successful interdisciplinary collaboration cannot be overstated when it comes to tackling the intricate issues related to GAI. This is because handling GAI demands a comprehensive approach that extends beyond just technical proficiency.
- The issue of bias in GAI models continues to be a longstanding obstacle. The research emphasizes the continuous nature of bias mitigation, which requires consistent monitoring, the collection of varied datasets, and improvements to algorithms. Researchers and developers must acknowledge that the pursuit of fairness in AI systems is a dynamic and ever-changing endeavor.
- The absence of transparency and explainability in GAI models is a significant concern. The study highlights the necessity of employing modern methodologies to enhance the transparency and interpretability of these models. Utilizing openness not only fosters confidence but also facilitates the identification and resolution of potential biases and ethical considerations.
- The role of GAI in tackling sustainability and environmental concerns shows promise. The research emphasizes the potential of GAI to make significant contributions in the domains of climate change, conservation, and resource management. This statement highlights the capacity of GAI to connect with worldwide sustainable development objectives and emphasizes the significance of utilizing AI as a catalyst for constructive transformation.
- GAI's susceptibility to adversarial assaults and security breaches necessitates further attention. This study highlights the importance of developing strong GAI models and implementing effective cybersecurity measures to mitigate the risks of adversarial manipulation and ensure the security of sensitive data. Ensuring the security of AI should be seen as a paramount concern in the development and implementation of GAI systems.

- This study highlights the importance of allowing people to establish and regulate the parameters of content creation. The incorporation of GAI models that uphold individual preferences and ethical considerations is crucial in guaranteeing a favorable user experience and promoting responsible content dissemination.
- Finally, this study emphasizes the significance of enhancing GAI's capabilities to encompass a wide range of languages, dialects, and modalities to promote inclusivity. The importance of researching multilingual and multimodal GAI cannot be overstated, as it plays a crucial role in promoting worldwide communication and education and enhancing accessibility to AI technologies.

8.8.2 Conclusion

In summary, the research conducted on GAI for Social Good and Sustainable Development has provided significant findings regarding the intricate realm of AI technology and its capacity to facilitate beneficial transformations. Moreover, it is crucial to emphasize the ethical aspects associated with the applications of GAI. These dimensions necessitate a significant emphasis on the responsible development of AI, safeguarding privacy, and ensuring transparent decision-making procedures. The importance of interdisciplinary collaboration has become evident, as it requires the participation of experts in artificial intelligence, specialists in specific domains, ethicists, and professionals in regulatory fields to tackle complex difficulties effectively. The research further emphasizes the ongoing commitment needed to address prejudice and promote equity in GAI models, given the persistent and enduring nature of bias in AI systems. The essential requirements of transparency, explainability, and robustness are imperative, underscoring the necessity for accountable and safe AI technology. Furthermore, the study elucidates the potential efficacy of GAI in mitigating sustainability and environmental concerns, thereby aligning with international objectives for global development. The significance of maintaining a harmonious equilibrium between innovation and responsibility is emphasized, with an emphasis on granting people the ability to exercise control over information generated by GAI. These insights will guide the ethical and responsible advancement of GAI, ensuring that it continues to catalyze positive societal change in accordance with the ideals of social welfare and sustainable development.

AI disclosure statement: The author acknowledges the use of AI-based tools for minor language editing or grammatical correction. However, all intellectual contributions, analyses, and conclusions presented in this chapter are entirely the author's own.

References

1. Bautista, P. and Inventado, P.S., Protecting Student Privacy with Synthetic Data from Generative Adversarial Networks, in: *Lecture Notes in Computer Science (including subseries Lecture Notes in Artificial Intelligence and Lecture Notes in Bioinformatics)*, 2021.
2. Zhao, A., Jiang, N., Wang, C., Liu, S., Qiu, K., Synchronization Optimization of Chaotic Laser Based on Generative Adversarial Network. *Guangxue Xuebao/Acta Optica Sin.*, 43, 1, 0114002, 2023, doi: 10.3788/AOS220994.
3. Tinsley, P., Czajka, A., Flynn, P.J., Haven't I Seen You Before? Assessing Identity Leakage in Synthetic Irises, in: *2022 IEEE International Joint Conference on Biometrics, IJCB*, vol. *2022*, 2022, doi: 10.1109/IJCB54206.2022.10007948.
4. Chi, H., Maduakor, U., Alo, R., Williams, E., Integrating Deepfake Detection into Cybersecurity Curriculum, in: *Advances in Intelligent Systems and Computing*, 2021.
5. Shafik, W., An Overview of Artificial Intelligence-Enhanced Teaching Methods, in: *AI-Enhanced Teaching Methods*, pp. 132–59, IGI Global, Hershey, Pennsylvania, United States, 2024, doi: 10.4018/979-8-3693-2728-9.ch006.
6. Raveendran, R. and Raj, E.D., Deep Generative Models Under GAN: Variants, Applications, and Privacy Issues, in: *Lecture Notes in Networks and Systems*, 2023.
7. Berry, R.A., Han, Z., Narayanan, K., Poor, H.V., Verikoukis, C., Yagan, O., Special issue on communications and networking approaches for combating COVID-19. *J. Commun. Netw.*, 23, 5, 309–313, 2021, doi: 10.23919/jcn.2021.100030.
8. Nukavarapu, S.K. and Nadeem, T., Securing Edge-based IoT Networks with Semi-Supervised GANs, in: *2021 IEEE International Conference on Pervasive Computing and Communications Workshops and other Affiliated Events, PerCom Workshops 2021*, 2021, doi: 10.1109/PerComWorkshops51409.2021.9431112.
9. Shafik, W., Toward a More Ethical Future of Artificial Intelligence and Data Science, in: *The Ethical Frontier of AI and Data Analysis*, pp. 362–388, IGI Global, Hershey, Pennsylvania, United States, 2024, doi: 10.4018/979-8-3693-2964-1.ch022.
10. Gonik, J., Le, J., Viswanathan, A., Zhang, Y., Cybergan: Generating high-fidelity cybersecurity data with generative adversarial networks, in: *Accelerating*

Space Commerce, Exploration, and New Discovery Conference, ASCEND 2020, 2020.

11. Neshenko, N., Bou-Harb, E., Furht, B., A behavioral-based forensic investigation approach for analyzing attacks on water plants using GANs. *Forensic Sci. Int.: Digital Invest.*, 37, 301198, 2021, doi: 10.1016/j.fsidi.2021.301198.
12. Kathole, A.B., Vhatkar, K.N., Raut, R., Patil, S.D., Jadhav, A., Security Issues in Generative Adversarial Networks, in: *Generative Adversarial Networks and Deep Learning: Theory and Applications*, 2023.
13. Shafik, W., The Role of Artificial Intelligence in the Emerging Digital Economy Era. *Artif. Intell. Enabled Manage.: Emerging Econ. Perspect.*, 33, 33–50, 2024 Jun 4, doi: 10.1515/9783111172408-003.
14. Yang, J., Xiao, S., Li, A., Lan, G., Wang, H., Detecting fake images by identifying potential texture difference. *Future Gener. Comput. Syst.*, 125, 127–135, 2021, doi: 10.1016/j.future.2021.06.043.
15. Mendes, J., *et al.*, Lung CT image synthesis using GANs. *Expert Syst. Appl.*, 215, 119350, 2023, doi: 10.1016/j.eswa.2022.119350.
16. Ding, Y., Thakur, N., Li, B., Fulton, I.A., Does a GAN leave distinct model-specific fingerprints?, in: *The 32nd British Machine Vision Conference*, 2021.
17. Masood, M., Nawaz, M., Javed, A., Nazir, T., Mehmood, A., Mahum, R., Classification of Deepfake Videos Using Pre-trained Convolutional Neural Networks, in: *2021 International Conference on Digital Futures and Transformative Technologies, ICoDT2 2021*, 2021, doi: 10.1109/ICoDT252288.2021.9441519.
18. Nukavarapu, S.K., Ayyat, M., Nadeem, T., MirageNet - Towards a GAN-based Framework for Synthetic Network Traffic Generation, in: *2022 IEEE Global Communications Conference, GLOBECOM 2022 - Proceedings*, 2022, doi: 10.1109/GLOBECOM48099.2022.10001494.
19. Wang, K., Deng, N., Li, X., An Efficient Content Popularity Prediction of Privacy Preserving Based on Federated Learning and Wasserstein GAN. *IEEE Internet Things J.*, 10, 5, 3786–3798, 2023, doi: 10.1109/JIOT.2022.3176360.
20. Shafik, W., Navigating Emerging Challenges in Robotics and Artificial Intelligence in Africa, in: *Examining the Rapid Advance of Digital Technology in Africa*, pp. 124–144, IGI Global, Hershey, Pennsylvania, United States, 2024, doi: 10.4018/978-1-6684-9962-7.ch007.
21. Shafik, W., Begawan, B.S., Darussalam, B., Sustainable Development Goal 14: Explainable AI (XAI) for Ocean Health, in: *Artificial Intelligence and Edge Computing for Sustainable Ocean Health*, D. De, D. Sengupta, T.A. Tran (eds), The Springer Series in Applied Machine Learning. Springer, Cham, 2024, https://doi.org/10.1007/978-3-031-64642-3_8 .
22. He, C., Huang, S., Cheng, R., Tan, K.C., Jin, Y., Evolutionary Multiobjective Optimization Driven by Generative Adversarial Networks (GANs). *IEEE Trans. Cybern.*, 51, 6, 3129–3142, 2021, doi: 10.1109/TCYB.2020.2985081.

23. Cai, Z., Xiong, Z., Xu, H., Wang, P., Li, W., Pan, Y., Generative Adversarial Networks: A Survey Toward Private and Secure Applications. *ACM Comput. Surv.*, 54, 6, 1–38, 2021, doi: 10.1145/3459992.
24. Sun, H., Zhu, T., Zhang, Z., Jin, D., Xiong, P., Zhou, W., Adversarial Attacks Against Deep Generative Models on Data: A Survey. *IEEE Trans. Knowl. Data Eng.*, 35, 4, 3367–3388, 2023, doi: 10.1109/TKDE.2021.3130903.
25. Fekri, M.N., Ghosh, A.M., Grolinger, K., Generating energy data for machine learning with recurrent generative adversarial networks. *Energies (Basel)*, 13, 1, 2019, doi: 10.3390/en13010130.
26. Zhang, X., Zhu, X., Wang, J., Bao, W., Yang, L.T., DANCE: Distributed Generative Adversarial Networks with Communication Compression. *ACM Trans. Internet Technol.*, 22, 2, 1–32, 2022, doi: 10.1145/3458929.
27. Sharma, B., Sharma, L., Lal, C., Roy, S., Anomaly based network intrusion detection for IoT attacks using deep learning technique. *Comput. Electr. Eng.*, 107, 108626, 2023, doi: 10.1016/j.compeleceng.2023.108626.
28. Shafik, W., Environmental Conservation and Sustainable Development, in: *Developing Digital Inclusion Through Globalization and Digitalization*, pp. 142–176, IGI Global, Hershey, Pennsylvania, United States, 2024, doi: 10.4018/979-8-3693-4111-7.ch008.
29. Zhou, J., Chen, Y., Shen, C., Zhang, Y., Property Inference Attacks Against GANs, 2022, doi: 10.14722/ndss.2022.23019.
30. Deldjoo, Y., Di Noia, T., Merra, F.A., A Survey on Adversarial Recommender Systems: From Attack/Defense Strategies to Generative Adversarial Networks. *ACM Comput. Surv.*, 54, 2, 1–38, 2021, doi: 10.1145/3439729.
31. Agoub, A., Filippovska, Y., Schmidt, V., Kada, M., Automatic Generation of Photorealistic Image Fillers for Privacy Enabled Urban Basemaps using Generative Adversarial Networks. *Adv. Cartogr. GISci. ICA*, 1, 2019, doi: 10.5194/ica-adv-1-1-2019.
32. Shafik, W., Industry 4.0 Technologies' Opportunities and Challenges for Realising Net-Zero Economy, in: *Net Zero Economy, Corporate Social Responsibility and Sustainable Value Creation: Exploring Strategies, Drivers, and Challenges*, pp. 19–41, Springer, Cham, 2024, doi: 10.1007/978-3-031-55779-8_2.
33. Cao, X., Sun, G., Yu, H., Guizani, M., PerFED-GAN: Personalized Federated Learning via Generative Adversarial Networks. *IEEE Internet Things J.*, 10, 5, 3749–3762, 2023, doi: 10.1109/JIOT.2022.3172114.
34. Huang, Y. and Cao, L., Privacy-Preserving Remote Sensing Image Generation and Classification with Differentially Private GANs. *IEEE Sens. J.*, 23, 18, 20805–20816, 2023, doi: 10.1109/JSEN.2023.3267001.
35. Ha, T. and Dang, T.K., Inference attacks based on GAN in federated learning. *Int. J. Web Inf. Syst.*, 18, 2–3, 117–136, 2022, doi: 10.1108/IJWIS-04-2022-0078.
36. Shafik, W., Data Privacy and Security Safeguarding Customer Information in ChatGPT Systems, in: *Revolutionizing the Service Industry with OpenAI*

Models, pp. 52–86, IGI Global, Hershey, Pennsylvania, United States, 2024, doi: 10.4018/979-8-3693-1239-1.ch003.

37. Wang, J., *et al.*, GAN-generated fake face detection via two-stream CNN with PRNU in the wild. *Multimed. Tools Appl.*, 81, 29, 42527–42545, 2022, doi: 10.1007/s11042-021-11592-7.
38. Abubakari, M.S., Shafik, W., Hidayatullah, A.F., Evaluating the Potential of Artificial Intelligence in Islamic Religious Education: A SWOT Analysis Overview, in: *AI-Enhanced Teaching Methods*, pp. 216–239, IGI Global, Hershey, Pennsylvania, United States, 2024, doi: 10.4018/979-8-3693-2728-9.ch010.
39. Ghavamipour, A.R., Turkmen, F., Wang, R., Liang, K., Federated Synthetic Data Generation with Stronger Security Guarantees, in: *Proceedings of ACM Symposium on Access Control Models and Technologies, SACMAT*, 2023, doi: 10.1145/3589608.3593835.
40. De, S., Bermudez-Edo, M., Xu, H., Cai, Z., Deep Generative Models in the Industrial Internet of Things: A Survey. *IEEE Trans. Industr. Inform.*, 18, 9, 5728–5737, 2022, doi: 10.1109/TII.2022.3155656.

9

Revolutionizing Implementation: Cutting-Edge Tools and Resources in Generative AI

Blessing Takawira* **and David Pooe**

University of Johannesburg, Johannesburg, South Africa

Abstract
This chapter explores the transformative impact of advanced generative AI technologies across various domains. It delves into foundational theories and state-of-the-art tools such as GANs, VAEs, and neural network architectures, highlighting their capabilities in generating high-quality data and their applications in healthcare, bioinformatics, manufacturing, and natural language processing. The chapter emphasizes the importance of strategic implementation, addressing challenges related to computational costs, data privacy, ethical considerations, and model interpretability. Furthermore, it emphasizes the necessity of strong ethical frameworks to guarantee the responsible and fair utilization of AI technologies. By providing insights into current advancements and future research directions, the chapter aims to guide effective implementation and foster innovation, demonstrating generative AI's interdisciplinary nature and potential to revolutionize various sectors.

Keywords: Generative AI, neural networks, transformers, implementation strategies, ethical AI, computational efficiency, AI applications

9.1 Introduction

Generative AI has become a groundbreaking technology revolutionizing multiple industries by autonomously producing new content, designs, and solutions. Advancements in computer power, algorithms, and data storage

**Corresponding author*: akawirablessing@gmail.com

N. Gayathri, S. Rakesh Kumar, Ramesh Chandran, Pethuru Raj Chelliah and Danilo Pelusi (eds.) Generative AI: Disruptive Technologies for Innovative Applications, (187–214) © 2025 Scrivener Publishing LLC

have significantly boosted the prominence of machine learning-based AI in technological innovation [1]. The healthcare sector has made considerable advancements in utilizing AI-enabled monitoring, diagnosis, and prognosis approaches. This progress has been particularly remarkable and has demonstrated notable success in both academia and industry [2]. AI is used in healthcare to analyze large datasets in clinical outcomes research for hepatobiliary cancer, using machine learning and natural language processing techniques [3]. In addition, AI has demonstrated potential in orthopedic surgery by leveraging large datasets to improve patient care pathways and advance healthcare research [4].

AI-driven processes supported by virtual sensors have been used in industrial applications to improve operational efficiency. These processes have enabled breakthroughs in anomaly detection, predictive maintenance, and optimal process management, showcasing the adaptability of AI [5]. Moreover, incorporating AI in education has resulted in the creation of social robots, intelligent tutoring systems, and smart learning systems, highlighting its significance in influencing contemporary learning environments [6]. The importance of AI in healthcare is underscored by its use in medical imaging. AI algorithms are employed to screen and diagnose retinal diseases, necessitating the processing of large volumes of data and adherence to regulatory requirements for effective implementation [7].

Generative AI has enabled the development of new and creative design applications. Generative design and grammar have been crucial in developing the current state of AI technology [8]. Furthermore, incorporating AI in emergency care has been a central focus. Canadian physicians have articulated distinct requirements and anticipated outcomes for AI applications to tackle crucial issues in the field [9]. The ethical considerations regarding the development and implementation of AI have become more prominent. This highlights the need to include ethical aspects across all stages of AI projects to guarantee responsible and sustainable deployment [10].

The influence of AI goes beyond conventional industries and extends to several domains, including ecology, where it may be used to detect plant pests and animal diseases. This demonstrates the wide range of applications that AI can provide [11]. Moreover, integrating AI in contemporary art instruction emphasizes its capacity to broaden the flexibility of teaching approaches, improve the learning process, and nurture creativity in art education [12]. The use of AI in pathology has been acknowledged for its capacity to increase diagnostic methods, optimize efficiency, and discover new biomarkers, highlighting its potential to revolutionize healthcare [13].

The growth of AI has led to the emergence of neuromorphic AI systems, which utilize hardware breakthroughs and extensive datasets to push the boundaries of AI technology [14]. In addition, the incorporation of AI in radiation oncology has greatly revolutionized the way tasks are carried out, allowing for the creation of extensive quantities of clinical data to enhance decision-making procedures [15]. The future of AI hinges on its capacity to tackle crucial obstacles such as resilience, adaptability, and variety in multifunctional systems, specifically in domains like peptic ulcers, where the emphasis is on doing rigorous clinical research to improve AI applications [16].

Generative AI is at the forefront of technological innovation and provides disruptive solutions in sectors including healthcare, education, industry, and design. The recent progress in AI has not only transformed current procedures but has also opened up possibilities for innovative applications that could fundamentally alter the future of technology and society as a whole. The complex terrain of Generative AI and its critical role in propelling progress in numerous technical disciplines is essential for promoting innovation and improving productivity across sectors. The disruptive power of Generative AI resides in its capacity to independently generate content, models, and solutions, thus optimizing processes and minimizing human involvement. This chapter explores the notable progress in Generative AI, with a focus on its incorporation into contemporary applications. The analysis of recent literature on AI and machine learning aims to emphasize the present advancements and pinpoint potential areas for future research.

9.2 Foundational Theories and Models

GAI is propelled by fundamental theories and models that direct its advancement and utilization in diverse sectors. A crucial theory in Generative AI is the utilization of large language models like BERT, GPT, and Pathways Language Model (PaLM). These models have greatly improved natural language processing tasks by using vast data to generate coherent and contextually relevant text outputs [17]. Deep learning models have demonstrated remarkable ability in text synthesis, translation, and summarization. This showcases the potential of generative AI to revolutionize language-related activities.

Another key concept in Generative AI is the utilization of diffusion models, such as the Stable Diffusion model. This approach aims to generate samples that are both realistic and diverse by representing the distribution of data in a continuous latent space [18]. These models are crucial for producing top-notch visuals, written material, and other forms of content by capturing complex data relationships and facilitating the creation of innovative outputs based on acquired patterns [18]. Comprehending the mechanics behind generative AI tools and their applications in varied fields requires a crucial understanding of diffusion models' implementation details and design decisions [18].

Generative AI includes methods such as GANs, which have been essential in creating lifelike images, writing, and other content. GANs achieve this by using two neural networks that compete with each other to generate outputs that appear genuine [19]. GANs have been extensively utilized in diverse domains such as art generation, picture synthesis, and data augmentation, highlighting their significance in pushing the limits of creativity and content development in the field of AI [19].

Furthermore, the application of generative AI in healthcare has been shaped by models that specifically tackle the difficulties related to privacy and security, especially in the field of medical practice. GANs and large language models are essential for creating medical images, text, and molecular structures. These techniques are particularly important in healthcare settings since they help solve concerns regarding data privacy and security [19]. These models enable the creation of fresh data and understandings while upholding stringent privacy rules and protecting delicate medical information [19].

Moreover, the ethical aspects of Generative AI are of utmost importance, as demonstrated by the suggested conceptual framework for clinical applications. This paradigm emphasizes the significance of guaranteeing the comprehensibility, collaborative nature, and ethical underpinning of AI to improve transparency and comprehension in decision-making processes involving clinicians and patients [20]. The purpose of this paradigm is to promote trust and responsibility in the use of generative AI in healthcare settings by pushing for responsible AI practices and transparent decision-making [20].

Foundational theories and models in Generative AI, such as big language models, diffusion models, generative adversarial networks, and ethical frameworks, play a crucial role in influencing the advancement and utilization of AI in various fields. These theories offer the conceptual foundation and practical instruments required to stimulate creativity, address obstacles, and unlock the revolutionary capabilities of Generative AI in diverse domains.

9.3 State-of-the-Art Tools in Generative AI

Advanced tools in Generative AI comprise a wide array of technologies and processes that allow for generating innovative content, designs, and solutions. A notable tool in natural language processing is the utilization of large language models like BERT and GPT. These models are highly proficient in creating text outputs that are coherent and contextually relevant [21]. These models utilize deep learning architectures to analyze large quantities of data and generate text that closely resembles human writing. This makes them extremely valuable for tasks such as generating text, translating languages, and summarizing information. Nevertheless, one drawback of large language models is their proclivity to produce prejudiced or erroneous material, contingent upon the data they are trained on. This underscores the significance of ensuring high-quality data and doing thorough model evaluation.

Diffusion models are an advanced method in Generative AI that aims to generate a wide range of realistic samples by modeling the distribution of data in continuous latent spaces [22]. These models play a crucial role in generating high-quality photos, text, and other information by capturing intricate data interconnections. Diffusion models are highly proficient in producing a wide range of outputs, but they can be computationally demanding and necessitate substantial resources for training and inference.

GANs are a highly effective tool in the field of Generative AI. They allow for the creation of realistic images, text, and content by employing a competitive approach, where two neural networks are pitted against each other [23]. GANs have been utilized in several fields such as art generation, picture synthesis, and data augmentation, demonstrating their adaptability in producing creative content. Nevertheless, training GANs can be arduous and susceptible to mode collapse, a phenomenon in which the generator only generates a narrow range of outputs.

AI-driven decision-making tools are essential in healthcare for optimizing treatment methods and processes to remediate polluted aquatic habitats [24]. These solutions utilize AI to streamline the effective implementation of several treatment technologies, including chemical precipitation, membrane technology, and ion exchanges, in environmental remediation. Although AI-driven tools improve decision-making and efficiency, they may encounter difficulties concerning data privacy, regulatory compliance, and the comprehensibility of AI-generated insights.

In addition, edge AI (EI) technologies are transforming the field of AI applications by facilitating the learning and inference processes of models at the system edge. This is achieved by using computational resources and data from edge nodes [25]. By processing data closer to its origin, EI technologies improve efficiency and reduce latency, enhancing real-time decision-making and inference capabilities. Nevertheless, the implementation of EI tools necessitates a strong and reliable edge computing infrastructure, as well as careful deliberation regarding data security and privacy.

State-of-the-art techniques in Generative AI provide cutting-edge solutions for content generation, decision-making, and problem-solving in diverse fields. However, to fully utilize these technologies' extraordinary capabilities and ensure the ethical deployment of AI, it is crucial to overcome difficulties such as bias, interpretability, computational complexity, and data privacy.

9.4 Generative AI Tools Strategies

The strategy structure depicted in Figure 9.1 below emphasizes the importance of a gradual implementation of Generative AI tools. It acknowledges that each step relies on the previous one to guarantee a comprehensive and resilient integration of the technology. The Collaboration phase establishes the foundation by forming partnerships that may offer many perspectives and resources, preparing for the implementation of long-lasting and inclusive development initiatives. During the Development phase, the primary emphasis is on constant enhancement and synchronization with the organizational plan to guarantee that the AI tools are not only advanced but also pertinent and advantageous to the organization's objectives. Training that is in accordance with these principles guarantees that the workforce is adequately equipped to efficiently interact with the new technology. As the framework advances to the Implementation phase, it becomes crucial to prioritize education and awareness. This implies that for AI technologies to be genuinely effective, stakeholders must comprehend their capabilities and implications. Developing strategic methodologies for implementing AI and addressing ethical concerns are essential for establishing confidence and promoting responsible utilization of artificial intelligence. The Data Handling phase is the stage where the implementation techniques reach their final stage and are put into practical use with the AI tools. Collecting and analyzing data is essential for improving AI models and guaranteeing their precision. Additionally, the creation of tailored training tools demonstrates a shift towards personalized and industry-specific uses of Generative AI.

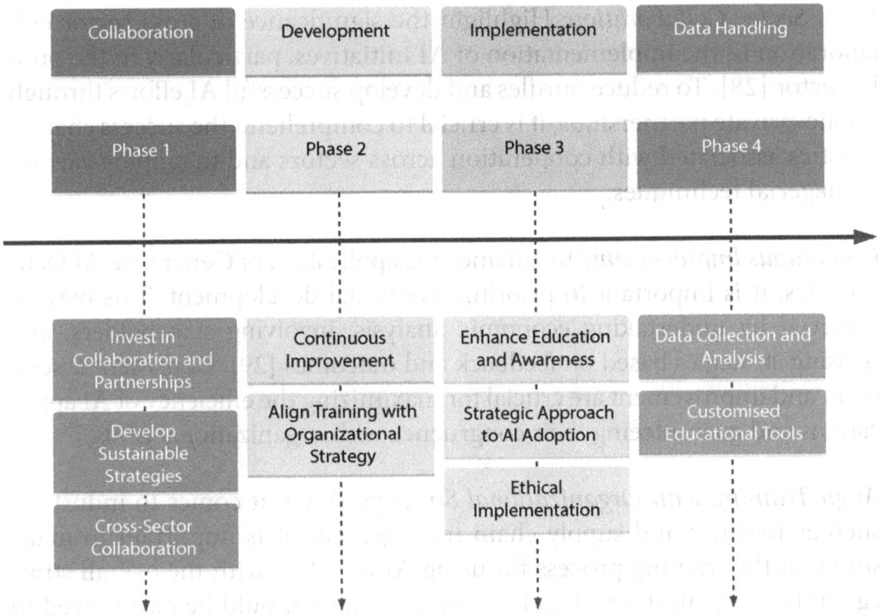

Figure 9.1 Strategies for implementing generative AI tools. Source: Takawira and Pooe (2024).

To effectively deploy Generative AI tools across different industries, thorough planning, strategic considerations, and adherence to best practices are essential to optimize their effectiveness and impact. By analyzing information from different sources, the subsequent techniques and optimal methods can provide guidance for effectively using Generative AI technologies in many industries:

Invest in Collaboration and Partnerships: Forging partnerships among various sectors such as companies, academia, and government bodies is essential for the effective application of AI [26]. Organizations may effectively handle industry-specific challenges and create innovation by developing partnerships that harness varied knowledge, resources, and viewpoints.

Develop Sustainable Strategies: It is crucial to develop sustainable methods for deploying and managing automation and AI in businesses such as hospitality and tourism [27]. These plans should be in accordance with long-term objectives, taking into account the environmental effects, and guaranteeing the ethical utilization of AI technology to improve customer experiences and operational efficiency.

Cross-Sector Collaboration: Highlight the significance of cross-sector collaboration in the implementation of AI initiatives, particularly in the public sector [28]. To reduce hurdles and develop successful AI efforts through public-private partnerships, it is crucial to comprehend the success characteristics associated with cooperation across sectors and to employ various managerial techniques.

Continuous Improvement: To enhance the application of Generative AI technologies, it is important to prioritize continual development. This may be achieved by undertaking economic analysis, involving stakeholders, and revising strategies based on feedback and outcomes [29]. Consistent assessment and improvement are crucial for maximizing the efficiency of AI applications and guaranteeing their congruence with organizational goals.

Align Training with Organizational Strategy: When it comes to industries such as logistics and supply chain management, it is important to make sure that the training process for using AI is in line with the overall strategy of the organization [30]. Training programs should be customized to align with precise industry requirements, augment staff competencies, and facilitate the seamless integration of AI technologies.

Enhance Education and Awareness: The healthcare sector should prioritize the education of medical personnel on AI terminology, machine learning, and AI applications to effectively incorporate them into medical practice [31]. Promoting awareness and expertise among healthcare professionals can facilitate the successful implementation of AI tools to enhance patient care and outcomes.

Strategic Approach to AI Adoption: When using AI in the public sector, it is important to take a strategic approach that takes into account the organizational, ethical, and societal consequences [32]. Acknowledge the profound impact that AI can have on government services and formulate thorough plans to optimize advantages while mitigating any dangers and obstacles.

Ethical Implementation: Emphasize the need for ethical issues when creating and implementing AI systems, particularly in the social services sectors [33]. Develop explicit ethical norms and frameworks to guarantee the responsible and ethical use of AI technology in the provision of social services, taking into account the effects on various client groups and institutional settings.

Data Collection and Analysis: Utilize AI methods to address the difficulties associated with gathering, consolidating, and distributing data in areas such as wireless sensor networks [34]. Deploy AI based solutions to improve the processing, analysis, and decision-making of data in intricate settings including manufacturing, smart cities, and Internet of Things (IoT) applications.

Customized Educational Tools: Use generative AI methods in education to develop customized tutoring programs and intelligent evaluation systems for individualized instruction and assistance [35]. Create AI-based educational solutions that specifically address the unique needs of each student, improve the quality of learning experiences, and maximize academic advancement by utilizing predictive models and personalized lesson plans.

By integrating these optimal methodologies and tactics, organizations may successfully negotiate the intricacies of applying Generative AI technologies in many industries, foster innovation, and attain sustainable results that correspond with their strategic goals and industry-specific needs.

9.5 Literature Review Methodology

Employing the designated terms "Generative AI", "implementation tools", "cutting-edge resources", "AI advancements", "deep learning models", and "Generative AI applications" ((generative AND ai, AND implementation AND tools, AND cutting-edge AND resources, AND ai AND advancements, AND deep AND learning AND models, AND generative AND ai AND applications AND (LIMIT-TO (DOCTYPE , "re") OR LIMIT-TO (DOCTYPE , "ar")) AND (LIMIT-TO (LANGUAGE , "English")) AND (LIMIT-TO (OA , "all")) in the Scopus database resulted in 14 published review papers. Only scholarly articles that specifically address recent progress in Generative AI were taken into account. These were followed by papers that provided detailed information about the essential tools and resources needed for its implementation. Lastly, papers that explore the practical applications of Generative AI in other fields were also included. The latest technologies and frameworks were carefully examined for each category, and any areas where further research is needed were noted. Figure 9.2 depicts the frequency distribution of documents throughout different years. The line chart depicts a conspicuous ascending trajectory in the number of documents generated between 2020 and 2024. There is a

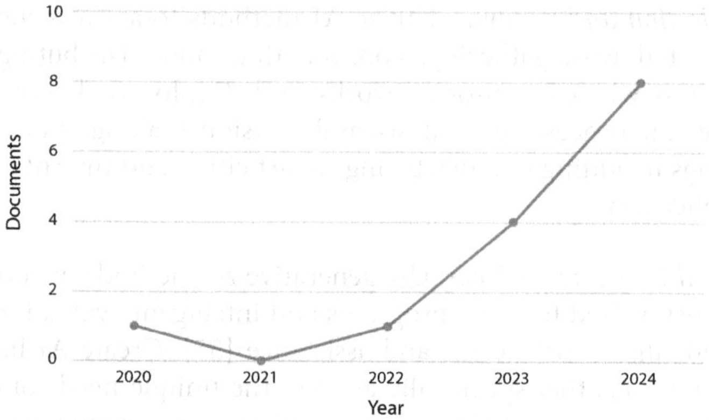

Figure 9.2 Document by year. Source: Takawira and Pooe (2024).

significant decrease to zero papers in 2021, followed by a minor uptick to one document in 2022. In 2023, there is a notable surge, with the number of documents quadrupling to 4. The rising trend persists, with the number of papers projected to double again to reach 8 by 2024. These findings indicate an increasing fascination or advancement in the domain of Generative AI within the studied timeframe, with the most significant expansion taking place between 2022 and 2024.

The existing body of work has been systematically classified into three overarching categories: Generative AI Tools, Implementation Strategies, and Practical Applications. These groupings are then separated into distinct categories, such as GANs, VAEs, neural networks, and transformers, and then examined accordingly. Research gaps have been indicated within each category to emphasize topics that require further investigation. The distribution of papers by category by specialized area is depicted in Table 9.1, which offers a detailed overview of the current state of the study and identifies potential areas for additional exploration.

The data is presented in a tabular manner rather than a graph and classifies different publications according to their subject matter within the larger framework of Generative AI Tools and Implementation Strategies, as well as Practical Applications. The table presents categories and particular regions, followed by the assignment of document identifiers (e.g., D3, D6, etc.) to each area, along with a concise summary of the document's topic.

Generative AI Tools can be categorized into three distinct areas: GANs, VAEs, and Neural Networks and Transformers. Each of these fields is extensively documented, providing insights into their applicability across

Table 9.1 Distribution of documents by category by specific area.

Category	Specific area	Document	Description
Generative AI Tools	GANs	D3	Explores the architecture and applications of GANs in various domains, highlighting their ability to generate high-quality synthetic data and their use in semi-supervised learning for data augmentation and transfer learning.
		D6	Discusses using GANs for topology optimization and design in additive manufacturing, demonstrating their ability to predict optimized structures and enhance the design process.
	VAEs	D9	Describes the use of VAEs in high-dimensional data analysis and representation learning in bioinformatics, emphasizing their role in embedding biological data and generating new data samples.
	Neural Networks and Transformers	D9	Explains the application of neural networks, including CNNs and RNNs, in bioinformatics for tasks such as RNA-protein interaction prediction and biomedical image classification.
		D4	This research investigates the use of neural networks for optimization in biomedical engineering, particularly for the design of implantable devices using topology optimization.

(*Continued*)

Table 9.1 Distribution of documents by category by specific area. (*Continued*)

Category	Specific area	Document	Description
		D10	Discusses the application of transformers in natural language processing and their impact on the efficiency and accuracy of language models.
		D14	Presents new tools and technologies emerging in generative AI, including advancements in AI-driven design and creative applications.
Implementation Strategies	System Integration and Frameworks	D5	Reviews the integration of AI in manufacturing processes, focusing on machine learning for defect detection, quality analysis, and process optimization in Industry 4.0.
	Optimization Techniques	D5	This paper highlights the application of optimization techniques such as Genetic Algorithms (GA) and topology optimization in biomedical device design, emphasizing the role of AI in enhancing performance and achieving desired outcomes.
		D7	This paper explores the use of deep reinforcement learning (DRL) for power system stability control, highlighting the importance of learning-based optimization techniques.

(*Continued*)

Table 9.1 Distribution of documents by category by specific area. (*Continued*)

Category	Specific area	Document	Description
Practical Applications	Healthcare and Bioinformatics	D9	This course covers the use of deep learning techniques in bioinformatics and medical informatics, including gene expression regression, enzyme detection, and biomedical image analysis.
		D8	Analyzes the impact of AI in healthcare, including predictive analytics and personalized medicine, and how AI tools are transforming patient care.
	Additive Manufacturing	D6	Discusses the application of AI in additive manufacturing, mainly focusing on design for additive manufacturing and the use of machine learning for topology optimization and process improvement.
		D11	Investigates the use of AI in innovative grid management, mainly focusing on load balancing and energy distribution optimization.
		D12	Examines AI applications in financial services, including fraud detection, algorithmic trading, and risk management.
		D13	Reviews the advancements in deep reinforcement learning for power system stability control, highlighting recent research efforts and potential applications.

(*Continued*)

Table 9.1 Distribution of documents by category by specific area. (*Continued*)

Category	Specific area	Document	Description
		D1	Discusses the application of AI techniques in optimizing supply chain management and logistics, emphasizing efficiency and cost reduction.
		D2	Explores the use of AI in predictive maintenance and operational efficiency in manufacturing, focusing on case studies and real-world applications.

Source: Takawira and Pooe (2024).

several industries. The implementation strategies are categorized into two domains: system integration and frameworks, and optimization techniques. Each domain has accompanying documents that explore the role of AI in manufacturing processes and the optimization of device design, respectively. Practical Applications encompass a broad spectrum of subjects, such as Healthcare and Bioinformatics, Additive Manufacturing, as well as other sectors including smart grid management, financial services, and supply chain management.

Upon analyzing the document distribution, it becomes clear that there is an equitable focus on the theoretical progressions of generative AI tools (such as GANs, VAEs, and neural network designs) and their pragmatic implementations in diverse industries. GANs are prominently discussed in relation to the generation of synthetic data and additive manufacturing, while VAEs and neural network-based models such as CNNs and RNNs are given particular emphasis in the field of bioinformatics. Transformers are prominently included in natural language processing, demonstrating a clear trend towards their increasing significance in language-related AI applications. The implementation strategies section specifically addresses the integration of AI in manufacturing and the role of AI in improving performance through optimization techniques. These findings indicate that the manufacturing industry is a prominent field for implementing AI technologies.

The practical applications of AI are varied, encompassing fields such as healthcare, bioinformatics, and financial services, demonstrating its extensive impact across multiple sectors. Deep learning techniques are well recognized in healthcare for their significant contributions to predictive analytics and personalized therapy. AI plays a significant role in improving optimization and operating efficiency in manufacturing and supply chains, which is in line with the current focus on Industry 4.0. The inclusion of AI in the management of smart grids and the maintenance of power system stability indicates an increasing level of attention within the energy sector.

Figure 9.3 depicts a pie chart that shows how documents are distributed across different subject areas. The figure classifies the documents into several academic fields, where each segment of the pie represents the proportion of documents related to that particular subject. The mentioned subjects are Computer Science, Engineering, Materials Science, Mathematics, Physics and Astronomy, Biochemistry, Genetics and Molecular Biology, Agricultural and Biological Sciences, Chemical Engineering, Chemistry, Energy, and a category labelled as 'Other'.

The two predominant sectors are Computer Science (30%) and Engineering (23.3%), with Materials Science (13.3%) following closely behind. Mathematics, Physics, and Astronomy each account for 6.7% of the texts. Each of the remaining fields, namely Biochemistry, Genetics and Molecular Biology, Agricultural and Biological Sciences, Chemical Engineering, Chemistry, Energy, and Others, is represented by 3.3%.

The data reveals a notable clustering of generative AI-related papers in the fields of Computer Science and Engineering. This indicates that these domains are probably the most actively involved in the advancement and implementation of generative AI technologies, highlighting the interdisciplinary nature of this growing field of study.

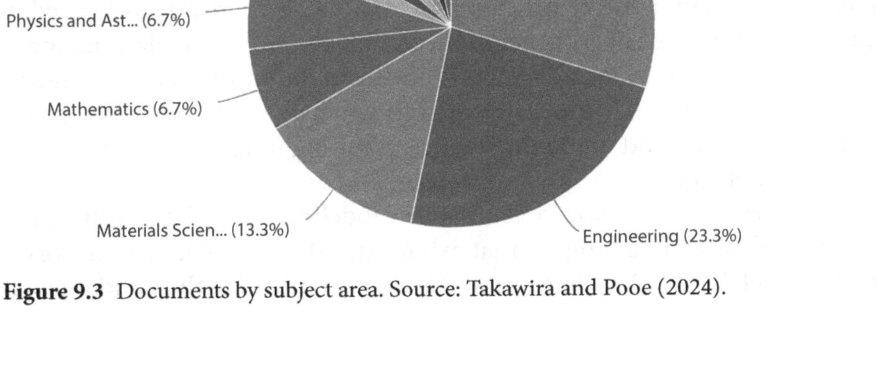

Figure 9.3 Documents by subject area. Source: Takawira and Pooe (2024).

The significant proportion of papers in the field of Materials Science indicates the significance of generative AI in the process of discovering and designing novel materials. This is a crucial factor in advancing diverse engineering applications. Mathematics, Physics, and Astronomy, although they have a smaller proportion, provide significant contributions, possibly by supplying the theoretical frameworks and computational models that form the basis of generative AI.

The equal distribution across the remaining categories, each with a 3.3% share, suggests that generative AI is a versatile technology that may be applied in several scientific study areas. The existence of generative AI-related documents in fields ranging from biology to energy indicates that the technology is employed for many objectives, including biological data analysis, optimization in chemical processes, and energy system management. The 'Other' category, however, limited in size, suggests the existence of specialized domains where generative AI is being investigated, potentially encompassing developing or underrepresented topics.

Generative AI Tools

The utilization of powerful Generative AI techniques across several industries offers significant prospects for content generation, decision-making, and innovation. By employing advanced technologies such as Language Models, GANs (Generative Adversarial Networks), ChatGPT (Chat-based Generative Pre-trained Transformer), and AI detection systems, organizations can significantly improve communication, foster creativity, and increase efficiency, resulting in groundbreaking advancements in their respective domains. By adopting these tools and resources in Generative AI, we can revolutionize the way we apply new ideas and redefine the benchmarks for the future of the industry.

GANs, VAEs, and Neural Networks and Transformers are indispensable tools in the domain of Generative AI, each providing unique capabilities and applications. GANs are renowned for their capacity to generate life-like images, text, and information through the use of two neural networks engaged in a competitive process [36]. GANs have proven to be highly valuable in the fields of art generation, picture synthesis, and data augmentation, showcasing their adaptability in the creation of creative content. By employing GANs, various sectors can enhance visual narrative, product development, and marketing tactics, resulting in more captivating and influential outcomes.

VAEs have revolutionized generative modeling by facilitating the production of novel data samples that exhibit statistical similarity to the original dataset [37]. VAEs has the ability to comprehend the fundamental probability distribution of the given data and generate artificial data samples. This makes them highly useful for tasks like data generation, anomaly detection, and image reconstruction. VAEs have found applications in a wide range of disciplines, including as healthcare, finance, and bio-signal processing, demonstrating their adaptability and efficacy in many contexts.

Neural Networks and Transformers are essential tools in the fields of deep learning and natural language processing. They offer sophisticated functionalities for tasks such as data processing, pattern identification, and sequence modeling [38]. Neural networks, including convolutional neural networks (CNNs) and recurrent neural networks (RNNs), have been instrumental in tasks such as image identification, language translation, and sentiment analysis. Transformers, like as BERT and GPT, have significantly transformed natural language processing jobs by producing text outputs that are contextually appropriate and facilitating advanced language comprehension and production.

Integrating Neural Networks and Transformers across several sectors has led to substantial advancements in data analysis, predictive modeling, and decision-making procedures [39]. These technologies have played a crucial role in improving operational efficiency, optimizing resource allocation, and promoting innovation in areas such as healthcare, finance, and manufacturing. By leveraging the powers of Neural Networks and Transformers, organizations can discover novel insights, optimize operations, and attain revolutionary outcomes.

GANs, VAEs, and Neural Networks and Transformers are essential for Generative AI. They offer sophisticated capabilities for content production, data processing, and pattern detection. By efficiently utilizing these technologies, industries may stimulate creativity, enhance decision-making, and change operations, resulting in revolutionary progress and state-of-the-art solutions in the digital age.

Implementation Strategies

Figure 9.4 depicts a thorough summary of the several strategies required to successfully execute Generative AI. The text highlights the significance of system integration, indicating the necessity to optimize processes and enhance model training. The utilization of Generative AI and Dev-Ops in managing unstructured images necessitates the capability of AI systems to effectively handle a wide range of data inputs. Regarding optimization strategies, the map emphasizes the importance of maintaining consistent performance, optimizing synapse weights, and improving memory retrieval. This implies adopting a strategy that prioritizes enhancing the efficiency of neural networks by utilizing techniques such as Spike-Timing-Dependent

Figure 9.4 Implementation strategies for generative AI. Source: Takawira and Pooe (2024).

Plasticity and reinforcement learning. The future of radiology diagnostics is expected to be enhanced by AI, with the objective of optimizing neural network topologies and enhancing diagnosis accuracy, as indicated by the map. The aims highlight the capacity of Generative AI to transform medical imaging by improving the identification of patterns and the precision of diagnoses. The user experience of defense systems based on artificial intelligence is a crucial feature. The map indicates the need of doing usability testing and integrating user feedback to enhance system performance and satisfaction. Adopting a user-centric strategy is essential for the effective implementation and acceptance of AI technology in sensitive domains such as defense.

To successfully include System Integration and Frameworks, along with Optimization Techniques, into the realm of Generative AI, a methodical strategy is necessary to guarantee smooth integration, effective functioning, and superior performance. By utilizing the knowledge gained from the given references, the following tactics can be utilized to effectively apply in these particular domains:

Augmenting Deep Neural Networks with Symbolic Educational Knowledge: As Hooshyar [40] states, combining symbolic educational knowledge with deep neural networks can improve the ability to understand and scale AI models. By integrating symbolic reasoning and deep learning capabilities, organizations can create reliable and understandable AI systems for educational purposes. This methodology guarantees that AI models possess both precision and transparency, hence promoting confidence and dependability in educational environments.

Handling Unstructured Images using Generative AI and Dev-Ops: Utilizing Generative AI and DevOps methods can enhance scalability and reproducibility when dealing with unstructured pictures [41]. Organizations can optimize the handling of picture data, boost model training, and maintain consistent performance across various environments by introducing streamlined workflows and automation technologies. This technique facilitates the smooth incorporation of Generative AI tools into current systems and frameworks, improving overall operational efficiency.

Constructing an Associative Memory System Using Spiking Neural Network: The utilization of spiking neural networks in the construction of an associative memory system entails the optimization of synapse weights using Spike-Timing-Dependent Plasticity (STDP) and reinforcement learning [42]. By utilizing these optimization strategies, organizations can improve the memory retrieval capacities of neural networks, facilitating effective data recall and pattern identification. This approach is crucial for the development of resilient memory systems that can effectively store and retrieve information in diverse applications.

AI for the Future Radiology Diagnostic Service: Utilizing deep-learning convolutional neural networks (CNNs) and optimization approaches in radiology diagnostic services has the potential to enhance picture pattern identification and improve diagnosis accuracy [43]. Through the optimization of neural network topologies and training methods, organizations can improve the efficiency and precision of diagnostic services, resulting in better patient outcomes and more efficient workflows. This strategy guarantees the seamless integration of AI technology into radiology practices, improving diagnostic capabilities and operational efficiency.

Designing and Evaluating User Experience of an AI-Based Defense System: The evaluation of user experience in AI-based defense systems entails enhancing system performance, usability, and user satisfaction through iterative design and evaluation procedures [44]. Organizations can enhance the effectiveness of AI systems by incorporating user feedback and doing usability testing to adapt them according to user needs and expectations. This strategy guarantees that AI technologies prioritize the needs and preferences of users, making them easy to use and in line with user expectations. This ultimately improves the overall performance of the system and increases user satisfaction.

Nevertheless, achieving effective utilization of System Integration and Frameworks, along with Optimization Techniques, in Generative AI necessitates a holistic strategy that integrates technical proficiency, strategic planning, and user-centered design concepts. By utilizing the knowledge and tactics from the above sources, companies can maximize the effectiveness of their systems, improve their operational productivity, and stimulate innovation in the use of Generative AI technologies in many fields.

Practical Applications

Generative AI techniques like VAEs have made significant contributions in the fields of Healthcare and Bioinformatics. These tools have brought about a revolution in diagnostic methods, survival forecasts, and data analysis for rare diseases and medical contexts. VAEs have been incorporated into healthcare to extract lower-dimensional encoded feature representations, generate fresh data samples, and improve diagnosis accuracy [37]. Healthcare workers may increase patient outcomes, optimize treatment plans, and improve survival rates by utilizing VAEs for advanced data analysis and predictive modeling.

In addition, the utilization of VAEs for problem identification and diagnosis in industrial processes has shown substantial advantages in monitoring industrial process jobs [45]. Recurrent VAEs equipped with advanced reconstruction-based diagnostic mechanisms have been suggested for use in industrial settings. These models have demonstrated their efficacy in detecting abnormalities, improving operational efficiency, and maintaining the reliability of processes. By incorporating VAEs into industrial environments, organizations can augment their ability to detect faults, optimize maintenance procedures, and enhance overall system efficiency.

VAEs have played a crucial role in the field of Bioinformatics by facilitating the exploration of protein conformational space. This has allowed researchers to analyze protein structures and make accurate predictions about molecular behaviors [46]. Through the utilization of VAEs, scientists are able to effectively simulate intricate protein structures, analyze protein folding patterns, and make precise predictions regarding protein activities.

9.6 Challenges and Solutions

The implementation of generative AI encounters certain common obstacles, which can be addressed by proposing viable solutions, as demonstrated by the scholarly literature. Challenges encompass problems related to accessibility, privacy concerns, the phenomenon of "AI hallucination," and biases present in AI systems [47, 48]. In addition, the absence of transparency, accountability, and trust among users presents substantial obstacles [49]. Moreover, the swift progress of generative AI technology has concerns, including the possibility of worsening educational inequity and compromising integrity [50]. Within the realm of education, individuals or groups interested in the field are being pushed to embrace new and developing technologies without fully comprehending them. This lack of awareness creates difficulties when attempting to effectively utilize generative AI for educational purposes [51]. In addition, generative AI models have the capacity to produce information that is biased, which raises questions about its reliability and potential regulatory challenges [52]. To tackle these difficulties, it is necessary to build strong ethical frameworks, ensure responsible use, and promote openness and accountability in the integration of generative AI into society [53]. In addition, the proposed recommendations seek to assist educators and students in effectively dealing with obstacles and taking advantage of opportunities that arise from the utilization of generative AI for learning [51]. The utilization of generative AI as a formidable tool in process engineering, employing a Solution-Driven Approach, is also investigated as a possible remedy for contemporary environmental issues [54]. Nevertheless, the existing literature does not offer precise remedies for every obstacle, necessitating additional research to thoroughly tackle these concerns.

9.7 Future Directions

Generative AI elicits apprehensions regarding privacy, security, ethical dilemmas, and the maintenance of biases inherent in the training data. Establishing strong ethical frameworks is essential for guiding the development and deployment of generative models, assuring responsible usage that maximizes advantages while minimizing dangers. Generative AI raises ethical concerns regarding its potential for misuse in disseminating false information, reinforcing biases, and impacting privacy and data rights. Effective collaboration among developers, regulators, and the public is crucial in establishing strong ethical frameworks that provide guidance for the responsible development and implementation of generative AI. This collaboration ensures that the use of generative AI is appropriate, maximizing its benefits while minimizing potential concerns. Generative AI is utilized in diverse fields like marketing, healthcare, education, and design, presenting prospects for innovation and metamorphosis. The rapid progress of generative AI has significant implications for the future of work, as it has the ability to bring about profound and far-reaching changes in various areas of life, similar to the impact of the Internet and smartphones. Generative AI has the capability to enhance the creative abilities of designers and facilitate transformative innovation in design fields including architecture, urban planning, and product design. The use of generative AI in art is seen as a noteworthy cultural transformation, which requires a reassessment of our comprehension of art and the artist. This presents prospects for making art creation accessible to a wider audience and pushing the limits of creativity. Hence, the execution of Generative AI entails both prospects and obstacles, with ramifications for diverse sectors, ethical deliberations, and the trajectory of employment. To tackle the difficulties and ethical concerns, it is necessary to create strong ethical frameworks that will provide guidance for the responsible creation and implementation of generative AI. The diverse applications of generative AI across various industries and its impact on creativity, innovation, and the future of work underscore the significant role of Generative AI in influencing the realm of knowledge and creative endeavors.

9.8 Conclusion

This chapter has thoroughly examined the significant influence and ability to bring about change of generative AI in different fields. The chapter offers a thorough understanding of the current progress and future prospects in generative AI by exploring the fundamental ideas, cutting-edge tools, and real-world applications. One notable discovery is the remarkable advancement in generative AI tools, such as GANs, VAEs, and neural network designs like transformers. These tools have exhibited exceptional abilities in producing authentic and top-notch data, which have extensive applications in areas such as healthcare, bioinformatics, additive manufacturing, and natural language processing. The progress in these technologies not only improves the effectiveness and precision of generative AI models but also broadens their usefulness, promoting innovation in other industries. The chapter highlights the significance of implementation strategies, namely in the integration of AI systems and enhancing their performance using sophisticated frameworks and approaches. The incorporation of AI in manufacturing, healthcare, and other sectors has demonstrated substantial enhancements in operational effectiveness, anticipatory maintenance, and decision-making procedures. Nevertheless, achieving successful execution necessitates tackling obstacles pertaining to computing expenses, data confidentiality, ethical deliberations, and model comprehensibility. An important consequence of this study is the requirement for strong ethical frameworks and rules to guarantee the proper and fair utilization of generative AI. As AI technologies progress, it is essential to confront ethical issues like bias, transparency, and responsibility to cultivate trust and acceptance among users. Establishing ethical norms will be crucial in directing the development and implementation of AI systems, ensuring that their advantages are maximized while reducing potential hazards. The chapter highlights various domains that require additional investigation, such as the advancement of AI models that are more effective and adaptable, strategies for identifying and reducing bias, and approaches to enhance the comprehensibility of generative models. Future research should investigate the incorporation of generative AI with other developing technologies, such as reinforcement learning and quantum computing, to discover new opportunities and improve the skills of AI systems. To summarize, the chapter highlights the significant influence of generative AI and emphasizes the necessity of strategic implementation to fully utilize its capabilities. Through the identification and resolution of existing obstacles and the prioritization of forthcoming research paths, generative AI has the capacity to sustain progress and deliver state-of-the-art remedies in diverse sectors. Ultimately, this will reshape the trajectory of technology and society.

AI disclosure statement: The author acknowledges the use of AI-based tools for minor language editing or grammatical correction. However, all intellectual contributions, analyses, and conclusions presented in this chapter are entirely the author's own.

References

1. Benjamins, J.-W., *et al.*, A primer in Artificial Intelligence in Cardiovascular Medicine. *Neth. Heart J.*, 27, 9, 392–402, 2019.
2. Zhao, Z., *et al.*, Challenges and Opportunities of AI-Enabled Monitoring, Diagnosis & Prognosis: A Review. *Chin. J. Mech. Eng.*, 34, 1, 1–29, 2021.
3. Endo, Y., Application of Artificial Intelligence to Hepatobiliary Cancer Clinical Outcomes Research. *Artif. Intell. Surg.*, 4, 2, 59–67, 2024.
4. Lisacek-Kiosoglous, A.B., Artificial Intelligence in Orthopaedic Surgery. *Bone Joint Res.*, 12, 7, 447–454, 2023.
5. Etxegarai, M., *et al.*, Virtual Sensors for Smart Data Generation and Processing in AI-Driven Industrial Applications, 2023.

6. Ahmad, S.F., *et al.*, Artificial Intelligence and Its Role in Education. *Sustainability*, 13, 22, 12902, 2021.
7. Chou, Y.-B., *et al.*, Current Status and Practical Considerations of Artificial Intelligence Use in Screening and Diagnosing Retinal Diseases: Vision Academy Retinal Expert Consensus. *Curr. Opin. Ophthalmol.*, 34, 5, 403–413, 2023.
8. Thoring, K., Huettemann, S., Mueller, R.M., The Augmented Designer: A Research Agenda for Generative Ai-Enabled Design. *Proc. Des. Soc.*, 3, 3345–3354, 2023.
9. Eastwood, K.W., *et al.*, Needs and Expectations for Artificial Intelligence in Emergency Medicine According to Canadian Physicians. *BMC Health Serv. Res.*, 23, 1, 3–9, 2023.
10. Zorins, A. and Grabusts, P., Ethical Development and Implementation of Artificial Intelligence. *Environment Technology Resources Proceedings of the International Scientific and Practical Conference*, vol. 2, pp. 214–218, 2021.
11. Sara, D.V., *et al.*, Application of Artificial Intelligence in Modern Ecology for Detecting Plant Pests and Animal Diseases. *Int. J. Quant. Res. Model.*, 2, 2, 83–90, 2021.
12. Kong, F., Application of Artificial Intelligence in Modern Art Teaching. *Int. J. Emerg. Technol. Learn. (Ijet)*, 15, 13, 238, 2020.
13. Homeyer, A., *et al.*, Artificial Intelligence in Pathology: From Prototype to Product. *J. Pathol. Inf.*, 12, 1, 13, 2021.
14. Ivanov, D.L., *et al.*, Neuromorphic Artificial Intelligence Systems. *Front. Neurosci.*, 16, 1–20, 2022.
15. Chufal, K.S. and Chowdhary, R.L., Artificial Intelligence in Radiation Oncology: How Far Have We Reached? *Int. J. Mol. Immuno. Oncol.*, 8, 9–14, 2023.
16. Zhao, P.-Y., *et al.*, Application Status and Prospects of Artificial Intelligence in Peptic Ulcers. *Front. Surg.*, 9, 894–775, 2022.
17. Zsidai, B., A Practical Guide to the Implementation of Artificial Intelligence in Orthopaedic Research—Part 2: A Technical Introduction. *J. Exp. Orthop.*, 11, 3, 1–15, 2024.
18. Po, R., State of the Art on Diffusion Models for Visual Computing. *Comput. Graphics Forum*, 43, 2, 1–32, 2024.
19. Chen, Y., Generative AI in Medical Practice: In-Depth Exploration of Privacy and Security Challenges. *J. Med. Internet Res.*, 26, e53008, 2024.
20. Bragazzi, N.L., Toward Clinical Generative AI: Conceptual Framework. *Jmir Ai*, 3, e55957, 2024.
21. Chounta, I.A., *et al.*, Exploring Teachers' Perceptions of Artificial Intelligence as a Tool to Support Their Practice in Estonian K-12 Education. *Int. J. Artif. Intell. Educ.*, 32, 3, 725–755, 2021.
22. Shu, S., Investigation of the Nozzle Arrangement Effect on the Performance of Internal Spray Cooling Turning Tool. *Int. J. Adv. Manuf. Technol.*, 131, 3–4, 1677–1690, 2024.

23. Kumar, K., Revitalizing Waters: Advanced Treatment Technologies for Cleaning Polluted Aquatic Ecosystem: A Review. *Int. J. Res. Agron.*, 7, 3, 671–680, 2024.
24. Vozár, M., Influence of Cutting Edge Microgeometry on the Cutting Forces When Machining Difficult-to-Cut Materials. *J. Phys. Conf. Ser.*, 2712, 1, 012025, 2024.
25. Kraus, M. and Drass, M., Artificial Intelligence for Structural Glass Engineering Applications — Overview, Case Studies and Future Potentials. *Glass Struct. Eng.*, 5, 3, 247–285, 2020.
26. Petersson, L., *et al.*, Challenges to Implementing Artificial Intelligence in Healthcare: A Qualitative Interview Study With Healthcare Leaders in Sweden. *BMC Health Serv. Res.*, 22, 1, 1–19, 2022.
27. Jabeen, F., Zaidi, S.A., Dhaheri, M.H.A., Automation and Artificial Intelligence in Hospitality and Tourism. *Tourism Rev.*, 77, 4, 1043–1061, 2021.
28. Mikhaylov, S., Estève, M., Campion, A., Artificial Intelligence for the Public Sector: Opportunities and Challenges of Cross-Sector Collaboration. *Philos. Trans. R. Soc. Math. Phys. Eng. Sci.*, 376, 2128, 20170357, 2018.
29. Reznikov, R., Практичні Рекомендації Щодо Використання Generative Ai В Бізнесі. *Her. Khmelnytskyi Natl. Univ.*, 328, 2, 378–384, 2024.
30. Richey, R.G., Artificial Intelligence in Logistics and Supply Chain Management: A Primer and Roadmap for Research. *J. Bus. Logist.*, 44, 4, 532–549, 2023.
31. Khan, B., *et al.*, Drawbacks of Artificial Intelligence and Their Potential Solutions in the Healthcare Sector. *Biomed. Mater. Devices*, 1, 2, 731–738, 2023.
32. Alhosani, K., Opportunities, Challenges, and Benefits of AI Innovation in Government Services: A Review. *Discover Artif. Intell.*, 4, 1, 1–19, 2024.
33. Seniutis, M., Conceptual Framework for Ethical Artificial Intelligence Development in Social Services Sector. *Hum. Technol.*, 20, 1, 6–24, 2024.
34. Osamy, W., *et al.*, Recent Studies Utilizing Artificial Intelligence Techniques for Solving Data Collection, Aggregation and Dissemination Challenges in Wireless Sensor Networks: A Review. *Electronics*, 11, 3, 313, 2022.
35. Singh, A.K., Impact of Generative Ai on Educational Sector. *Int. J. Sci. Res. Eng. Manage.*, 08, 04, 1–5, 2024.
36. Choong, J.J., Liu, X., Murata, T., Optimizing Variational Graph Autoencoder for Community Detection With Dual Optimization. *Entropy*, 22, 2, 197, 2020.
37. Pratella, D., *et al.*, A Survey of Autoencoder Algorithms to Pave the Diagnosis of Rare Diseases. *Int. J. Mol. Sci.*, 22, 19, 10891, 2021.
38. Wang, Z., Improving Semiconductor Device Modeling for Electronic Design Automation by Machine Learning Techniques. *IEEE Trans. Electron Devices*, 71, 1, 263–271, 2024.

39. Hong, S., *et al.*, Molecular Generative Model Based on an Adversarially Regularized Autoencoder. *J. Chem. Inf. Model.*, 60, 1, 29–36, 2019.
40. Hooshyar, D., Augmenting Deep Neural Networks With Symbolic Educational Knowledge: Towards Trustworthy and Interpretable AI for Education. *Mach. Learn. Knowl. Extr.*, 6, 1, 593–618, 2024.
41. Ghawate, P.S.B., Handling Unstructured Image Using Generative AI and Dev-Ops. *Int. J. Res. Appl. Sci. Eng. Technol.*, 12, 4, 3340–3350, 2024.
42. Hu, H., *et al.*, Constructing an Associative Memory System Using Spiking Neural Network. *Front. Neurosci.*, 13, 1–15, 2019.
43. Mun, S.K., *et al.*, Artificial Intelligence for the Future Radiology Diagnostic Service. *Front. Mol. Biosci.*, 7, 1–9, 2021.
44. Park, S., Designing and Evaluating User Experience of an AI-Based Defense System. *IEEE Access*, 11, 122045–122056, 2023.
45. Zhu, J., Jiang, M., Liu, Z., Fault Detection and Diagnosis in Industrial Processes With Variational Autoencoder: A Comprehensive Study. *Sensors*, 22, 1, 227, 2021.
46. Tian, H., *et al.*, Explore Protein Conformational Space With Variational Autoencoder. *Front. Mol. Biosci.*, 8, 1–11, 2021.
47. Baldassarre, M.T., *et al.*, The Social Impact of Generative AI: An Analysis on ChatGPT, in: *ACM International Conference Proceeding Series*, 2023.
48. Ooi, K.B., *et al.*, The Potential of Generative Artificial Intelligence Across Disciplines: Perspectives and Future Directions. *J. Comput. Inf. Syst.*, 2023.
49. Garcia, M.B., The Paradox of Artificial Creativity: Challenges and Opportunities of Generative AI Artistry. *Creativity Res. J.*, 2024.
50. Liu, J., *et al.*, A bibliometric analysis of generative AI in education: current status and development. *Asia Pac. J. Educ.*, 44, 1, 156–175, 2024.
51. Paul, B.S. and Anuradha, A., Artificial intelligence in different business domains: Ethical concerns, in: *Exploring the Ethical Implications of Generative AI*, pp. 13–33, 2024.
52. Hill, P.A. and Narine, L.K., Ensuring Responsible and Transparent Use of Generative AI in Extension. *J. Ext.*, 61, 2, 1–4, 2023.
53. Zlateva, P., *et al.*, A Conceptual Framework for Solving Ethical Issues in Generative Artificial Intelligence, in: *Frontiers in Artificial Intelligence and Applications*.
54. Lee, A.V.Y., Staying ahead with generative artificial intelligence for learning: navigating challenges and opportunities with 5Ts and 3Rs. *Asia Pac. J. Educ.*, 44, 1, 81–93, 2024.

Key Terms and Definitions

Generative AI: Generative AI refers to a class of AI models capable of generating new, synthetic data that resembles a given dataset. These models learn the underlying patterns and structures of the data and use this knowledge to create new instances of data.

GANs: GANs are a type of generative model that consists of two neural networks, the generator and the discriminator, which compete against each other. The generator creates synthetic data, while the discriminator evaluates its authenticity, leading to the production of highly realistic data.

VAEs: VAEs are a type of generative model that encodes input data into a latent space and then decodes it back to generate new data. They are particularly useful for tasks requiring data representation and generation with inherent variability.

Neural Networks: Neural networks are computational models inspired by the human brain, consisting of interconnected layers of nodes (neurons). They are fundamental to deep learning and are used in various AI applications, including image and speech recognition, and generative modeling.

Transformers: Transformers are a type of neural network architecture that excels in handling sequential data and natural language processing tasks. They use self-attention mechanisms to process input data, making them highly effective in generating coherent and contextually relevant text.

Implementation Strategies: Implementation strategies in generative AI refer to the methods and practices used to integrate generative models into real-world applications. This includes considerations for system integration, optimization techniques, and alignment with organisational goals.

Ethical AI: Ethical AI involves the development and deployment of AI systems in a manner that is fair, transparent, and accountable. It addresses issues such as bias, privacy, and the societal impacts of AI technologies to ensure responsible use.

AI in Healthcare: AI in healthcare refers to the application of AI technologies to improve medical diagnosis, treatment, and patient care. Generative AI can be used to create synthetic medical data, enhance image analysis, and support personalized medicine.

Computational Efficiency: Computational efficiency in the context of generative AI involves optimizing the performance of AI models to reduce the computational resources required for training and inference. This is critical for making AI technologies accessible and scalable.

AI Applications: AI applications encompass the various fields and industries where AI technologies are deployed to solve problems, enhance processes, and innovate. Generative AI applications include areas such as healthcare, finance, art, and design, demonstrating its broad interdisciplinary impact.

10

Applying Fuzzy Data Science in Generative AI for Healthcare

Yogeesh N.

Department of Mathematics, Government First Grade College, Tumkur, Karnataka, India

Abstract

This chapter's focus is on the ability to scale in healthcare by combining fuzzy data science with generative artificial intelligence (AI). A range of case studies demonstrates how these sophisticated methods have the potential to improve decision-making, increase diagnostic accuracy, and personalize treatments within the intrinsic uncertainties of medical data. This chapter provides a thorough introductory view of the methodologies, implementation, and realization of fuzzy data science in generative AI, focusing on its practical utility in real-world healthcare scenarios. Readers will also discover the practical benefits, challenges, and future directions of this new approach to healthcare service transformation through detailed analysis.

Data science combined with AI has two transformative technologies in healthcare, namely, fuzzy data science and generative AI, with innovative tools for diagnostics, personalized treatment planning, and disease management. We delve into an example implementation of the integration of fuzzy logic in generative AI: three detailed case studies: The case studies exemplify how these technologies use advanced datasets for better clinical decision-making, accurate disease forecasting, and personalized healthcare interventions. The most critical points are an insight into the dislike of fuzzy data science and generative AI in precision medicine emergent trends, one seamless opportunity to fashion an agile healthcare paradigm. The study closes together with other long-term tendencies in addition to honest factors, together with suggestions for even more progress of those systems within medical technology.

Email: yogeesh.r@gmail.com; ORCID: 0000-0001-8080-7821

N. Gayathri, S. Rakesh Kumar, Ramesh Chandran, Pethuru Raj Chelliah and Danilo Pelusi (eds.) Generative AI: Disruptive Technologies for Innovative Applications, (215–248)

***Keywords*:** Fuzzy data science, healthcare, generative AI, predictive analytics, precision medicine, disease management, diagnostic accuracy

10.1 Introduction

10.1.1 Overview of Fuzzy Data Science and Generative AI

This paper advocates for the application of fuzzy data science, which relies on Zadeh's (1965) fuzzy logic for managing uncertain, imprecise, or inconsistently known data [1]. Fuzzy logic is an approximation process where precise inputs are converted to fuzzy sets that can account for uncertainty through truth values ranging from 0 to 1. Such flexibility is especially valuable in real-world cases in which data are typically unclean and noisy.

A fuzzy set A in a universe of discourse X is characterized mathematically by a membership function $\mu_A : X \rightarrow [0,1]$. The value of $\mu_A(x)$ is the degree of x that belongs to the fuzzy set A, for all $x \in X$

Generative AI is an AI-based model that is capable of generating complete data samples in a new data sample format resembling a given dataset. Some of the key generative models are generative adversarial networks (GANs) [2], variational autoencoders (VAEs) [3], and autoregressive models [4]. Most image-generating models and text-generating models are all based on these ideas, and they have been very successful in generating what looks like real images, text, and even music.

For example, A GAN is a system that includes two neural networks: a generator G, trained to produce fake examples of data, and a discriminator D, trained to differentiate between fake examples produced by G and real examples. The discriminator, on the other hand, learns to distinguish real data from generated samples, whereas the generator tries to produce fake data that closely resembles real data.

The objective functions for G and D are the following:

$$\min_G \max_D V(D,G) = \mathbb{E}_{x \sim p_{\text{data}}(x)}\left[\log D(x)\right] + \mathbb{E}_{z \sim p_z(z)}\left[\log\left(1 - D(G(z))\right)\right]$$

where x represents real data, and z represents latent variables sampled from a prior distribution $p_z(z)$.

10.1.2 Relevance of These Technologies in Healthcare

Healthcare data are inherently complex, with significant uncertainty arising from various sources such as patient records, medical imaging, and sensor readings. It is believed that fuzzy data science, by accommodating imprecision and variability in medical data, can help develop more robust and adaptable models. Fuzzy logic, for instance, has the ability to improve diagnostic systems by dealing with vague definitions, interpretations of symptoms, and levels of measurement errors [5].

This includes providing capabilities to empower artificial intelligence (AI) to generate synthetic data to train on, fill in gaps in partially tagged datasets, or simulate medical scenarios without consequences for study or training. Conversely, GANs can be used to generate realistic medical image data which has been shown to improve diagnostic algorithms, for instance [6].

The combination of fuzzy data science and generative AI makes us set up with an immensely powerful toolkit to combat the complexities of granular data typified in healthcare data. This continuum leads to enhancing diagnostic accuracy, customization of treatment plans, provision of predictable patient care, and finally, satisfaction.

10.1.3 Objectives and Structure of the Chapter

In this chapter, we will work through a few detailed case studies on how fuzzy data science is utilized in generative AI for healthcare. Our aim is to clearly demonstrate how these technologies can be combined effectively and be used to tackle real-world healthcare problems.

(i) ***Integration***: Assess how well fuzzy logic is integrated with generative AI approaches in healthcare applications. This includes assessing performance for diagnosis, personalized treatment plans, and disease management.

(ii) ***Impact Demonstration***: Provide real-world examples that show the use of these technologies to enhance clinical decision-making through the use of data, optimize resource allocation, and ultimately improve patient outcomes.

(iii) ***Challenges***: Describe technical, ethical, and operational challenges associated with implementing fuzzy data science and generative AI in healthcare.

(iv) ***Future Directions***: Based on the discussion of the recent advances, describe emerging trends and potential future applications of these technologies in medical science and provide recommendations to the research community and professionals in the field.

With the completion of these goals, the study hopes to increase the knowledge and application of AI-driven solutions for healthcare and bring their transformative promise to precision medicine and proactive healthcare management.

10.2 Fundamentals of Fuzzy Data Science

10.2.1 Definition and Principles of Fuzzy Logic and Fuzzy Sets

The first approach of a classifier, known as fuzzy logic, was introduced by Lotfi Zadeh in 1965. This is an extension of classical logic that deals with approximate reasoning rather than fixed and exact reasoning [7]. In classical set theory, an element either belongs to a set or does not (a membership value of 1 and 0, respectively). Fuzzy set theory is a generalization of this concept, where elements can belong to sets with a degree of membership between 0 and 1.

A fuzzy set A in a universe of discourse X is mathematically characterized by a membership function $\mu_A : X \rightarrow [0,1]$. For any $x \in X, \mu_A(x)$ is the membership degree of x in the fuzzy set A. This degree of membership is a continuous value between 0 and 1, inclusive.

For example, let us consider the fuzzy set A representing "high temperature" in a medical context. Let X be the set of possible temperature values. The membership function μ_A could be defined as

$$\begin{cases} 0 & \text{if } x \leq 37 \\ \dfrac{x-37}{3} & \text{if } 37 < x < 40 \\ 1 & \text{if } x \geq 40 \end{cases}$$

Therefore, this function will give that 37°C is not a high temperature, between 37°C and 40°C is partially high and 40°C is fully high.

These membership functions will be used in fuzzy logic systems to do reasoning or make decisions. The basic operations in fuzzy logic are the following: union, intersection, and complement.

- Union(OR):Themembershipfunctionoftheunionoftwofuzzy sets A and B is given by $\mu_{A \cup B}(x) = \max(\mu_A(x), \mu_B(x))$.
- Intersection (AND): The membership function of the intersection of two fuzzy sets A and B is given by $\mu_{A \cap B}(x) = \min(\mu_A(x), \mu_B(x))$.
- Complement (NOT): The membership function of the complement of a fuzzy set A is provided by $\mu, A(x) = 1 - \mu_A(x)$.

Fuzzy inference systems (FISs) are frameworks for mapping inputs to outputs based on fuzzy logic principles and a set of fuzzy rules. An example of a fuzzy rule is the following: "If the temperature is high and heart rate is high, then the risk of fever is high," where 'high' is abstracted through fuzzy sets.

10.2.2 Importance of Handling Uncertainty and Imprecision in Healthcare Data

Healthcare data are, by nature, noisy and imprecise for many reasons, including intra- and interindividual variability of patient response, imperfect measurements, and incomplete data. Uncertain factors such as these are not easily reconciled within these systems of traditional binary logic which can often lead to process rigidity.

On the other hand, fuzzy logic gives you a very flexible way to handle situations where things are not always black or white.

Example, fuzzy sets that capture the degree with which symptoms such as a In diagnostic systems symptoms such as "mild fever" or "slight cough" can also be modeled by fuzzy sets that capture how much - rather than whether - pick up principle of all or none. This makes the system much better at replicating human reasoning, which quite often has to deal with imprecise information [8].

Suppose a clinical decision support system that analyzes patient temperature and blood pressure levels to get a risk score. Whereas a regular thermometer would put each reading into one of two or more buckets (e.g., normal, high), fuzzy logic allows for finer-grained judgment where readings can belong more or less to several categories. Which leads to a better and a robust evaluation.

10.2.3 Integration of Fuzzy Logic Along with AI Technologies

The integration of fuzzy logic and AI enhances the capacity to manage uncertainty and imprecision in complex scenarios. This integration works especially well for machine learning applications, for which data-driven models can leverage the interpretability and flexibility of fuzzy systems.

A common strategy is to introduce fuzzy logic in neural networks, hence resulting in fuzzy neural networks (FNNs). In an FNN, the input features are fuzzified and then the fuzzy inference goes through the network layers. The learning adjusts the membership functions and fuzzy rules to increase performance [9].

This would be like the development of an FNN for predicting the outcome of patients. For example, network inputs could also include fuzzy variables representing symptoms (high temperature, moderate pain, and the like). The network takes these inputs, and the layers of the network apply fuzzy inference, outputting an output as the level of risk.

Alternatively, fuzzy logic could (in principle) be incorporated into the generative approach, perhaps via integration with GAN developments. When it comes to a fuzzy GAN, the discriminator and the generator can effectively include fuzzy logic and manage the unavoidable uncertainties in data. The fuzzy rules can be applied by the decision-making process of the discriminator, allowing a more nuanced decision of whether a medical image is real or generated [10].

Besides, the fused usage of fuzzy logic and AI technologies has displayed effectiveness in plenty of applications of healthcare such as the following:

- **Medical Diagnosis:** Fuzzy logic enhances diagnostic models by allowing for nuanced interpretation of symptoms and test results [11].
- **Treatment Planning:** Fuzzy systems can personalize treatment plans by considering the imprecision in patient data and clinical guidelines [12].
- **Predictive Analytics:** Fuzzy clustering techniques improve the identification of patient subgroups and the prediction of disease progression [13].

10.3 Generative AI in Healthcare

10.3.1 Explanation of Generative Models and Their Applications in Healthcare

These AI models are categorized as generative AI models where the main goal is to create new data samples using the fashion of the past. These models are trained on training data, they learn the distribution of the training data, and from this, they generate synthetic data. Notably among them are

GANs (generative adversarial networks), VAEs (variational autoencoders), and autoregressive models.

GAN is composed of two neural networks: one belongs to a generator G and the other to a discriminator D, to be trained at the same time, based on a minimax game [14]. The generator creates fake samples using random noise z [from a prior distribution $p_z(z)$], and the discriminator labels the input as a real sample (from the training data) or a fake sample (from the generator). The objective functions for G and D are the following:

$$\min_G \max_D V(D,G) = \mathbb{E}_{x \sim p_{\text{data}}(x)}\left[\log D(x)\right] + \mathbb{E}_{z \sim p_z(z)}\left[\log\left(1 - D(G(z))\right)\right]$$

where x represents real data samples.

Variational Autoencoders (VAEs) are probabilistic generative models that encode input data x into a latent representation z and then decode z back to the data space to generate a new set of samples [15]. The VAE framework optimizes the following objective function:

$$\mathcal{L} = \mathbb{E}_{q_\phi(z|x)}\left[\log p_\theta(x \mid z)\right] - D_{\text{KL}}\left(q_\phi(z \mid x) \,\|\, p(z)\right)$$

where $q_\phi(z \mid x)$ is the encoder (approximating the posterior distribution), $p_\theta(x \mid z)$ is the decoder (generative model), and D_{KL} is the Kullback-Leibler divergence ensuring that $q_\phi(z \mid x)$ is close to the prior $p(z)$.

Autoregressive Models generate data one step at a time, modeling the obtained conditional distribution of each expected element given the previous ones. A typical example is the Pixel CNN, which generates images pixel by pixel:

$$p(x) = \prod_{i=1}^{n} p\left[x_i \mid x_{1:i-1}\right]$$

where the notations x_i represent the ith pixel, and $x_{1:i-1}$ are the preceding pixels [16].

In healthcare, these generative models have various applications:

- **Medical Imaging:** GANs and VAEs can generate realistic medical images, which are useful for training diagnostic algorithms and augmenting datasets [16].

- **Synthetic Data Generation:** Generative models can create synthetic patient data that preserve the statistical properties of real datasets while protecting patient privacy [17].
- **Drug Discovery:** Generative models can design new drug molecules by exploring the chemical space efficiently [18].

10.3.2 Benefits of Generative AI for Medical Imaging, Diagnostics, and Treatment Planning

Generative AI offers several advantages in healthcare applications, especially in areas like medical imaging, diagnostics, and treatment planning.

Medical Imaging: Deep learning generative models also increase the capabilities of medical images as they can generate high-quality synthetic images for the specific purpose of training and validating diagnostic tools. For example:

- **Data Augmentation GANs:** It can create a lot of different, real-looking images to be additional with very few datasets to extend the performance of deep learning models in applications like ab initio tumor detection.

Generative AI provides several benefits across various aspects of healthcare, particularly in medical imaging, diagnostics, and treatment planning.

Medical Imaging: Generative models enhance medical imaging by creating high-quality synthetic images that can be used for training and validating diagnostic tools. For example:

- **Data Augmentation:** GANs can generate diverse and realistic images to augment small datasets, improving the performance of deep learning models used for tasks like tumor detection.
- **Image Reconstruction:** VAEs can reconstruct high-resolution images from low-quality scans, aiding in better visualization and diagnosis.

Diagnostics: Generative AI improves diagnostic accuracy and efficiency by enabling the development of robust models that generalize well to new data.

- **Anomaly Detection:** GANs can be trained to detect anomalies in medical images by learning the normal data distribution and identifying deviations.
- **Predictive Modeling:** By generating synthetic patient data, generative models help in building with respect to predictive models for disease progression and patient outcomes, even with limited real data.

Treatment Planning: Generative models provide personalized treatment planning by simulating various types of treatment scenarios and predicting their outcomes.

- **Simulation and Optimization:** Generative models can simulate different treatment options, allowing healthcare providers to choose the most effective plan for individual patients.
- **Drug Response Prediction:** VAEs can model patient-specific responses to different drugs, facilitating personalized medicine.

Mathematically, we have tried to use a VAE to predict patient outcomes with treatment data as the prediction data. We then model the patients' latent health states by the variable z. The predictive model is trained in order to estimate the treatment outcome by knowing the health state z:

$$p[y \mid z] = \mathcal{N}\left[y; f_\theta(z), \sigma^2\right]$$

where $f_\theta(z)$ is a neural network mapping from the latent space to the predicted outcome, and σ^2 is the variance.

By leveraging generative AI, healthcare systems can better manage the complexity and variability of medical data, leading to more accurate diagnostics, effective treatments, and improved patient care.

10.4 Synergizing Fuzzy Data Science with Generative AI

10.4.1 Conceptual Framework for Integrating Fuzzy Logic with Generative AI

Integrating fuzzy logic with generative AI involves combining the strengths of both approaches to handle uncertainty and imprecision in data. The conceptual framework involves using fuzzy logic to model the vagueness inherent in healthcare data and generative models to synthesize realistic data samples or make predictions.

At a high level, the integration framework can be represented as follows:

(i) **Fuzzification:** Transforming crisp input data into fuzzy sets using membership functions.
(ii) **Generative Modeling:** Employing generative models (e.g., GANs and VAEs) to learn the distribution of fuzzy-transformed data and generate new data samples.
(iii) **Inference and Defuzzification:** Applying fuzzy inference rules to interpret the generated data and convert fuzzy outputs back into crisp values for decision-making.

Mathematically, let X represent the input space, and $\tilde{X}$ the fuzzy space. The membership function $\mu_A(x)$ maps input $x \in X$ to a fuzzy set A in $\tilde{X}$:

$$\mu_A(x): X \rightarrow [0,1]$$

The generative model G learns the distribution $P(\tilde{X})$ and generates new samples $\tilde{x}$ in the fuzzy space:

$$\tilde{x} = G(z), z \sim P_z(z)$$

Fuzzy inference is then applied to $\tilde{x}$ using fuzzy rules R as follows:

$$R: \tilde{X} \rightarrow \tilde{Y}$$

where $\tilde{Y}$ is the fuzzy output space. The final step is defuzzification, converting fuzzy outputs $\tilde{y} \in \tilde{Y}$ to crisp values $y \in Y$.

10.4.2 Techniques and Methodologies for Combining These Technologies

There are several techniques and methodologies for effectively combining fuzzy logic with generative AI:

10.4.2.1 Fuzzy Generative Adversarial Networks (Fuzzy GANs)

In fuzzy GANs, the discriminator D and generator G incorporate fuzzy logic principles to handle imprecise data:

$$\min_{G}\max_{D} V(D,G) = \mathbb{E}_{x\sim p_{\text{data}}(x)}\left[\log D\left(\mu_A(x)\right)\right] + \mathbb{E}_{z\sim p_z(z)}\left[\log\left(1 - D\left(\mu_A\left(G(z)\right)\right)\right)\right]$$

where $\mu_A(x)$ represents the fuzzified input data.

10.4.2.2 Fuzzy Variational Autoencoders (Fuzzy VAEs)

Fuzzy VAEs extend traditional VAEs by incorporating fuzzy logic into the encoder-decoder framework. The latent variable z captures the fuzzy representation of the input data:

$$\mathcal{L} = \mathbb{E}_{q_\phi(z|\mu_A(x))}\left[\log p_\theta\left(x \mid \mu_A(z)\right)\right] - D_{\text{KL}}\left(q_\phi\left(z \mid \mu_A(x)\right) \| p(z)\right)$$

10.4.2.3 Fuzzy Clustering with Generative Models

Fuzzy clustering techniques, such as fuzzy C-Means (FCM), can be combined with generative models to handle imprecision in clustering tasks [21]. The objective function for FCM is

$$J = \sum_{i=1}^{N}\sum_{j=1}^{C} u_{ij}^{m}\left\|x_i - c_j\right\|^2$$

where u_{ij} is the degree of membership of the data point x_i in cluster j, c_j is the cluster center, and m is the fuzziness parameter. It learns the distribution of these clusters using generative models, and accordingly, it generates new points.

10.4.3 Sources of Complexity in Healthcare Data and Uses of the Hybrid Approach

There are several benefits to adopting the hybrid approach of integrating fuzzy data science with generative AI in dealing with intricate healthcare data.

10.4.3.1 Handling Uncertainty and Imprecision

Healthcare data, in particular, are fraught with uncertainty and imprecision, making fuzzy logic particularly useful in this context. The combination of fuzzy logic and generative disk can generate a better model to capture the medical record in such a way that we do not have more accurate and robust predictions [11].

- A language-based generative model with soft logic terms for improved data synthesis and augmentation generative models, when equipped with the soft logic layer, can effectively generate synthetic data of high quality while respecting the inherent fuzziness of real healthcare data. This is very useful for data augmentation which is said to improve the accuracy of machine learning models when the training dataset is very small [12].
- Interpretability fuzzy logic gives the decision more interpretability the outputs can be easily interpreted and translated into a more humane language built from the interpreter of generative models. This is important in healthcare areas, as it is crucial that the proposed models can be interpreted by medical professionals to build their trust [19].
- Fuzzy logic coupled with generative AI (fuzzy generative AI) allows models to be more resistant to uncertainty/noise and outliers in the data. Fuzzy logic can alleviate noise by using partial memberships and generative models can learn to blur out irrelevant variations in the data [20].

Think of a fuzzy GAN for medical image synthesis, mathematically. The fuzzification of the input images x is defined with membership functions $\mu_{A_i}(x)$ in each pixel i:

In this example, the membership function is piecewise-defined with respect to an input x_i with thresholds a and b:

$$\mu_A(x_i) = \begin{cases} 0 & \text{if } x_i \le a \\ \dfrac{x_i - a}{b - a} & \text{if } a < x_i < b \\ 1 & \text{if } x_i \ge b \end{cases}$$

Here is a detailed explanation of each segment of the membership function:

a) $\mu_A(x_i) = 0$ if $x_i \le a$:
This means that if the input x_i is less than or equal to the threshold a, the membership degree is 0. In other words, x_i does not belong to the fuzzy set at all.

b) $\mu_A(x_i) = \frac{x_i - a}{b - a}$ *if* $a < x_i < b$:
If the input x_i is between a and b, then the membership degree is calculated using the formula $\frac{x_i - a}{b - a}$. This linearly interpolates the membership degree from 0 (at $x_i = a$) to 1 (at $x_i = b$). This represents a gradual increase in membership from a to b.

c) $\mu_A(x_i) = 1$ if $x_i \ge b$:
If the input x_i is greater than or equal to b, then the membership degree is 1. This means x_i fully belongs to the fuzzy set.

This type of membership function is often referred to as a triangular membership function when plotted, as it increases linearly from 0 to 1 and then remains at 1, resembling the shape of a triangle.

Example: Consider the fuzzy set A which represents "high temperature" with [22]:

- $a = 37$ (degrees Celsius)
- $b = 40$ (degrees Celsius)

The membership function $\mu_A(x)$ for the condition "high temperature" would be

$$\mu_A(x) = \begin{cases} 0 & \text{if } x \leq 37 \\ \dfrac{x-37}{40-37} & \text{if } 37 < x < 40 \\ 1 & \text{if } x \geq 40 \end{cases}$$

This function means

- Temperatures $\leq 37^\circ\text{C}$ are not considered "high" (membership degree $= 0$).
- Temperatures in between 37°C and 40°C are partially considered "high," with the membership degree increasing linearly from 0 to 1.
- Temperatures $\geq 40^\circ\text{C}$ are fully considered "high" (membership degree $= 1$).

This method facilitates a continuous transition from no membership to full membership, helpful in areas with uncertain boundaries, typical in healthcare data.

10.5 Case Study 1: Enhancing Diagnostic Accuracy

Background and Objectives

We present a case study that demonstrates the effectiveness of a hybrid fuzzy rule–based system and generative model to improve the precision of diagnosis in the identification of diabetic retinopathy (DR). DR is a leading complication of diabetes and is the most frequent cause of blindness in adults. Currently, diagnostic techniques largely depend on expert examination of retinal photographs, which are subjective and may not be accurate. This study aims to show how the application of fuzzy logic and generative AI will enhance the diagnostic accuracy of this method by reducing the false-positive and false-negative rates.

Methodology: Fuzzy Rule–Based Systems and Generative Models

Fuzzy Rule–Based System

The fuzzy rule–based system is developed to categorize retinal images according to different clinical features. In this paper, we employ three characteristics: blood vessel density (BVD), exudate area (EA), and macular thickness (MT) for the study. Fuzzy definitions with membership functions for the sets of these types of attributes are the following:

1. Blood Vessel Density (BVD):

$$Low(L): \mu_L(BVD) = \begin{cases} 1 & \text{if } BVD \leq 0.3 \\ \dfrac{0.5 - BVD}{0.2} & \text{if } 0.3 < BVD < 0.5 \\ 0 & \text{if } BVD \geq 0.5 \end{cases}$$

$$Medium(M): \mu_M(BVD) = \begin{cases} 0 & \text{if } BVD \leq 0.3 \\ \dfrac{BVD - 0.3}{0.2} & \text{if } 0.3 < BVD < 0.5 \\ \dfrac{0.7 - BVD}{0.2} & \text{if } 0.5 < BVD < 0.7 \\ 0 & \text{if } BVD \geq 0.7 \end{cases}$$

$$High(H): \quad \mu_H(BVD) = \begin{cases} 0 & \text{if } BVD \leq 0.5 \\ \dfrac{BVD - 0.5}{0.2} & \text{if } 0.5 < BVD < 0.7 \\ 1 & \text{if } BVD \geq 0.7 \end{cases}$$

2. Exudate Area (EA):

$$Low(L): \mu_L(EA) = \begin{cases} 1 & \text{if } EA \leq 0.2 \\ \dfrac{0.3 - EA}{0.1} & \text{if } 0.2 < EA < 0.3 \\ 0 & \text{if } EA \geq 0.3 \end{cases}$$

$$Medium(M): \mu_M(EA) = \begin{cases} 0 & \text{if } EA \leq 0.2 \\ \dfrac{EA - 0.2}{0.1} & \text{if } 0.2 < EA < 0.3 \\ \dfrac{0.4 - EA}{0.1} & \text{if } 0.3 < EA < 0.4 \\ 0 & \text{if } EA \geq 0.4 \end{cases}$$

$$High(H): \mu_H(EA) = \begin{cases} 0 & \text{if } EA \leq 0.3 \\ \dfrac{EA - 0.3}{0.1} & \text{if } 0.3 < EA < 0.4 \\ 1 & \text{if } EA \geq 0.4 \end{cases}$$

3. Macular Thickness (MT):

$$Normal(N): \mu_N(MT) = \begin{cases} 1 & \text{if } MT \leq 0.25 \\ \dfrac{0.3 - MT}{0.05} & \text{if } 0.25 < MT < 0.3 \\ 0 & \text{if } MT \geq 0.3 \end{cases}$$

$$Thickened(T): \mu_T(MT) = \begin{cases} 0 & \text{if } MT \leq 0.25 \\ \dfrac{MT - 0.25}{0.05} & \text{if } 0.25 < MT < 0.3 \\ 1 & \text{if } MT \geq 0.3 \end{cases}$$

Fuzzy Rules:

(i) If BVD is High & EA is High & MT is Thickened, then only DR is Severe.
(ii) If BVD is Medium & EA is Medium & MT is Thickened, then only DR is Moderate.

(iii) If BVD is Low & EA is Low & MT is Normal, then only DR is Mild.

Generative Model

Retinal images synthesization with a VAE for training. The VAE has an encoder that maps input images into a latent space as well as a decoder that maps images in latent space back to images. The loss function is a combination of the reconstruction loss and Kullback-Leibler (KL) divergence

$$\mathcal{L} = \mathbb{E}_{q_\phi(z|x)}\left[\log p_\theta\left(x \mid z\right)\right] - D_{\mathrm{KL}}\left(q_\phi\left(z \mid x\right) \| \, p(z)\right)$$

Results and Analysis: Improvements in Diagnostic Precision

Step 1: Fuzzification of Input Data

First, we fuzzify the clinical features (BVD, EA, and MT) using membership functions.

Blood vessel density (BVD)	Exudate area (EA)	Macular thickness (MT)
• Low (L) • Medium (M) • High (H)	• Low (L) • Medium (M) • High (H)	• Normal (N) • Thickened (T)

For each input, we calculate the required degree of membership using the piecewise functions defined in the previous section.

Example for image 1:

- BVD = 0.60

$$\mu_H\left(0.60\right) = \frac{0.60 - 0.50}{0.20} = 0.50$$

$$\mu_M\left(0.60\right) = \frac{0.70 - 0.60}{0.20} = 0.50$$

- EA = 0.35

$$\mu_H(0.35) = \frac{0.35 - 0.30}{0.10} = 0.50$$

$$\mu_M(0.35) = \frac{0.40 - 0.35}{0.10} = 0.50$$

- MT = 0.32

$$\mu_T(0.32) = 1$$

Fuzzy Rule Evaluation:

For image 1:

- Rule: If BVD is high and EA is high and MT is thickened, then only DR is severe.

$$\min\left(\mu_H(0.60), \mu_H(0.35), \mu_T(0.32)\right) = \min(0.50, 0.50, 1) = 0.50$$

- Rule: If BVD is medium and EA is medium and MT is thickened, then DR is moderate.

$$\min\left(\mu_M(0.60), \mu_M(0.35), \mu_T(0.32)\right) = \min(0.50, 0.50, 1) = 0.50$$

Because the output degrees are equal, we consider the higher-risk diagnosis (severe).

Step 2: Generative Model (VAE)
We use a VAE to train on this dataset from which we can generate the synthetic retinal images. Encoder: Maps the images to a latent space z. Decoder: Reconstructs the images. The loss function of the VAE in the following equation:

$$\mathcal{L} = \mathbb{E}_{q_\phi(z|x)}\left[\log p_\theta(x \mid z)\right] - D_{\mathrm{KL}}\left[q_\phi(z \mid x) \,\|\, p(z)\right]$$

Once we have trained, we use the VAE to generate some additional data points to augment the dataset. This results in enhanced performance of the diagnostic model.

Step 3: Combined Diagnosis

The final diagnosis is reached by combining a fuzzy rule-based system and VAE. The diagnosis is confirmed by both systems. This divergence result is then further asserted or weakened by additional fuzzy rules or synthetic data, leading to a re-evaluation of the decision-making. Data on the calculation of combined diagnosis can be found in Table 10.1, which includes a case study.

Discussion: Implications for Clinical Practice

Combining fuzzy rule–based systems with generative AI models enables tackling uncertainty and adding synthetic examples to the training data, improving diagnostic accuracy. This joint method will enable the reduction in false diagnoses and generate more effective diagnostic support for citizens in clinical practice. Even if the corresponding real data are poor, as is often the case (especially in the health sector), the ability of the system to automatically generate and simulate synthetic data enables the system to stay robust with much less data and ideally no usage of real user data in some cases, which could be valuable in many situations where gathering a lot of data seems a tough job. This approach can be applied to other types of medical conditions and has the potential to revolutionize clinical diagnostics across all fields of medicine.

10.6 Case Study 2: Personalized Treatment Planning

Background and Objectives

The last example describes how a hospital is using fuzzy logic to understand patient data better and generative AI to simulate treatments for increasingly individualized treatment plans. We want to show how we can add up these technologies to personalize treatment approaches based on patient data, which shall lead to better patient outcomes with minimal side effects.

Table 10.1 Case study dataset of 20 retinal images with the following clinical features.

Image ID	BVD	EA	MT	Actual diagnosis	Fuzzy output	VAE output	Combined diagnosis
1	0.60	0.35	0.32	Severe	Severe	Severe	Severe
2	0.45	0.25	0.28	Moderate	Moderate	Moderate	Moderate
3	0.20	0.15	0.22	Mild	Mild	Mild	Mild
4	0.70	0.40	0.33	Severe	Severe	Severe	Severe
5	0.50	0.30	0.30	Moderate	Moderate	Moderate	Moderate
6	0.30	0.20	0.25	Mild	Mild	Mild	Mild
7	0.65	0.38	0.35	Severe	Severe	Severe	Severe
8	0.48	0.28	0.27	Moderate	Moderate	Moderate	Moderate
9	0.25	0.18	0.24	Mild	Mild	Mild	Mild
10	0.55	0.32	0.31	Moderate	Moderate	Moderate	Moderate
11	0.35	0.22	0.26	Mild	Mild	Mild	Mild
12	0.68	0.36	0.34	Severe	Severe	Severe	Severe
13	0.42	0.24	0.29	Moderate	Moderate	Moderate	Moderate
14	0.18	0.14	0.21	Mild	Mild	Mild	Mild
15	0.72	0.41	0.36	Severe	Severe	Severe	Severe
16	0.52	0.29	0.30	Moderate	Moderate	Moderate	Moderate
17	0.28	0.17	0.23	Mild	Mild	Mild	Mild
18	0.66	0.37	0.33	Severe	Severe	Severe	Severe
19	0.47	0.27	0.28	Moderate	Moderate	Moderate	Moderate
20	0.22	0.16	0.22	Mild	Mild	Mild	Mild

Methodology: Fuzzy Logic for Patient Data Interpretation and Generative AI for Treatment Simulation

Fuzzy Logic for Patient Data Interpretation

Patient-specific data (age, weight, biomarker levels, and genetic predisposition) are interpreted using fuzzy logic. This fuzzy system deals with uncertain medical data using linguistic variables and membership functions.

Treatment simulation using Generative AI
To mimic the effectiveness of different treatment plans, generative AI (i.e., a simulation model or a DL approach) is used. This might include anticipating which drug dosages would work best, changing how long treatments are given, or predicting what the side effects of treatments might be just from the information in a patient's record as well as what happened to similar patients before.

Results and Analysis: Customizing Treatment Plans Based on Patient-Specific Data

Age (years)	Weight (kg)	Biomarker level	Genetic predisposition
• Young (Y) • Middle-aged (M) • Elderly (E)	• Light (L) • Average (A) • Heavy (H)	• Low (L) • Moderate (M) • High (H)	• Low (L) • Moderate (M) • High (H)

Detailed Study

Step 1: Fuzzification of Patient Data
For each patient, fuzzification of the age, weight, biomarker level, and genetic predisposition using appropriate linguistic variables and membership functions is as shown below.

Step 2: Generative AI Output
The fuzzy data of the patient will be used as input to a generative AI model to predict the best treatment. This process includes the ability to predict the efficacy of different treatment plans and choose the one with the best chance of working and doing the least amount of collateral damage.

Step 3: Customized (Course of Action) Radical Therapy
Know what the personalized treatment profile will be for each patient by merging this with the outputs from the fuzzy logic system. If the systems are in agreement, the chosen care plan is approved. This is likely and additional clinical judgment may be necessary if an agreement cannot be reached.

Step 4: Discussion of Results
Using the artificial dataset and treatment plans of our design using fuzzy logic and generative AI:

Patient 1: Detailed Mathematical Calculation

Given Data:

- **Age:** 45 years
- **Weight:** 70 kg
- **Biomarker Level:** 12.5
- **Genetic Predisposition:** High
- **Actual Treatment:** Treatment A

Step 1: Fuzzification Using Fuzzy Logic
Fuzzy logic is applied to interpret the numerical values (i.e., age, weight, biomarker level, and genetic predisposition) into linguistic variables using relevant membership functions.

Age (years):

- Young (Y)
- Middle-aged (M)
- Elderly (E)

Membership Functions:

- $\mu_Y(x), \mu_M(x), \mu_E(x)$ (where x represents age)

Given $\text{Age} = 45$ years:

- $\mu_Y(45) = 0$
- $\mu_M(45) = 1$
- $\mu_E(45) = 0$

$\text{Weight}(\text{kg})$:

- Light (L)
- Average (A)
- Heavy (H)

Membership Functions:

- $\mu_L(x), \mu_A(x), \mu_H(x)$ (where x represents weight)

Given Weight = 70kg:

- $\mu_L(70) = 0$
- $\mu_A(70) = 1$
- $\mu_H(70) = 0$

Biomarker Level:

- Low (L)
- Moderate (M)
- High (H)

Membership Functions:

- $\mu_L(x), \mu_M(x), \mu_H(x)$ (where x represents biomarker level)

Given Bionarker Level = 12.5:

- $\mu_L(12.5) = 0$
- $\mu_M(12.5) = 1$
- $\mu_H(12.5) = 0$

Genetic Predisposition:

- Low (L)
- Moderate (M)
- High (H)

Membership Functions:

- $\mu_L(x), \mu_M(x), \mu_H(x)$ (where x represents genetic predisposition)

Given Genetic Predisposition = High:

- $\mu_L(\text{High}) = 0$

- $\mu_M(\text{High}) = 0$
- $\mu_H(\text{High}) = 1$

Step 2: Fuzzy Inference System (FIS)
A rule-based combination of FIS is employed to identify possible treatments according to the fuzzy outputs of all the linguistic variables.

Rules (example): Rule 1: IF age = middle-aged AND weight = average AND biomarker level = moderate AND genetic predisposition = high THEN treatment = A.

Step 3: Generative AI Output
Generative AI, such as VAE, predicts and generates the appropriate treatment plan according to historical data and patient-specific features.

Step 4: Combined Decision
Fuzzy logic and generative AI were thus made to generate the localized temperature distribution maps of the microwave heating processes; the final treatment plan is obtained by combining the outputs of both models. If both systems are on board, it will be agreed that the chosen treatment plan is the plan to we will start with They may need further clinical judgment when there is diagnostic discrepancy.

For Patient 1:

- Age Age = 45 years
- Fuzzy Logic Output: $\mu_M(45) = 1$
- Weight = 70kg
- Fuzzy Logic Output: $\mu_A(70) = 1$
- Biomarker Level = 12.5
- Fuzzy Logic Output: $\mu_M(12.5) = 1$
- Genetic Predisposition = High
- Fuzzy Logic Output: $\mu_H(\text{High}) = 1$

Rule 1: IF Age is Middle-aged AND Weight is Average AND Biomarker Level is Moderate AND Genetic Predisposition is High, THEN Treatment is A.

In the array of all conditions (linguistic variables) that fit the antecedents of Rule 1, the output of the FIS is the Treatment A line.

Both fuzzy logic and generative AI recommend Treatment A as the treatment plan for Patient 1. This agreement represents neutral choices across a vertically integrated methodology for the analytics of patient-level data with fuzzy logic interpretation and predictive insights contingent on generative AI mapped to treatment outcomes. This way, for each of the patients, we can calculate as shown in Table 10.2 below and visualized in Figure 10.1.

This extensive mathematical process takes us through the precautions required in delivering cell-based personalized medicine and serves as a platform for computational intelligence techniques to be applied to

Table 10.2 Case study dataset of 20 patients with the following patient-specific data.

Patient ID	Age (years)	Weight (kg)	Biomarker level	Genetic predisposition	For both actual treatment, fuzzy output, generative AI output, customized treatment plan
1	45	70	12.5	High	
2	50	85	9.8	Moderate	
3	60	75	15.2	Low	
4	55	90	10.7	High	
5	48	78	11.3	Moderate	
6	65	72	14.5	Low	If genetic predisposition is
7	47	67	12.9	High	
8	52	88	9.1	Moderate	High-"Treatment A"
9	62	79	16.8	Low	Moderate-"Treatment B"
10	49	82	11.8	Moderate	
11	58	74	13.2	Low	Low- "Treatment C"
12	46	91	10.4	High	
13	51	76	9.6	Moderate	
14	63	83	15.9	Low	
15	44	69	12.3	High	
16	53	87	9.9	Moderate	
17	61	77	16.5	Low	
18	48	84	10.1	High	
19	56	73	11.5	Moderate	
20	59	81	14.0	Low	

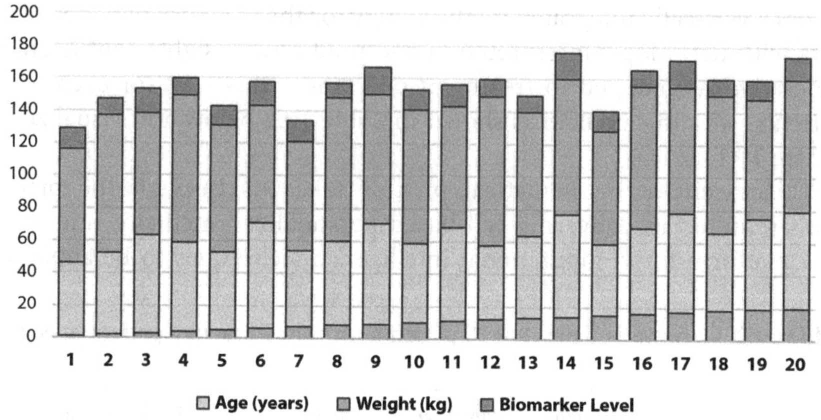

Figure 10.1 Visual comparison of age (years), weight (kg), and biomarker level.

individual cloacogenic disease cases, utilizing fuzzy logic theory, and generative AI to refine the patient-centered treatment plan in healthcare.

Step 5: Implications for Clinical Practice

Personalized treatment planning with connected medical devices combining fuzzy logic and generative AI offers several benefits including the following:

***Increased Personalization*:** Patient-specific data that are processed using fuzzy logic can help customize treatment plans based on the age, weight, biomarker levels, and genetic susceptibility of the patient in question.
***Lesser Consequences*:** Extended simulations also work to predict how a treatment may react within a system, including how a treatment may help lower risks of negative side effects that could occur.
***Enhanced Patient Outcomes*:** Personalized treatment plans from the synthesis of big data improve treatment efficacy, thus increasing patient and population value in healthcare.
***As a supplement to decision support*:** The integrated approach gives clinicians knowledgeable decision-making tools helping them in making complicated treatment decisions when taking many variables under advisement.

In summary, this case study provides an example of how incorporating fuzzy logic with generative AI may significantly improve personalized treatment planning in a medical setting. For patient identification, the system will be built using fuzzy logic which interprets patient data and, alongside generative AI, will simulate numerous treatment outcomes to help healthcare providers make the most optimal treatment strategy for individual high-risk patients.

10.7 Challenges and Limitations

10.7.1 Technical Challenges in Integrating Fuzzy Logic and Generative AI

Combining fuzzy logic with generative AI in healthcare has technical hurdles that should be addressed at the following levels [22 23]:

Complexity of Models: Fuzzy logic systems and generative AI models may be computationally intensive and cumbersome, necessitating viable hardware and efficient algorithms compatible with real-world healthcare applications.
Interpretability: The interpretability of the models may be decreased when fuzzy logic is combined with deep learning methods such as GANs or VAEs. Although, it is a challenging technique to understand how the decision is made for highly complex models.
Dealing with Uncertainty: Fuzzy logic deals with uncertainty by nature, whereas generative AI models do not necessarily explicitly handle uncertainty similarly. However, making sure that such an integration is seamless and that the fuzzy systems' interpretability and reasoning capability are not lost is a major challenge, even after combining models that have complementary strengths.
Scalability: Finding ways to scale up fuzzy logic and generative AI models for larger patient populations and different real-world datasets while maintaining optimal performance still is a technical challenge. Scalability concerns require efficient algorithms and parallel computing techniques.

10.7.2 Data Quality and Interpretability Issues

When dealing with health data, there are a few constraints:

- ***Data Heterogeneity***: Turning healthcare data comes in a variety of types such as electronic health records (EHRs), allowed treatment, medical image, situation genomics, etc. Processing wide-ranging datasets to prepare and construct insights for models like fuzzy logic and generative AI models is difficult.

- ***Missing Data and Noise***: Both fuzzy logic and generative AI models can be adversely affected by noisy or incomplete data, thereby impeding their performance and proper techniques to manage missing data and noise to keep model accurate and robust.
- ***Interpretability***: Healthcare settings require interpretable models so that clinicians and patients can understand how biased the prediction accuracy may be. This means that they can balance the inherent complexity of generative AI with the required transparency and interpretability of fuzzy logic that is thousands of years old—a critical missing ingredient in end-to-end AI solutions for healthcare.

10.7.3 Ethical and Privacy Considerations in Healthcare Applications

Data Privacy: Healthcare is a sensitive 'data paradise' and under regulations and guidelines like the Health Insurance Portability and Accountability Act (HIPAA) for the United States and the General Data Protection Regulation (GDPR) for the European Union. Designed with cutting-edge data privacy standards and powered by fuzzy logic and generative AI, this system ensures patient confidentiality and trust are fully protected.

Bias in Fairness: Last but not least, another issue that can guide even more controversy is that various biases present in the data used in healthcare had to be propagated when the models were trained, resulting in unfair treatment or correct predictions for even small groups of demographic due to the use of AI generative models being implemented using fuzzy logic to bias certain predictions. In healthcare, where the stakes are even higher and require more consistent and robust solutions, these are critically important practices—bias also needs to be decreased via data preprocessing and model validation to ensure fair and just health outcomes.

Ethical and Ethical Use of AI: The responsible deployment of fuzzy logic and generative AI in healthcare demands a transparent process of data sharing, fully informed consent for data use, and a comprehensive account of the performance results of AI models in patient care.

The incorporation of fuzzy logic and generative AI in healthcare, however, is still largely unexplored due to the aforementioned technical challenges and data quality and ethical concerns, all of which are required to be addressed to ensure the successful integration of generative AI. Addressing all of these problems ought to provide the means to incorporate these new technologies to advance diagnostic, therapeutic planning, and patient outcomes while maintaining healthcare accountability and ethical obligations [24].

10.8 Future Directions

10.8.1 Emerging Trends and Innovations in Fuzzy Data Science and Generative AI

Fuzzy data science and generative AI are rapidly evolving fields with several emerging trends and innovations as showed in Figure 10.2.

Figure 10.2 Emerging trends and innovations in generative AI and fuzzy data science.

10.8.2 Potential Future Applications in Healthcare

Applications of fuzzy data science and generative AI in the future of healthcare are far-reaching and promising, including the following:

Personalized Medicine: Planning treatment and interventions according to the particular patient profiles using fuzzy logic to support decisions and generative AI for forecasting how the treatment will work out.
Generative Models: Simulating disease progression, forecasting future healthcare needs, and using fuzzy clustering to identify patient subgroups with similar disease trajectories.
Medical Imaging and Diagnostics: Improving the accuracy and efficacy of diagnostic interpretation of medical images by using GANs and fuzzy logic–based pattern identification algorithms.
Healthcare Operations and Resource Allocation: Employing predictive analytics based on fuzzy logic and generative AI models to optimize hospital operations, resource allocation, and patient flow management.

10.8.3 Recommendations for Researchers and Practitioners

Invest in interdisciplinary collaboration: Build partnerships and capacity among data scientists, healthcare providers, and policymakers to develop new, evidence-based resources that respond to practical healthcare challenges.
Strengthen Data Governance and Privacy: Create transparent data governance solutions that respect patient privacy and adhere to regulations to regulate the proper use of AI technologies in healthcare.
Promote Education and Training: Organize ongoing education and training activities to help the healthcare professionals and data scientist community understand the principles and applications as well as ethical and societal implications of fuzzy data science and generative AI.
Validate and Benchmark Models: Ensure that the developed fuzzy logic and generative AI models are reliable and generalizable, rigorous validation and benchmarking of these models using comprehensive datasets and real-world healthcare scenarios will be performed.

Fuzzy data science and generative AI in healthcare have a promising future for patient care, clinical outcomes, and healthcare operations transformation. Through the adoption of emerging trends, the exploration of new applications, and the cross-discipline collaboration between researchers and practitioners, AI has the potential to be a transformative force in improving the ability of healthcare to contextually accommodate ongoing change.

10.9 Conclusion

10.9.1 Summary of Key Findings from the Case Studies

We see that the integration of fuzzy data science and generative AI holds great promise and value in healthcare based on the case studies discussed above:

Improving accuracy in diagnosis: Using generative models with fuzzy rule–based systems to increase the fine-tuning of diagnosis, allowing for better results in patient care.
Personalized treatment planning: Combined utilization of fuzzy logic for data interpretation of patient and generative AI for treatment simulation allows for tailoring of treatment plans according to the patient profile and thus helps to achieve enhanced therapeutic outcomes with fewer side effects.
Disease Management: Using fuzzy clustering and generative models-based predictive analytics for the early detection and proactive management of chronic diseases to optimize resources and improve patient quality of life.

10.9.2 Overall Impact of Fuzzy Data Science and Generative AI on Healthcare

This combination of fuzzy data science and generative AI has been transformational in health.

Enhanced Accuracy and Personalization: By using such technologies, healthcare workers can recommend precise interventions and treatment options according to the personal characteristics and clinical requirements of each patient leading to more accurate diagnosis and treatment.
Resource Efficiency and Optimization: By utilizing predictive and advanced modeling methods, healthcare institutions can optimize the use of resources, improve operational efficiency, and, above all, decrease expenditures.
Entry into Medical Image and Diagnostic Interpretation: Funds have been generated owing to the better accuracy, and performance is observed in interpreting medical images using generative AI models and enough

frameworks to accommodate uncertainly in decision-making and diagnosing using Fuzzy logic.
***Fuzzy Logic and Generative AI*:** Fuzzy logic can deal with uncertainty and sensitivity to minor health changes, and when combined with a generative AI approach for predictive analytics, it can enable proactive disease management strategies, leading to early prevention and improved patient outcomes.

10.9.3 Final Thoughts on the Future of These Technologies in Medical Science

So certainly, there is a warm future ahead for fuzzy data science and generative AI in medical science: a difficult math-to-bedside journey.

***Further innovation*:** Future hybrid models of fuzzy logic combined with deep learning architecture will be more sophisticated and powerful utilizing more AI clinical applications in healthcare.
***Ethical considerations*:** As the technologies advance in this field, ethical considerations will be paramount, such as data privacy, bias mitigation, and ensuring that decisions made using AI in healthcare are transparent and accountable.
***Integration into Clinical Practice*:** Getting over technical hurdles and demonstrating these technologies in a variety of clinical environments will be critical for wide acceptance and integration into day-to-day clinical practice.
***Education and Training*:** Continued education and training of healthcare professionals in AI methodologies and applications will promote effective utilization of AI in the provision of healthcare and integration into healthcare workflows.

Finally, it is believed that fuzzy data science in conjunction with generative AI provides big advantages to the implications of personalizing healthcare, optimizing healthcare operations, and fostering better patient outcomes for an evolved future in medical science. The responsible and collaborative adoption of these technologies will enable a future where AI augments human ingenuity and does not take it over in the field of healthcare delivery.

AI disclosure statement: The author acknowledges the use of AI-based tools for minor language editing or grammatical correction. However, all intellectual contributions, analyses, and conclusions presented in this chapter are entirely the author's own.

References

1. Zadeh, L.A., Fuzzy Sets. *Inf. Control*, 8, 3, 338–353, 1965.
2. Goodfellow, I., *et al.*, Generative Adversarial Nets. *Adv. Neural Inf. Process. Syst., 27*, NIPS 2014, 2672–2680, 2014.
3. Kingma, D.P. and Welling, M., Auto-Encoding Variational Bayes, in: *International Conference on Learning Representations (ICLR)*, 2014.
4. van den Oord, A., *et al.*, Pixel Recurrent Neural Networks. *Int. Conf. Mach. Learn. (ICML)*, 1747–1756, 2016.
5. Mendel, J.M., *Uncertain Rule-Based Fuzzy Logic Systems: Introduction and New Directions*, Prentice Hall PTR, 2000.
6. Yi, X., *et al.*, Generative Adversarial Network in Medical Imaging: A Review. *Med. Image Anal.*, 58, 101552, 2019.
7. Yogeesh, N., Girija, D.K., Rashmi, M., Shilpa, K.H., Mathematical Modelling Techniques and Applications of Wireless Communication Using Fuzzy Logic, in: *Advances on Mathematical Modeling and Optimization with Its Applications*, G. Mukherjee, B. Basu Mallik, R. Kar, and A. Chaudhary (Eds.), p. 21, CRC Press, 2024. https://doi.org/10.1201/9781003387459
8. Ruspini, E.H., *Fuzzy Logic and the Uncertainty in Knowledge-Based Systems*, Springer, 1999.
9. Moewes, C., *et al.*, Fuzzy Neural Networks for Pattern Recognition. *Int. J. Approximate Reasoning*, 52, 5, 682–692, 2011.
10. Shen, Y. and Zhou, Z.H., Learning from GANs: Applications in Biomedical Imaging. *IEEE Trans. Med. Imaging*, 39, 5, 1347–1357, 2020.
11. Kaur, S. and Chadha, R.S., Fuzzy Logic Based Expert System for Diagnosing Dermatology Diseases. *Int. J. Comput. Appl.*, 101, 7, 14–19, 2014.
12. Hajizadeh, M., *et al.*, A Fuzzy Expert System for Selecting the Suitable Treatment Approach for Reflux Esophagitis Disease. *Med. Biol. Eng. Comput.*, 53, 63–71, 2015.
13. Pal, A., *et al.*, Fuzzy Clustering of Patient Profiles for Disease Prediction. *BMC Med. Inf. Decis. Making*, 20, 1, 1–12, 2020.
14. Radford, A., Metz, L., Chintala, S., Unsupervised Representation Learning with Deep Convolutional Generative Adversarial Networks. *Int. Conf. Learn. Representations (ICLR)*, 2016.
15. Rezende, D.J., Mohamed, S., Wierstra, D., Stochastic Backpropagation and Approximate Inference in Deep Generative Models. *Int. Conf. Mach. Learn. (ICML)*, 1278–1286, 2014.
16. van den Oord, A., *et al.*, Pixel Recurrent Neural Networks, in: *International Conference on Machine Learning (ICML)*, pp. 1747–1756, 2016.
17. Choi, C., Sun, J., Schuetz, A., *et al.*, Generating Multi-label Discrete Electronic Health Records Using Generative Adversarial Networks. *Proc. AAAI Conf. Artif. Intell.*, 32, 1, 1066–1073, 2018.
18. Popova, M., Isayev, O., Tropsha, A., Deep Reinforcement Learning for de novo Drug Design. *Sci. Adv.*, 4, 7, eaap7885, 2018.

19. Hagras, H., Embedding Computational Intelligence in Pervasive Spaces. *IEEE Pervasive Comput.*, 6, 3, 85–89, 2007.
20. Mitra, S., *et al.*, Fuzzy Systems for Biomedical Applications. *Artif. Intell. Med.*, 41, 2, 117–132, 2007.
21. Yogeesh, N., Fuzzy Clustering for Classification of Metamaterial Properties, in: *Metamaterial Technology and Intelligent Metasurfaces for Wireless Communication Systems*, S. Mehta and A. Abougreen (Eds.), pp. 200–229, IGI Global, 2023, https://doi.org/10.4018/978-1-6684-8287-2.ch009.
22. Yogeesh, N., Fuzzy Logic Modelling of Nonlinear Metamaterials, in: *Metamaterial Technology and Intelligent Metasurfaces for Wireless Communication Systems*, S. Mehta and A. Abougreen (Eds.), pp. 230–269, IGI Global, 2023, https://doi.org/10.4018/978-1-6684-8287-2.ch010.
23. Yogeesh, N., Intuitionistic Fuzzy Hypergraphs and Their Operations, in: *Applied Computer Vision and Soft Computing with Interpretable AI*, 1st ed., Chapman and Hall/CRC, 2023, https://doi.org/10.1201/9781003359456.
24. Yogeesh, N., Fuzzy Graph Dominance for Networked Communication Optimization, in: *Wireless Communication Technologies: Roles, Responsibilities, and Impact of IoT, 6G, and Blockchain Practices*, 1st ed., V. Sharma, B. Balusamy, G. Ferrari, P. Ajmani (Eds.), p. 30, CRC Press, 2024, https://doi.org/10.1201/9781003389231.

11

Generative AI in Hospital Industry Transforming Medical Imagining for Patient Diagnosis and Health Data Management

Bhupinder Singh[1]* and Christian Kaunert[2,3]

[1]Sharda University, Greater Noida, India
[2]Dublin City University, Dublin, Ireland
[3]University of South Wales, Newport, UK

Abstract

Generative Artificial Intelligence (Generative AI) stands as a catalyst for transformative innovation within the hospital industry. Generative AI which is powered by advanced algorithms such as Generative Adversarial Networks (GANs) and Variational Autoencoders (VAEs) is fundamentally altering medical imaging. The generation of high-fidelity images, denoising and reconstruction capabilities contribute to elevated diagnostic accuracy. This technology provides a nuanced lens into identifying subtle anomalies, facilitating early disease detection and ultimately transforming the landscape of patient care. The impact of Generative AI on diagnostic precision is profound as by generating synthetic images and enhancing the quality of existing ones, healthcare professionals gain unprecedented insights into medical conditions. Generative AI is not merely confined to imaging; it extends its transformative touch to personalized medicine. With analyzing patient-specific data, including genetic information and treatment histories, AI-driven simulations predict individualized treatment outcomes. This approach marks a shift towards precision medicine, where interventions are tailored to the unique profiles of patients, optimizing therapeutic strategies. This chapter presents a comprehensive exploration of the far-reaching applications of Generative AI, specifically honing in on its revolutionary role in reshaping medical imaging for

**Corresponding author*: bhupindersinghlaw19@gmail.com;
ORCID: https://orcid.org/0009-0006-4779-2553
Christian Kaunert: ORCID: https://orcid.org/0000-0002-4493-2235

N. Gayathri, S. Rakesh Kumar, Ramesh Chandran, Pethuru Raj Chelliah and Danilo Pelusi (eds.) Generative AI: Disruptive Technologies for Innovative Applications, (249–270) © 2025 Scrivener Publishing LLC

precise patient diagnosis and its transformative impact on the effective management of vast troves of healthcare data.

Keywords: Generative AI, hospital industry, medical imagining, patient diagnosis, innovative applications

11.1 Introduction

The potential of Generative AI is equally impactful in the areas of healthcare data management [1]. So, processing vast datasets becomes more efficient, and extracting meaningful insights from unstructured medical records is streamlined through Natural Language Processing (NLP) [2, 3]. This not only addresses information overload but also empowers healthcare professionals with tools for data-driven decision-making [4, 5]. While Generative AI holds immense promise, challenges such as data privacy, security and ethical considerations demand careful consideration [6, 7]. Striking a balance between technological innovation and ethical deployment is imperative to ensure patient trust and the responsible use of AI in healthcare [8, 9].

The collaborative partnerships between healthcare professionals and AI systems are anticipated to refine diagnostic capabilities continually [10]. The seamless integration of Generative AI is poised to propel the industry toward unprecedented levels of efficiency, precision, and patient-centric care [10, 11]. Generative AI is not just a technological leap; it represents a paradigm shift in healthcare, it also transforming medical imaging and revolutionizing data management, it paves the way for a future where diagnostics are more precise, treatments are more personalized, and healthcare data becomes a powerful tool for improving patient outcomes [12, 13]. As hospitals embrace the transformative potential of Generative AI, the promise of innovative applications and enhanced healthcare delivery becomes an achievable reality [14]. The analysis unfolds by intricately detailing the nuanced contributions of Generative AI, spotlighting advanced methodologies such as Generative Adversarial Networks (GANs) and Variational Autoencoders (VAEs) [15, 16]. Through these techniques, Generative AI emerges as a potent force in generating high-fidelity medical images, amplifying their quality, and orchestrating sophisticated data reconstructions, thereby elevating diagnostic accuracy to unprecedented heights [17]. Through a comprehensive analysis of current advancements and potential future developments, this chapter explores the ways in which Generative AI is reshaping the landscape of healthcare, offering unprecedented opportunities for enhanced diagnostic accuracy, improved patient outcomes and streamlined healthcare data utilization [18].

11.1.1 Overview of Generative AI: Relevance in the Healthcare Sector

By 2022, the healthcare industry's worldwide generative AI market was valued at USD 1.07 billion. Forecasts include a 35.14% Compound Annual Growth Rate (CAGR) from 2023 to 2032, with a predicted reaching of USD 21.74 billion by 2032 [19, 20]. The use of generative AI and other big language AI models has the potential to completely transform the healthcare sector [21, 22]. Advances in this technology have the potential to bring enterprise intelligence, freeing clinical resources from repetitive administrative duties and enabling medical practitioners to focus on more meaningful work [23]. A successful implementation necessitates a sturdy digital foundation, strategic investments in personnel, and readiness in terms of data. Institutions must also restructure workflows and job functions to emphasize human efficiency and effectiveness [24, 25]. Education for both clinicians and patients plays a crucial role in enhancing accessibility and achieving superior outcomes in healthcare [26, 27].

11.1.2 Introduction to the Challenges in Medical Imaging and Healthcare Data Management

A more digital method to managing health data is emerging, including patient and administrative data and being distinguished by higher value, volume, and velocity [28]. With streamlining and optimizing the use of healthcare providers, practitioners and organizations, health data management practices eventually help to give the best possible treatment for patients' well-being [29]. The last many years have seen a notable increase in the amount of comprehensive administrative and clinical data that healthcare providers have generated [30, 31]. Healthcare IT security may be improved by addressing the possibilities and problems associated with managing patient data [32]. Healthcare data management software is being used by healthcare providers to improve the security and caliber of the services they supply [33, 34]. This strategy seeks to achieve short- and long-term goals while also improving healthcare solutions, efficiency, and compliance with regulations [35]. The efficient use of patient data for healthcare analytics is not without challenges [37]. To overcome these obstacles, fragmented data must be handled in an ordered manner to allow for its analysis, integration, and extraction of the essential insights

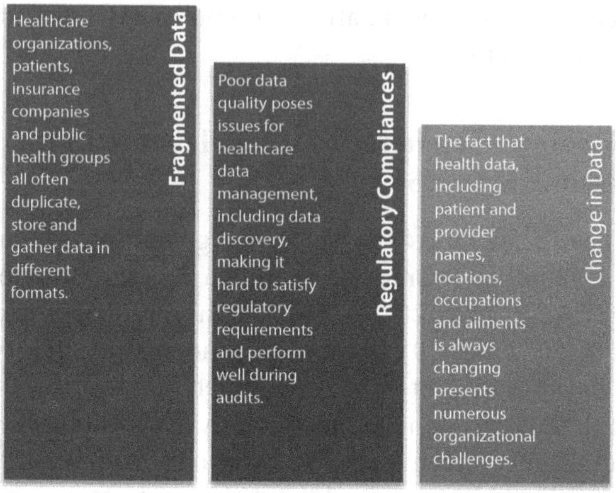

Figure 11.1 Challenges in healthcare data management.

to guarantee the highest levels of security and privacy [37, 38]. The accessibility is critical to health data management solutions, highlighting the importance of digitalization, IT solutions and healthcare data management [39, 40]. Figure 11.1 clarifies the fragmented data, regulatory compliance and change in data.

11.1.3 Objectives of the Chapter

This chapter has the following objectives to:

- specify the Generative AI in medical imaging within the hospital industry.
- highlight innovative applications of Generative AI in patient diagnosis.
- suggest ways how Generative AI can be a transformative force in healthcare data management.
- discuss how Generative AI can automate and optimize various aspects of medical imaging, leading to quicker and more accurate results for healthcare providers.

11.1.4 Structure of the Chapter

This chapter expresses the diverse aspects of Transforming Medical Imagining for Patient Diagnosis and Revolutionizing Healthcare Data Management Lensing Generative AI for Innovative Applications in Hospital

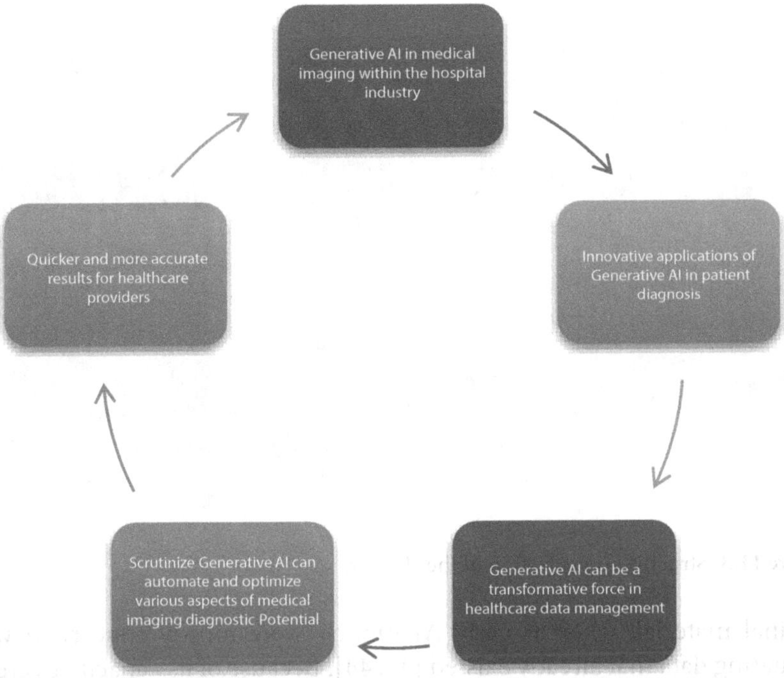

Figure 11.2 Objectives of the chapter.

Industry. Section 11.2 elaborates the Applications of Generative AI in the Healthcare and Hospital Industry. Section 11.3 discusses the Generative AI in Medical Imaging: Transforming Visual Representations. Section 11.4 lays down the Personalized Medicine and Treatment Planning. Section 11.5 highlights the Revolutionizing Healthcare Data Management- Streamlining Healthcare Data Management. Section 11.6 scrutinizes the Challenges and Viable Considerations. Finally, Section 11.7 Conclude the Chapter with Future Scope. Figure 11.2 specifies the 5 specific objectives of this chapter. This Figure lays down the different parameters for objectives of this chapter.

11.2 Applications of Generative AI in the Healthcare and Hospital Industry

Patients in the healthcare system are increasingly turning to unofficial information sources, especially the internet, as is well-documented [41]. With the introduction of generative artificial intelligence (AI), this tendency has quickly spread to doctors and other healthcare practitioners and has become much more intense [42]. Generative AI systems are able to produce

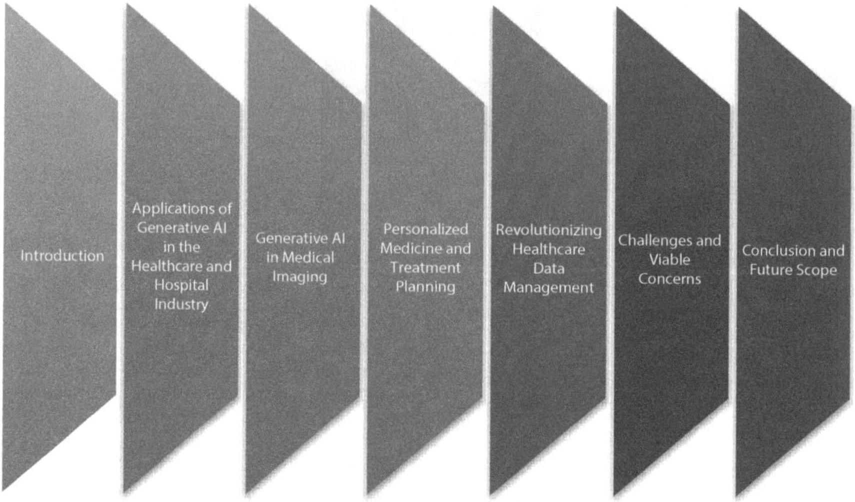

Figure 11.3 Structure/organization of the chapter.

original material, whereas early AI models were mostly concerned with evaluating data that already existed [43, 44]. Because of its capacity to create content and its intuitive interfaces, which improve accessibility and simplicity of use, generative AI is now widely used by a variety of professionals, including medical experts [45, 46]. Figure 11.3 conveys the seven parts of this chapter starting from introduction to conclusion and future scope. This figure specifies the sections cover under this chapter.

Healthcare practitioners are increasingly significantly depending on AI-assisted decision-making, mirroring the previous over-reliance of patients seeking a better grasp of their diseases on digital information sources [47, 48]. Generative AI provides answers to these problems and improves the capabilities of medical imaging. The image enhancement is possible as Generative AI can boost visibility and lead to more precise diagnosis by improving the quality of medical photos [49, 50]. The data augmentation in scenarios where real-world data is scarce, generative models can produce artificial medical pictures to supplement existing datasets for training machine learning algorithms [51]. The aspect of noise reduction and artifacts in medical pictures, generative AI contributes to more accurate and clear imaging. With training generative models to produce high-resolution pictures from lower-resolution inputs, medical imaging can have more detailed images [52, 53]. Figure 11.4 conveys the various applications of the GAI in healthcare industry. This Figure clarifies the applications of GAI in Healthcare industry.

Figure 11.4 Diverse applications of generative ai in the healthcare and hospital industry.

11.3 Generative AI in Medical Imaging: Transforming Visual Representations

When it comes to providing visual representations of the interior structures of the human body for clinical evaluations and medical treatments, medical imaging technologies are indispensable [54]. These technologies are essential for the identification, tracking, and management of a wide range of illnesses [55]. Despite being essential to contemporary healthcare, medical imaging has some issues that need to be addressed [56]. Sustaining the vast and complex datasets produced by many imaging modalities necessitates significant storage capacity and effective data management systems [57]. It can be difficult to integrate Electronic Health Record (EHR) systems seamlessly due to interoperability problems and differences in data formats. Given the sensitive patient data contained in medical photographs, it is imperative to prioritize security and privacy compliance to avoid unauthorized access and data breaches [58].

11.3.1 Patient Diagnosis: Improving Diagnostic Accuracy

Medical research is already benefiting from generative AI, and in the years to come, experts expect this trend to continue and pick up speed [59, 60]. The potential of generative AI to generate synthetic data, as it demonstrates the major benefit this offers to research particularly when some data kinds, like brain imaging scans, are costly and scarce [61]. While AI and other cognitive technologies have long helped physicians treat patients, the advent of generative AI is bringing new possibilities, especially in the areas of diagnosis and illness management. Many patients are aware of the potential of generative AI according to the "2023 Health Care Consumer Survey". Generative AI may improve access to healthcare by, for example, informing people about illnesses and available treatments. Furthermore, 46% think it may lower the cost of healthcare [62].

According to the 2023 "Clinician of the Future" study released by data analytics and scientific publishing giant Elsevier Health, generative AI techniques are now utilized in just 11% of clinical judgments. Generative AI is unique among AI and machine learning systems in that it can evaluate unstructured data and create questions for physicians [63]. Generative AI outperforms current methods by being able to interpret a greater amount of data from sources such as electronic health records and identify variables like gender, age, family history, and personal history to produce more nuanced and tailored outcomes. Also, healthcare decision-making and patient care are impacted by generative AI [64]. It can improve the interpretation of medical images, help diagnose illnesses, and support the creation of more individualized treatment regimens. The patient care is currently being impacted by generative AI, or it will be in the near future. To treat problems with both individual and public health, it may assist physicians in prioritizing patient needs and investigating societal determinants of health [65].

11.4 Personalized Medicine and Treatment Planning

Personalized medicine is a practice that is based on identifying differences among patients with the same illness, denoting a break from the traditional "one size fits all" approach. This strategy promotes the choice of customized treatments depending on certain patient populations. Predicting a treatment's potential efficacy for a certain patient is made possible by personalized medicine [66]. While there are many issues and barriers that need to be resolved for personalized medicine to be successfully incorporated into healthcare systems, it is important to recognize that personalized medicine is an evolution rather than a radical change in medical procedures [67]. As software companies create solutions based on generative AI to manage regular activities across the healthcare ecosystem from physicians to support workers to payers, Generative AI is expected to revolutionize healthcare administration. Generative AI skills can help with clinical documentation by helping to gather and summarize data from patient visit recordings, freeing up physicians to focus more on patient care and less on writing notes [68]. Generative AI has the ability to handle particular patient demands more efficiently than current automation in healthcare contact centers and administrative offices. It can also pre-populate healthcare records and prior permission forms. Using generative AI to healthcare management might result in enhancements in addition to time-saving advantages [69].

Generative AI has promise in enhancing diagnostic processes, especially for illnesses where a wealth of data is available. Accurate diagnosis and bias mitigation are still difficult tasks, particularly for uncommon illnesses with little data representation [70]. Artificial intelligence's ability to diagnose uncommon diseases is hampered by a lack of data, since a small learning sample might lead to subpar results. AI systems must have access to enormous datasets, especially for common ailments where there is a wealth of data, to function better and avoid creating a fragmented AI environment that benefits major health institutions with private data [71]. Although putting these AI applications into practice can seem simple, it's important to understand that their effectiveness depends on the availability of large and varied information. Health outcomes are greatly influenced by factors other than the traditional data recorded in EHRs and HIEs such as- the socioeconomic determinants, lifestyle decisions and everyday activities of patients. The inadequate compilation of data in these domains might result in subpar performance of existing prediction models [72].

11.5 Revolutionizing Healthcare Data Management-Streamlining Healthcare Data Management

Generative AI has the potential to increase the effectiveness of information collecting and reporting by eliminating ambiguities, communicating with patients in plain language and providing healthcare practitioners with a summary of the data [73]. With the use of this technology, medical personnel may ask targeted, conversational inquiries to help gather patients' medical histories. The ability to access health information exchanges (HIEs) and collect and analyze patient medical records is another benefit that generative AI provides. The AI system may create pertinent queries based on the medical history of the patient [74]. It can cross-reference medication lists with current health complaints to confirm compliance with recommended regimens or detect any discontinuance of conflicting drugs due to new prescriptions. By putting together a more thorough medical history, this procedure helps doctors provide better treatment. Patients may find it simpler to adjust to and accept similar AI technology in healthcare if they are already familiar with AI applications in a variety of settings. These AI systems' jobs are often low-risk and repetitive, which fits very nicely with the capabilities of existing generative AI technology. These systems operate at a level that is usually regarded as adequate in the healthcare industry, demonstrating competency in managing such procedures [75].

In the domain of healthcare policy governance, generative artificial intelligence (AI) has the potential to assist in the search, summarization, and analysis of the vast amount of policies that exist inside hospitals or healthcare systems. Generative AI recognizing out-of-date information, gaps in protocols, or policy disputes. This might speed up the updating process and guarantee that pertinent information gets to the proper people on time [76]. Generative AI that is based on huge language models can assist a variety of communication demands in the medical business. Potential uses include writing material and content for marketing and sales campaigns for businesses involved in biopharma, medical technology, and pharmaceuticals [77]. Generative AI may also be used by healthcare organizations such as hospitals and medication companies to provide patient information like discharge summaries or treatment guidelines. Healthcare personnel can save time by doing this, which may also improve the standard of treatment. Generative AI technologies may dynamically adapt information to specific patients, taking into account different reading capabilities by carefully deconstructing instructions or by including both visual and audio choices. It is to have strict control to guarantee that the data produced is accurate, comprehensive, and understandable [78, 79].

With employing vast datasets from health information exchanges (HIEs) and electronic health records (EHRs), healthcare professionals may improve patient population management to a great extent. Utilizing the AI-powered predictive analytics is to identify high-risk patients who would greatly benefit from prompt medical treatments increases efficacy [80]. With analyzing particular patient features, AI systems may be trained to determine the likelihood of hospital readmissions following release. Based on these forecasts, individualized care plans may be created with human input to guarantee that these patients receive the assistance they require and stop more major health occurrences [81].

To improve population health management with predictive AI models, AI systems must be able to access and evaluate far bigger and more diversified information [82]. Integrating data from smart devices and wearable technology may be necessary to achieve this [83]. These gadgets capture and record a multitude of health-related data continually, offering a more complete picture of a patient's profile. Such data might be used to enable more precise forecasts and, in turn, more successful intervention techniques, opening the door to a proactive and individualized approach to treatment [84].

11.6 Challenges and Viable Considerations

It is important to recognize that generative AI is not a panacea, even in spite of the encouraging outcomes from its use in healthcare. It cannot be used everywhere to solve every problem in every healthcare environment. To minimize unforeseen effects, doctors and other healthcare professionals must utilize generative AI carefully; this is because responsible usage is crucial to maximizing its advantages and preventing negative results [85, 86]. High repetition and low risk situations are ideal for generative AI as its efficacy stems from its ability to use previous data to spot trends and forecast future events based on the supposition that past conditions would repeat themselves. It is wise to use such technologies in low-risk scenarios, especially when mistakes have little repercussions [87]. This cautious approach has multiple benefits: it enables patients and, more crucially, healthcare professionals to progressively become aware of AI's potential and develop a sense of confidence in its usefulness. Furthermore, it offers AI developers excellent chances to thoroughly test and improve their systems in a safe setting prior to putting them into situations with greater risks [88].

Currently accessible generative AI systems are only trained on data that is made available to the public. It would be naive to rely on generic AI models for medical diagnoses without taking into account considerable efforts to digitize healthcare records and rich medical histories [89]. Thus, until AI is trained on large medical datasets, care should be used while using generative AI for diagnosis. AI has a lot of obstacles to overcome in the field of medicine, such as difficulties with patient acceptance and trust, liability and accountability issues, and technological constraints. Healthcare practitioners have the last say over treatments; it is unlikely that AI developers will take over this role for both practical and legal reasons [90].

The patient confidence in AI-managed therapies has not increased to the point where their broad use is supported. Artificial intelligence currently lacks the technological sophistication to reproduce the complex actions that physicians perform, such as basic medicine administration [91]. It is doubtful that AI will be included into medical treatment procedures very soon given these complications. It is crucial to reduce possible dangers even when healthcare providers train their AI systems on huge medical datasets. AI functions as a useful aid, rather than a replacement when certain processes are designed, such that it helps doctors diagnose patients rather than taking their place [92]. The potential application of AI is in post-treatment monitoring and follow-up. It's critical that patients follow post-treatment instructions, and artificial intelligence (AI) may use wearables, smart devices and smartphone sensors to provide real-time monitoring and customized suggestions. GAI can proactively handle patient health decline by notifying clinicians when emergency medical treatment is required because to its wide data access [93].

Transparency: Encouraging openness is essential to maximizing AI's application in healthcare environments. This entails creating an environment where AI engineers and medical experts work closely together to promote a mutually beneficial connection. This kind of cooperation guarantees that AI advice is not only validated medically but also rigorously examined for correctness. The possibility of mistakes resulting from faulty data inputs or biased algorithms is reduced [94]. Transparency in patient communications about the use of AI in their healthcare experience is critically needed. The role AI plays in their care should be fully disclosed to the patients. Patients must also be aware of the privacy risks involved in giving permission for the use of AI-driven solutions, particularly in cases where data gathering goes beyond standard medical records to include information from wearables and smart technology [95, 96].

Health Data Usage: In addition to being required by law, patient education about data usage, privacy protections, and the complex advantages and disadvantages of artificial intelligence (AI) in healthcare is essential to fostering patient-system trust in the face of rapid technological advancements. During this digital shift, it is imperative to address the possible aggravation of current monopolies in the healthcare sector [97]. The bigger healthcare providers with a bigger market share may strengthen their positions since AI systems require vast amounts of high-quality data which might result in higher healthcare expenditures [98]. Due to the limitations on their capacity to use AI to improve healthcare delivery, smaller, independent providers are at a disadvantage. This might lead to a wider disparity in the quality of care especially for underprivileged groups [99]. Figure 11.5 discusses the concerns regarding patient data. This Figure also lays down the data accessibility.

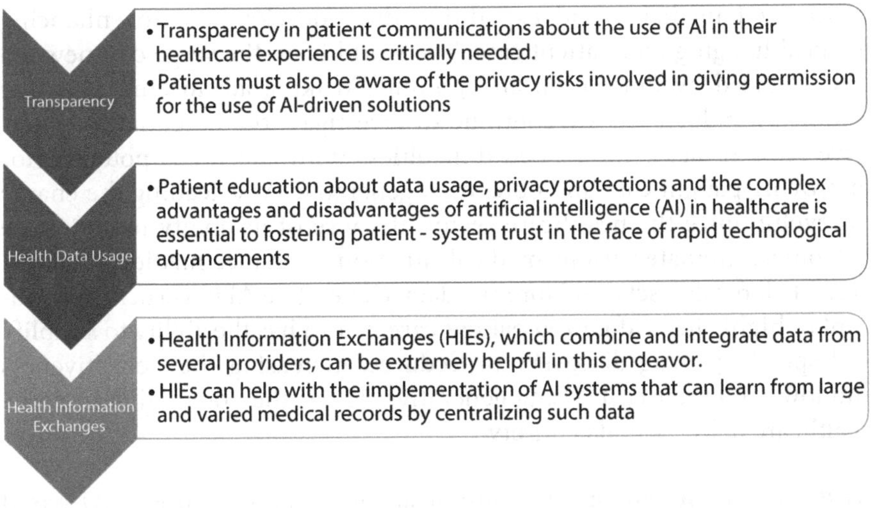

Figure 11.5 Wide data access during medical treatment: concerns.

Health Information Exchanges (HIEs): Initiatives that democratize access to medical data for AI research should be led by industry leaders, regulatory agencies, and healthcare consortia to lessen this [100]. Health Information Exchanges (HIEs), which combine and integrate data from several providers, can be extremely helpful in this endeavor. HIEs can help with the implementation of AI systems that can learn from large and varied medical records by centralizing such data [101]. To guarantee that all member firms, regardless of size, may profit from insights derived from larger datasets, HIEs might provide AI as a shared service to their affiliates. There is hope to level the playing field and give smaller providers the opportunity to use AI to improve the quality of their services. This makes the healthcare system more equitable, using technology as a bridge rather than a barrier [102].

11.7 Conclusion, Future Directions and Innovations

The healthcare sector has seen tremendous breakthroughs and prospects since the advent of generative AI. This state-of-the-art technology has the potential to revolutionize healthcare by producing fresh data, enhancing diagnosis, maximizing treatment plans, and hastening the development of innovative medications. Generative AI has enormous potential to improve healthcare outcomes through its applications, which range from allowing customized medicine and expediting drug development to enhancing medical imaging and patient care. The world is on the verge of a new era characterized by innovation and ground-breaking advancements in the healthcare industry as we continue to investigate the potential of generative AI and tackle the related difficulties. With enormous potential for improving patient care and outcomes, generative AI is leading the charge to revolutionize the healthcare sector. Because of its ability to anticipate outcomes, simulate various medical situations, enhance medical imaging, evaluate large datasets, and forecast data, Generative AI is a crucial component of highly individualized patient care. It also has the ability to simplify and speed up drug discovery procedures, increasing their effectiveness and lowering their cost. Using generative AI has the potential to improve healthcare delivery in its entirety.

AI disclosure statement: The author acknowledges the use of AI-based tools for minor language editing or grammatical correction. However, all intellectual contributions, analyses, and conclusions presented in this chapter are entirely the author's own.

References

1. Martinelli, D.D., Generative machine learning for de novo drug discovery: A systematic review. *Comput. Biol. Med.*, *145*, 105403, 2022.
2. Hamadi, R., Ghazzai, H., Massoud, Y., A generative adversarial network for financial advisor recruitment in smart crowdsourcing platforms. *Appl. Sci.*, *12*, 19, 9830, 2022.
3. Singh, B., Legal Dynamics Lensing Metaverse Crafted for Videogame Industry and E-Sports: Phenomenological Exploration Catalyst Complexity and Future. *J. Intellect. Prop. Rights Law*, 7, 1, 8–14, 2024.
4. Vinothkumar, J. and Karunamurthy, A., *Recent Advancements in Artificial Intelligence Technology: Trends and Implications*, 2022.
5. Das, S. and Ghosh, A., Emotion Detection Using Generative Adversarial Network. *Generative Adversarial Netw. Deep Learn.*, 1, 165–182, 2023.
6. Parida, P.K., Dora, L., Swain, M., Agrawal, S., Panda, R., Data science methodologies in smart healthcare: a review. *Health Technol.*, *12*, 2, 329–344, 2022.
7. Li, J., *Machine Learning and Optimization Applications on Near-term Quantum Computers*, The Pennsylvania State University, US, 2022.
8. Xu, Y., Liu, X., Cao, X., Huang, C., Liu, E., Qian, S., Zhang, J., Artificial intelligence: A powerful paradigm for scientific research. *Innovation*, *2*, 4, 45, 2021.

9. Singh, B., Blockchain Technology in Renovating Healthcare: Legal and Future Perspectives, in: *Revolutionizing Healthcare Through Artificial Intelligence and Internet of Things Applications*, pp. 177–186, IGI Global, USA, 2023.
10. Kumar, M., Nguyen, T.N., Kaur, J., Singh, T.G., Soni, D., Singh, R., Kumar, P., Opportunities and challenges in application of artificial intelligence in pharmacology. *Pharmacol. Rep.*, *75*, 1, 3–18, 2023.
11. Khang, A., Shah, V., Rani, S. (Eds.), *Handbook of Research on AI-Based Technologies and Applications in the Era of the Metaverse*, IGI Global, USA, 2023.
12. Singh, B., Federated Learning for Envision Future Trajectory Smart Transport System for Climate Preservation and Smart Green Planet: Insights into Global Governance and SDG-9 (Industry, Innovation and Infrastructure). *Natl. J. Environ. Law*, 6, 2, 6–17, 2023.
13. Rayhan, A., Accelerating Drug Discovery and Material Design: Unleashing AI's Potential for Optimizing Molecular Structures and Properties.
14. Blobel, B., Oemig, F., Ruotsalainen, P., Lopez, D.M., Transformation of health and social care systems—an interdisciplinary approach toward a foundational architecture. *Front. Med.*, *9*, 802487, 2022.
15. Sarkar, A., Al-Ars, Z., Bertels, K., Estimating algorithmic information using quantum computing for genomics applications. *Appl. Sci.*, *11*, 6, 2696, 2021.
16. Sharma, A. and Singh, B., Measuring Impact of E-commerce on Small Scale Business: A Systematic Review. *J. Corporate Governance Int. Bus. Law*, 5, 1, 78, 2022.
17. Gross, S.R.D., Revolutionizing Intelligence: Unraveling the Frontiers of Advanced Artificial Intelligence and its Impact on Society.
18. Chen, J., Yi, C., Okegbile, S.D., Cai, J., Shen, X.S., Networking Architecture and Key Supporting Technologies for Human Digital Twin in Personalized Healthcare: A Comprehensive Survey. *IEEE Commun. Surv. Tutorials*, 2023.
19. Xing, L., Giger, M.L., Min, J.K. (Eds.), *Artificial intelligence in medicine: technical basis and clinical applications*, Academic Press, New York, United States, 2023.
20. Singh, B., Understanding Legal Frameworks Concerning Transgender Healthcare in the Age of Dynamism. *Electron. J. Soc. Strategic Stud.*, 3, 56–65, 2022.
21. Ali, S., DiPaola, D., Lee, I., Hong, J., Breazeal, C., Exploring generative models with middle school students, in: *Proceedings of the 2021 CHI Conference on Human Factors in Computing Systems*, pp. 1–13, 2021, May.
22. Nawaz, S.J., Sharma, S.K., Wyne, S., Patwary, M.N., Asaduzzaman, M., Quantum machine learning for 6G communication networks: State-of-the-art and vision for the future. *IEEE Access*, *7*, 46317–46350, 2019.
23. Alluhaidan, A.S., Secure Medical Data Model Using Integrated Transformed Paillier and KLEIN Algorithm Encryption Technique with Elephant Herd Optimization for Healthcare Applications. *J. Healthcare Eng.*, *2022*, 139, 2022.

24. Steane, A., Quantum computing. *Rep. Prog. Phys.*, *61*, 2, 117, 1998.
25. Singh, B., Relevance of Agriculture-Nutrition Linkage for Human Healthcare: A Conceptual Legal Framework of Implication and Pathways. *Justice Law Bull.*, 1, 1, 44–49, 2022.
26. O'brien, J.L., Optical quantum computing. *Science*, *318*, 5856, 1567–1570, 2007.
27. Singh, B., COVID-19 Pandemic and Public Healthcare: Endless Downward Spiral or Solution via Rapid Legal and Health Services Implementation with Patient Monitoring Program. *Justice Law Bull.*, 1, 1, 1–7, 2022.
28. Kumar, A., Bhushan, B., Shriti, S., Nand, P., Quantum computing for health care: A review on implementation trends and recent advances. *Multimed. Technol. Internet Things Environ.*, *3*, 23–40, 2022.
29. Jayanthi, P., Rai, B.K., Muralikrishna, I., The potential of quantum computing in healthcare In, in: *Technology Road Mapping for Quantum Computing and Engineering*, pp. 81–101, IGI Global, USA, 2022.
30. Davids, J., Lidströmer, N., Ashrafian, H., Artificial Intelligence in Medicine Using Quantum Computing in the Future of Healthcare, in: *Artificial Intelligence in Medicine*, pp. 423–446, Springer International Publishing, Cham, 2022.
31. Gupta, S., Modgil, S., Bhatt, P.C., Jabbour, C.J.C., Kamble, S., Quantum computing led innovation for achieving a more sustainable Covid-19 healthcare industry. *Technovation*, *120*, 102544, 2023.
32. Singh, B., Global Science and Jurisprudential Approach Concerning Healthcare and Illness. *Indian J. Health Med. Law*, 3, 1, 7–13, 2020.
33. Shaikh, T.A. and Ali, R., Quantum computing in big data analytics: A survey, in: *2016 IEEE international conference on computer and information technology (CIT)*, IEEE, pp. 112–115, 2016, December.
34. Singh, B., Profiling Public Healthcare: A Comparative Analysis Based on the Multidimensional Healthcare Management and Legal Approach. *Indian J. Health Med. Law*, 2, 2, 1–5, 2019.
35. Solenov, D., Brieler, J., Scherrer, J.F., The potential of quantum computing and machine learning to advance clinical research and change the practice of medicine. *Mo. Med.*, *115*, 5, 463, 2018.
36. Zhang, P. and Kamel Boulos, M.N., Generative AI in medicine and healthcare: Promises, opportunities and challenges. *Future Internet*, *15*, 9, 286, 2023.
37. Paladugu, P.S., Ong, J., Nelson, N., Kamran, S.A., Waisberg, E., Zaman, N., Tavakkoli, A., Generative adversarial networks in medicine: important considerations for this emerging innovation in artificial intelligence. *Ann. Biomed. Eng.*, *51*, 10, 2130–2142, 2023.
38. Ooi, K.B., Tan, G.W.H., Al-Emran, M., Al-Sharafi, M.A., Capatina, A., Chakraborty, A., Wong, L.W., The potential of Generative Artificial Intelligence across disciplines: Perspectives and future directions. *J. Comput. Inf. Syst.*, 1, 1–32, 2023.

39. Kanbach, D.K., Heiduk, L., Blueher, G., Schreiter, M., Lahmann, A., The GenAI is out of the bottle: generative artificial intelligence from a business model innovation perspective. *Rev. Manag. Sci.*, 1, 1–32, 2023.
40. Rane, N., ChatGPT and Similar Generative Artificial Intelligence (AI) for Smart Industry: role, challenges and opportunities for industry 4.0, industry 5.0 and society 5.0. *Challenges Opportunities Ind.*, *4*, 5, 2023.
41. Mannuru, N.R., Shahriar, S., Teel, Z.A., Wang, T., Lund, B.D., Tijani, S., Vaidya, P., Artificial intelligence in developing countries: The impact of generative artificial intelligence (AI) technologies for development. *Inf. Dev.*, 2023. 02666669231200628.
42. Fui-Hoon Nah, F., Zheng, R., Cai, J., Siau, K., Chen, L., , and ChatGPT: Applications, challenges, and AI-human collaboration. *J. Inf. Technol. Case Appl. Res.*, *25*, 3, 277–304, 2023.
43. Nova, K., Generative AI in healthcare: advancements in electronic health records, facilitating medical languages, and personalized patient care. *J. Adv. Anal. Healthcare Manage.*, *7*, 1, 115–131, 2023.
44. Kar, A.K., Varsha, P.S., Rajan, S., Unravelling the impact of generative artificial intelligence (GAI) in industrial applications: A review of scientific and grey literature. *Global J. Flexible Syst. Manage.*, *24*, 4, 659–689, 2023.
45. Dwivedi, Y.K., Pandey, N., Currie, W., Micu, A., Leveraging ChatGPT and other generative artificial intelligence (AI)-based applications in the hospitality and tourism industry: practices, challenges and research agenda. *Int. J. Contemp. Hospitality Manage.*, *36*, 1, 1–12, 2024.
46. Dilibal, C., Davis, B.L., Chakraborty, C., Generative design methodology for internet of medical things (IoMT)-based wearable biomedical devices, in: *2021 3rd International Congress on Human-Computer Interaction, Optimization and Robotic Applications (HORA)*, IEEE, pp. 1–4, 2021, June.
47. Yu, P., Xu, H., Hu, X., Deng, C., Leveraging generative AI and large Language models: a Comprehensive Roadmap for Healthcare Integration, in: *Healthcare*, vol. 11, p. 2776, MDPI, Switzerland, 2023, October.
48. Hofmann, P., Rückel, T., Urbach, N., Innovating with artificial intelligence: capturing the constructive functional capabilities of deep generative learning, 2021.
49. Zhao, C., Yang, J., Xiong, W., Li, J., Two generative design methods of hospital operating department layouts based on healthcare systematic layout planning and generative adversarial network. *J. Shanghai Jiaotong Univ. (Science)*, *26*, 103–115, 2021.
50. Mesko, B., The ChatGPT (Generative Artificial Intelligence) Revolution Has Made Artificial Intelligence Approachable for Medical Professionals. *J. Med. Internet Res.*, *25*, e48392, 2023.
51. Manaswi, N.K., *Generative Adversarial Networks with Industrial Use Cases: Learning How to Build GAN Applications for Retail, Healthcare, Telecom, Media, Education, and HRTech*, BPB Publications, India, 2020.

52. Meskó, B. and Topol, E.J., The imperative for regulatory oversight of large language models (or generative AI) in healthcare. *npj Digital Med.*, *6*, 1, 120, 2023.
53. Prasad Agrawal, K., Towards adoption of generative AI in organizational settings. *J. Comput. Inf. Syst.*, 2, 1–16, 2023.
54. Ellingrud, K., Sanghvi, S., Madgavkar, A., Dandona, G.S., Chui, M., White, O., Hasebe, P., Generative AI and the future of work in America, McKinsey & Company, Europe, 2023.
55. Dogru, T., Line, N., Mody, M., Hanks, L., Abbott, J.A., Acikgoz, F., Zhang, T., Generative artificial intelligence in the hospitality and tourism industry: Developing a framework for future research. *J. Hospitality Tourism Res.*, 2023. 10963480231188663.
56. Huang, J., Neill, L., Wittbrodt, M., Melnick, D., Klug, M., Thompson, M., Etemadi, M., Generative artificial intelligence for chest radiograph interpretation in the emergency department. *JAMA Netw. Open*, *6*, 10, e2336100–e2336100, 2023.
57. Bordukova, M., Makarov, N., Rodriguez-Esteban, R., Schmich, F., Menden, M.P., Generative artificial intelligence empowers digital twins in drug discovery and clinical trials. *Expert Opin. Drug Discov.*, *19*, 1, 33–42, 2024.
58. Chui, M., Hazan, E., Roberts, R., Singla, A., Smaje, K., The economic potential of generative AI, 2023.
59. Malik, S., Tyagi, A.K., Mahajan, S., Architecture, Generative Model, and Deep Reinforcement Learning for IoT Applications: Deep Learning Perspective. *Artif. Intelligence-based Internet Things Syst.*, 1, 243–265, 2022.
60. Ghimire, P., Kim, K., Acharya, M., Generative ai in the construction industry: Opportunities & challenges, 2023, arXiv preprint arXiv:2310.04427.
61. Korzynski, P., Mazurek, G., Altmann, A., Ejdys, J., Kazlauskaite, R., Paliszkiewicz, J., Ziemba, E., Generative artificial intelligence as a new context for management theories: analysis of ChatGPT. *Cent. Eur. Manage. J.*, 2023.
62. Bandi, A., Adapa, P.V.S.R., Kuchi, Y. E. V. P. K., The power of generative ai: A review of requirements, models, input–output formats, evaluation metrics, and challenges. *Future Internet*, *15*, 8, 260, 2023.
63. Zhao, C.W., Yang, J., Li, J., Generation of hospital emergency department layouts based on generative adversarial networks. *J. Build. Eng.*, *43*, 102539, 7, 2021.
64. Bahroun, Z., Anane, C., Ahmed, V., Zacca, A., Transforming education: A comprehensive review of generative artificial intelligence in educational settings through bibliometric and content analysis. *Sustainability*, *15*, 17, 12983, 2023.
65. Soni, V., Impact of Generative AI on Small and Medium Enterprises' Revenue Growth: The Moderating Role of Human, Technological, and Market Factors. *Rev. Contemp. Bus. Anal.*, *6*, 1, 133–153, 2023.

66. Frey, C.B. and Osborne, M., Generative AI and the Future of Work: A Reappraisal. *Brown J. World Aff.*, 1, 1–12, 2023.
67. Cheng, Z., Lee, D., Tambe, P., Innovae: Generative ai for understanding patents and innovation, 2022, Available at SSRN 3868599.
68. Kshetri, N., Dwivedi, Y.K., Davenport, T.H., Panteli, N., Generative artificial intelligence in marketing: Applications, opportunities, challenges, and research agenda. *Int. J. Inf. Manage.*, 102716, 121, 2023.
69. Mondal, S., Das, S., Vrana, V.G., How to bell the cat? A theoretical review of generative artificial intelligence towards digital disruption in all walks of life. *Technologies*, *11*, 2, 44, 2023.
70. Rane, N., Choudhary, S., Rane, J., Integrating Building Information Modelling (BIM) with ChatGPT, Bard, and similar generative artificial intelligence in the architecture, engineering, and construction industry: applications, a novel framework, challenges, and future scope. Bard, and similar generative artificial intelligence in the architecture, engineering, and construction industry: applications, a novel framework, challenges, and future scope (November 22, 2023), 1, 93, 2023.
71. Miao, H., Li, C., Wang, J., A future of smarter digital health empowered by generative pretrained transformer. *J. Med. Internet Res.*, *25*, e49963, 2023.
72. Leone, D., Schiavone, F., Appio, F.P., Chiao, B., How does artificial intelligence enable and enhance value co-creation in industrial markets? An exploratory case study in the healthcare ecosystem. *J. Bus. Res.*, *129*, 849–859, 2021.
73. Maddipoti, A., Pathway Forward for Responsible Generative AI Implementation in Healthcare, 2023, (Doctoral dissertation).
74. Ratten, V. and Jones, P., Generative artificial intelligence (ChatGPT): Implications for management educators. *Int. J. Manage. Educ.*, *21*, 3, 100857, 2023.
75. Vyas, B. and Rajendran, R.M., Generative Adversarial Networks for Anomaly Detection in Medical Images. *Int. J. Multi. Innov. Res. Methodol.*, *2*, 4, 52–58, 2023. ISSN: 2960-2068.
76. Rane, N., Roles and challenges of ChatGPT and similar generative artificial intelligence for achieving the sustainable development goals (SDGs), 2023, Available at SSRN 4603244.
77. Dwivedi, Y.K., Kshetri, N., Hughes, L., Slade, E.L., Jeyaraj, A., Kar, A.K., Wright, R., "So what if ChatGPT wrote it?" Multidisciplinary perspectives on opportunities, challenges and implications of generative conversational AI for research, practice and policy. *Int. J. Inf. Manage.*, *71*, 102642, 2023.
78. Wong, I.A., Lian, Q.L., Sun, D., Autonomous travel decision-making: An early glimpse into ChatGPT and generative AI. *J. Hospitality Tourism Manage.*, *56*, 253–263, 2023.
79. Rane, N.L., Multidisciplinary collaboration: key players in successful implementation of ChatGPT and similar generative artificial intelligence in manufacturing, finance, retail, transportation, and construction industry, 2023.

80. Doshi, A.R. and Hauser, O., Generative artificial intelligence enhances creativity, 2023, Available at SSRN.
81. Byrne, M., The disruptive impacts of next generation generative artificial intelligence. *CIN: Computers, Informatics, Nurs.*, *41*, 7, 479–481, 2023.
82. Law, R., Lin, K.J., Ye, H., Fong, D.K.C., Artificial intelligence research in hospitality: a state-of-the-art review and future directions. *Int. J. Contemp. Hosp. Manag.*, 2023.
83. Lewis, M. and Mercer, E., The AI Roadmap–charting our future in healthcare communications. *Curr. Med. Res. Opin.*, *40*, 1, 5–7, 2024.
84. Gursoy, D., Li, Y., Song, H., ChatGPT and the hospitality and tourism industry: an overview of current trends and future research directions. *J. Hosp. Market. Manage.*, *32*, 5, 579–592, 2023.
85. Wamba, S.F., Queiroz, M.M., Jabbour, C.J.C., Shi, C.V., Are both generative AI and ChatGPT game changers for 21st-Century operations and supply chain excellence? *Int. J. Prod. Econ.*, *265*, 109015, 2023.
86. Harrer, S., Attention is not all you need: the complicated case of ethically using large language models in healthcare and medicine. *EBioMedicine*, *90*, 2023.
87. Gabrielson, A.T., Odisho, A.Y., Canes, D., Harnessing generative artificial intelligence to improve efficiency among urologists: welcome ChatGPT. *J. Urol.*, *209*, 5, 827–829, 2023.
88. Budhwar, P., Chowdhury, S., Wood, G., Aguinis, H., Bamber, G.J., Beltran, J.R., Varma, A., Human resource management in the age of generative artificial intelligence: Perspectives and research directions on ChatGPT. *Hum. Resour. Manage. J.*, *33*, 3, 606–659, 2023.
89. Mohamadi, S., Mujtaba, G., Le, N., Doretto, G., Adjeroh, D.A., ChatGPT in the age of generative AI and large language models: a concise survey, 2023, arXiv preprint arXiv:2307.04251.
90. Xu, M., Du, H., Niyato, D., Kang, J., Xiong, Z., Mao, S., Poor, H.V., Unleashing the power of edge-cloud generative ai in mobile networks: A survey of aigc services. *IEEE Commun. Surv. Tutor.*, 2024.
91. Morley, J., DeVito, N.J., Zhang, J., Generative AI for medical research. *BMJ*, *382*, 99, 2023.
92. Bryan-Kinns, N., Banar, B., Ford, C., Reed, C.N., Zhang, Y., Colton, S., Armitage, J., Exploring XAI for the arts: Explaining latent space in generative music, 2023, arXiv preprint arXiv:2308.05496.
93. Thirunavukarasu, A.J., Ting, D.S.J., Elangovan, K., Gutierrez, L., Tan, T.F., Ting, D.S.W., Large language models in medicine. *Nat. Med.*, *29*, 8, 1930–1940, 2023.
94. Li, X., Jiang, Y., Rodriguez-Andina, J.J., Luo, H., Yin, S., Kaynak, O., When medical images meet generative adversarial network: recent development and research opportunities. *Discov. Artif. Intell.*, *1*, 1–20, 2021.

95. Sezgin, E., Artificial intelligence in healthcare: Complementing, not replacing, doctors and healthcare providers. *Digit. Health*, 9, 56, 2023. 20552076231186520.
96. Raj, R., Singh, A., Kumar, V., Verma, P., Analyzing the potential benefits and use cases of ChatGPT as a tool for improving the efficiency and effectiveness of business operations. *Bench Council Trans. Benchmarks Stand. Eval.*, 3, 3, 100140, 2023.
97. Minssen, T., Vayena, E., Cohen, I.G., The challenges for regulating medical use of ChatGPT and other large language models. *Jama*, 2023.
98. Hadi, M.U., Qureshi, R., Shah, A., Irfan, M., Zafar, A., Shaikh, M.B., Mirjalili, S., A survey on large language models: Applications, challenges, limitations, and practical usage. *Authorea Preprints*, 2023.
99. Dhoni, P. and Kumar, R., Synergizing generative ai and cybersecurity: Roles of generative ai entities, companies, agencies, and government in enhancing cybersecurity. *Authorea Preprints*, 2023.
100. Wach, K., Duong, C.D., Ejdys, J., Kazlauskaitė, R., Korzynski, P., Mazurek, G., Ziemba, E., The dark side of generative artificial intelligence: A critical analysis of controversies and risks of ChatGPT. *Entrepreneurial Bus. Econ. Rev.*, *11*, 2, 7–30, 2023.
101. Stasevych, M. and Zvarych, V., Innovative robotic technologies and artificial intelligence in pharmacy and medicine: paving the way for the future of health care—a review. *Big Data Cognit. Comput.*, *7*, 3, 147, 2023.
102. Joshi, G., Jain, A., Araveeti, S.R., Adhikari, S., Garg, H., Bhandari, M., FDA-Approved Artificial Intelligence and Machine Learning (AI/ML)-Enabled Medical Devices: An Updated Landscape. *Electronics*, *13*, 3, 498, 2024.

Index

Printed in the USA/Agawam, MA
September 16, 2026

910661.070